Aries/Mars
Think like a man of action and act like a man (

Taurus/Venus
Money not only changes hands, it changes people ~ Anon

Gemini/Mercury
Conversation is a contest in which the first person to draw a breath
is declared the listener ~ Anon

Cancer/Moon
Most mothers are instinctive philosophers ~ Harriet Beecher Stowe

Leo/Sun
In this life we cannot do great things.
We can only do small things with great love ~ Mother Teresa

Virgo/Mercury
A critic is a man who knows the way but can't drive the car ~ Kenneth Tynan

Libra/Venus
Diplomacy is the art of letting someone else have your way ~ Anon

Scorpio/Pluto
As far as sex, women need a reason; men need a location ~ Anon

Sagittarius/Jupiter
To mistake the map for the territory is to mistake the menu for the meal
~ Greg Bateson

Capricorn/Saturn
Be someone, not something ~ Coco Chanel

Aquarius/Uranus
Cherish forever what makes you unique,
'cuz you're really a yawn if it goes! ~ Bette Midler

Pisces/Neptune
Music is grace made audible and a rainbow over suffering
~ David Hayward (D.H.)

... the cause and purpose of God's intervention and gift to us of sight was that we should see the revolutions of intelligence in the heavens and use their untroubled course to guide the troubled revolutions in our understanding, which are akin to them.

~ Plato

The more you add to the horoscope, the more you're admitting your inability to communicate with it.

~ Michael Lutin

The horoscope is a one-page outline of your potential autobiography.

~ D.H.

The final mystery is oneself. When one has weighed the Sun in the balance, and measured the steps of the Moon, and mapped out the seven heavens star by star, there still remains oneself. Who can calculate the orbit of his own soul?

~ Oscar Wilde

shorthand of the soul

the quotable horoscope

volume 1

david hayward

Flare Publications

Flare Astro-Links series
1999

www.flareuk.com

First published in 1999 by Flare Publications.

A catalogue record for this book is available from the British Library.

ISBN 0-9530261-2-4

Design: **Daniel St.John Smith**
Index: Garry Heaton
Horoscope Wheel Design: Charles Dvorak

Astrological charts generated using Io Edition
Astrological calculations produced by Esoteric Technologies' Solar Fire v4 - www.esotech.com.au/

Printed by Biddles, Woodbridge Park Estate, Woodbridge Road, Guildford, Surrey GU1 1DA

Every effort has been made to credit individuals whose words appear in this book.
If we have accidentally omitted your name, please contact us
and we'll update the source in the next edition.
In addition, there may be mistakes, both typographical and in content,
we would appreciate hearing from you if you discover any errors.

About the Artist:

The Artwork is taken from the collection, Aquallucinations
Pictures and Paintings by Olivier Keuchel
c/o Place de l'église, 07700 St. Just d'Ardèche, France
00 33 (0) 4 75 98 67 36
http://perso.club-internet.fr/lekeuch
lekeuch@club-internet.fr

To Write to the Author:

To contact David Hayward, or to receive details of his astrological consultations, bodywork therapy or
future seminars, please write to: Hayward & Associates, 15237 Sunset Boulevard STE. 116, Pacific
Palisades, CA 90272, USA, or e-mail: willisjoy@aol.com

For more information about David Hayward, please see pages 252-3

Visit our website at: **www.flareuk.com**

Flare Publications
P.O. Box 10126, London NW3 7WD, England
Head Office: 29 Dolben Street, London SE1 0UQ, England

For My Wife Joy
And
My Daughter Heather

who honor by living Joseph Campbell's metaphor:

"If there's a path before you,
It's not yours -
and you are not on The Journey."

As sidekicks to each other's souls we witness, once again,
the unfolding garden of love's journey

Contents

Acknowledgements

My life itself, and the best heart of it,
Thanks you for this great care
Shakespeare, Henry VIII

Experience has taught me that all sincere prayers are answered. In the assembling and writing of this book, I have tried to keep the doors open to the world of spirit where our great, departed astrological brethren whisper tidbits of tantalising insights in our ears. I want to offer my deepest thanks to all who have nurtured this creative project, both here on earth and beyond.

John Clyman (Taurus ♉), not only a great trumpet teacher, a powerful and loving influence in my teens and for the rest of my life. He showed me how to harness discipline, to be tough and yet have an open heart and mind.

Sonny Rollins (Virgo ♍ - 7 September 1930, approx. 11:40 am EST, Brooklyn, NY - data from his sister) - rarely are we given a gift that keeps giving on a daily basis. Mine was a seven-month association, both professional and personal, with Sonny Rollins, the Titan of the tenor sax, and one of the handful of modern jazz geniuses. Our friendship through the years since our first gig at Shelly's Mannehole in Hollywood in December 1964 has been a great source of inspiration and intellectual stimulation to both my wife and myself. So, I was given a grace that has left its permanent mark on my soul. I stood next to my hero in the full flower of his journey and was showered by the amazing fountain of his gift. Though we talk less often in recent years, and he knows I'm into other things, he always makes a point of asking in a serious tone, "You're still playing your horn, aren't you?" A reminder from the master that without our horns, we are not whole. Thank you, Newk ... I still put "the plumbing on my face".

Ann Ree Colton (Leo ♌), the great teacher of the soul's unfolding. Shortly before her passing in 1984 she stated, "I will be with you more when I am gone." I sense a presence on my left shoulder at times like a weightless dove has alighted and coos in my ear. She saw me as a dedicated, but eclectic, student of the inner life. She knew my path was different. She had a deep rich vein of knowledge, occult and yet highly spiritual. More than anyone, she taught we are not alone.

Barbara Frigillana (Aquarius ♒), was my first serious private astrology teacher. She tirelessly extended lessons to three and four hours. Her patience with my turtle-slow learning of the more technical aspects I shall always appreciate.

Marion March (Aquarius ♒), whose Master Class was the spawning ground for my passion for phrases, philosophical and farcical. The atmosphere dedicated to a lively exchange of concepts helped me to see how to bridge astrologese with language. Always the indefatigable and enthusiastic learner and teacher, "Madame Fullcharge" has been a great example of loving service to her belief in astrology as well as the life of culture and intellectual studies. My deep gratitude to all members of her Thursday Master Class for putting up with my occasionally outlandish asides. Thank you Marion for being who you are!

<u>Marge Rosen</u> (Leo ♌) has always been there for me. I truly feel there are no "dumb questions" I could ask her. This Leo does have the open heart and I've been a huge recipient of its bounty of experience and love. She remains, from her early days with Barbara Watters to the present, a great example of the perennial student with a fascination for learning and deep love of Astrology.

<u>Noel Tyl</u> (Capricorn ♑), whose response to my "sampler" was immediate and very enthusiastic. He shares the vision of this concept with me and sees the potential as a learning tool for students and professionals. He was the one who suggested I do the chart of a famous person. I chose Winston Churchill, then Noel, then Marion March, to apply astrological aphorisms to each planet. His help will always be appreciated along with Marion's, who suggested I show it to him.

<u>Arthyr Chadbourne</u> (Leo ♌), "the Cosmic Rascal," as I call him, has been relentless in his determination to get this book published. I love the fact that he grew up with astrology and may have "forgotten more than I've learned," as the saying goes. His humor is a great attraction for me.

<u>Paul Farrell</u> (Pisces ♓). His creativity and brilliance always shower me with possibilities, never negatives. Thank you for your encouragement.

<u>Samantha</u> (Taurus ♉) and <u>Allen Cameron</u>, and <u>Mary Williams</u> (Virgo ♍). These three friends share the love of language, the poetic experience of feelings and concepts put into "shorthand" as I think of it. Encouraging and trusting of my personal process, I can't thank them enough for the quality of their loving.

<u>Becky Bascom</u> (Aries ♈), who is responsible for the original format and setting to disk of my dreadful long-hand scratchings. She tactfully referred to my handwriting as having "character". I am deeply grateful for her invaluable assistance, experience, and excitement on this project.

<u>Frank C. Clifford</u> (Aries ♈). Publishing has been characterized as "the guessing game with ulcers". Each of our trans-oceanic phone calls has been dotted with laughter as well as learning. I can only offer my deepest THANK YOU to the man willing to guess there are sufficient others with whom to share this original concept. My hope is that, as a result of his brash decision, he may be spared any gastrological events.

Introduction

I admit to being a full-blown "maximholic" - one addicted to the shorthand of meaning. Gathering quips and quotes to share in Marion March's Master Class in Astrology was the beginning. Having come up with so many pithy sayings and asides for the principles we were learning, I saw a book unfolding, one that would give astrologers, and all others in love with words and symbols, a fresh approach to the unique snowflake that is each individual chart. I set to work, placing aphorisms, snippets from poems, within the planets, signs, and houses where I thought they fit best. For example, here's what I give to the Sun in Pisces in the 12th House (☉♓12):

> "Every time I think I know who I am,
> I end up in the lost and found."
> ~ Heather Hayward

Or this, for Venus in Scorpio in the 5th House (♀♏5):

> "No time to marry. No time to settle down.
> I'm a young woman, and I ain't done runnin' 'round."
> ~ Bessie Smith

As the book began to take shape it occurred to me that the professional astrologer might find it useful as a type of Astro Desk Reference, an "A.D.R", if you will, reminiscent of the Physician's Desk Reference, or "P.D.R." I thought of the many times when I sit with the chart before my client's arrival, the same old keywords and phrases dancing in my head, and I think: What's a more interesting or provocative way to express, say, Saturn in Libra in the 12th House? With this book as a handy reference, I might turn to the Capricorn/Saturn/10th House chapter, and W.H. Auden's: "Time watches from the shadows and coughs when you would kiss." The immediate sense of a forbidden pleasure, or a too costly one would then spring to mind. If this direct quote or idea were shared during the consultation, it might allow the client to see a pattern of energy, or a cycle with a new twist to it, perhaps unlocking old beliefs about "do's" and "don'ts", or about all pleasures needing to be earned.

These are but a few of the ways this work could be used by the professional consulting astrologer, as well as by teachers, students, or the casual reader interested in exploring wordplay as a path to meaning. Let me make it clear that the choices of rulerships for a given quotation are subjective, not written in stone. You as the reader may think a quote symbolises a completely different set of astrological combinations. Great! The whole point is to ignite the reader's interest in symbolism, which for Carl Jung was "the connecting point between man and divinity."

With regard to the issue of the metaphorical meaning as opposed to literal connotation, let me use a commercial to make it clear. The audience sees an egg being fried in the pan. The voice-over says, and I paraphrase: "This is your brain on drugs." The literal egg is now transformed into the symbol of the brain and a metaphor is born.

For astrologers, on a more technical note: there are some problems which arise from a "cookbook", rulership-orientated work. For example, I have included mundane and horary rulerships among my personal and humanistic references. The choice of sign, planet, or house assigned to a given phrase is based on what I deem the essence of the quote itself, i.e., the author's subject, context, and intent. An example can be drawn from T.S. Eliot's *The Love Song of J. Alfred Prufrock*:

> "... midnight shakes the memory as a madman
> shakes a dead geranium..."

I give this to Mars in Scorpio in the 4th House (♂♏4). Conveniently, in this case, Mars rules shaking, geraniums, and madmen, Scorpio rules death and psychology, and the 4th House rules midnight and our roots in the past. The word "midnight" is my keyword to the essence of the author's intention. Hence, I would categorise this quote under Cancer/Moon/4th House.

The astrological references to quotations in this book do not, unless stated as such, refer to the horoscopes of their authors. The quotations themselves are used as astrological references, and several are repeated elsewhere in the book. The exceptions to this are in the three horoscopes in the final chapters on Winston Churchill, and astrologers Noel Tyl and Marion March. These charts are used with specific quotations to fit each planet, sign and house combination in their horoscopes.

A Note on Rulerships:
I use, for the most part, the modern planet/sign rulerships in my counseling work. For the purposes of the book, and for simplicity sake, I've used the modern rulerships exclusively. This work is already quite sophisticated without mixing traditional, or ancient, rulerships with modern ones. So, for present purposes, Pluto (♇) rules Scorpio, Uranus (♅) rules Aquarius, and Neptune (♆) rules Pisces.

My dream is for this work to be of lasting value as a reference for professional astrological counselors, teachers, students, writers, and all others in love with words and symbols. Aside from astrology, I see it as a book of collected thoughts that aims to amuse, inspire, and educate.

This work is a unique form of what used to be called a "commonplace book", in which one records passages and comments to be especially remembered or referred to, with or without arrangement.

In fact, this book is a sort of coded autobiography in that I reach back to people who have rung my personal bell, so to speak, if for only a sentence. These choices then become ciphers on the map of my personal planet. **Therefore, I should like the work to stand by itself as a collection of thoughts, others and my own, aside from astrology and the symbolism thereof, though that surely gives this compilation of quotes its distinctive tone.** Have fun with it!

David Hayward

Publisher's Note

Italicised poems at the beginning of each main chapter are by **Joseph Addison**.
D.H. signifies David Hayward.
For those of you unaware or unsure of your **Sun Sign**,
please refer to the lists on pages 227-231.

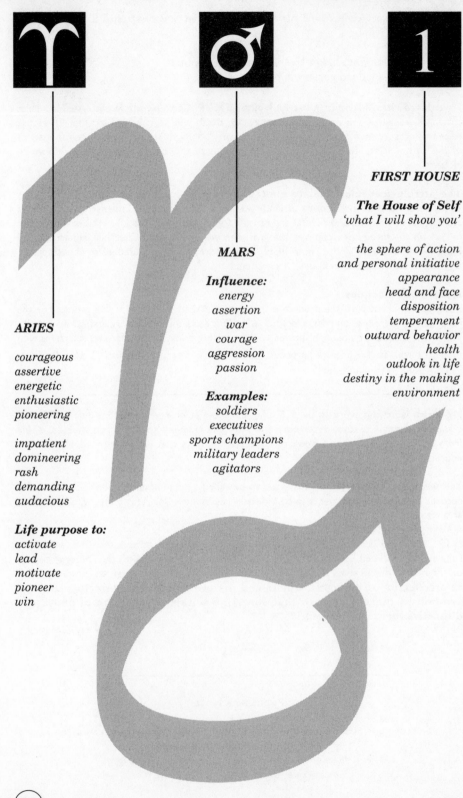

ARIES

courageous
assertive
energetic
enthusiastic
pioneering

impatient
domineering
rash
demanding
audacious

Life purpose to:
activate
lead
motivate
pioneer
win

MARS

Influence:
energy
assertion
war
courage
aggression
passion

Examples:
soldiers
executives
sports champions
military leaders
agitators

FIRST HOUSE

The House of Self
'what I will show you'

the sphere of action
and personal initiative
appearance
head and face
disposition
temperament
outward behavior
health
outlook in life
destiny in the making
environment

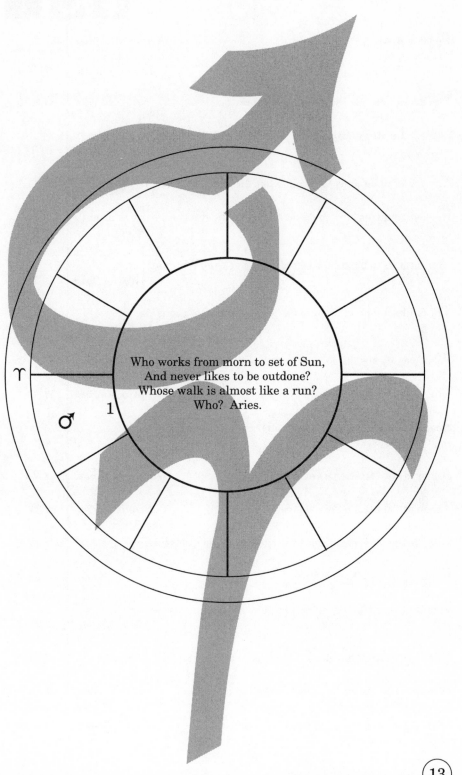

Who works from morn to set of Sun,
And never likes to be outdone?
Whose walk is almost like a run?
Who? Aries.

♈

♂   1

♈ ♂ 1

To be is to do.	*John Stuart Mill*	
To do is to be.	*Jean Paul Sartre*	
Do be, do be, do.	*Frank Sinatra*	♂ ♈ 1

You cannot escape the demand for courage.   *Emerson*   ♄ ♓ 1

I will go anywhere provided it be forward.
    David Livingston   ♂ ♈

The secret of doing is knowing when NOT to do.   *Carlos Castaneda*   ♄ ♈ 12

It doesn't matter how bold you are when the dangerous age is past.
    Noel Coward   ♄ ♈ 4

(Aries tends to be) a human doing rather than a human being.
    Wayne Dyer   ♂ ♈ 1

Think like a man of action and act like a man of thought.
    Henri Bergson   ☿ ♈ 1

What you do speaks so loud I cannot hear what you say.   *Emerson*   ☿ ♈ 7

The Lord is a man of war.   *Exodus 15:3*   ♂ ♈ 9

Speak when you're angry and you'll make the best speech
you'll never forget.   *Anon*   ♄ ♈ 3

Anger is one letter short of danger.   *Anon*   ♂ ♏ 3

Teach self control before self-esteem.   *Dennis Prager*   ♂ ♑ 1

The illusion of separation is the illusion of powerlessness.   *D.H.*   ♆ ♒ 1

Force without faith is a farce.   *Anon*   ♂ ♐ 12

War makes rattling good history, but peace is poor reading.
    Thomas Hardy   ♂ ♑ 3

Life fires at us point-blank.   *Santayana*   ♂ ♏ 1

Where is the life we have lost in the living?   *T.S. Eliot*   ♆ 1

Courage is the product of accepted discipline.   *Ann Ree Colton*   ♄ ♈ 6

Be in the present moment. The future is but the next
present moment. *Anon* | ♅ 1

Each venture is a new beginning, a raid on the inarticulate. *T.S. Eliot* | ☿ ≈ 1

Every day and each moment is a microcosm of the macrocosm
of destruction and creation acting out in our lives. *D.H.* | ♇ 1

We only get two messages from the body, one of comfort and the
other discomfort. Spirituality is extremely sensual, you need only
tune in to the body for the message of God in present time speaking
through your body. *Deepak Chopra* | ☽ ♓ 1

Know thyself, presume not God to scan; the proper study
of mankind is man. *Pope, after Plutarch* | ☿ ♏ 1

A ruffian entered my boudoir with a fowling piece. *W.C. Fields* | ♂ ♋ 12

I'm not much but I'm all I think about. *Anon* | ☿ ♓ 1

Monitor behaviour, not motives. Good motives insure nothing. *Dennis Prager* | ♄ ♍ 1

Enthusiasm can be the fire that burns away cynicism. *David Steindl-Rast* | ♂ ♑ 5

Seek to deepen and open the EXPERIENCE of life
rather than just explain its meaning. *Joseph Campbell* | ☉ ♏ 1

(On Joseph Campbell): **A**t eighty, he looked sixty; still erect
and alert, vital, and full of fun even into the last year of his life.
[Campbell had ☉ ♃ ☿ at 6° ♈ in 6th House.] *Larsen* | ☉ ♈ 6

Action, not reaction. *Krishnamurti* | ♂ ♈ 1

Our appointment with life is in the present moment. *Thich Nhat Hanh* | ♄ 1

It is true I am only one, but I am one. The fact that I cannot
do everything will not prevent me from doing what I can do. *Edward Hale* | ♃ ♑ 1

Reality comes through us, not to us. *D.H.* | ♅ 1

If you've heard the way (the Tao) in the morning,
You're ready to die in the evening.   *Confucius*   ♃ ♏ 1

If we don't get angry with those that deserve it we'll
express it to those that don't.   *Dennis Prager*   ♂ ♐ 7

The present is the only thing that never ends.   *Anon*   ♅ 1

The present contains whole case histories and
future determinations.   *Chogyam Trungpa*   ♄ ♐ 1

It may be that we've all lived before and died,
and this is hell.   *A.L. Prusick*   ♀ ♏ 1

Look out for #1 and don't step in #2.   *Rodney Dangerfield*   ♀ ♌ 1

Courage is not simply one of the virtues, but
the form of every virtue at the testing point.   *C.S. Lewis*   ♂ ♑ 9

Who are I? ... Only he who has selves has self.   *Anais Nin*   ♃ ♎ 1

There's nothing worse than a "now" look with a "then" face.
                    Dave Falk   ♄ ♒ 1

Wearing a ribbon on your lapel is moral exhibitionism.
                    William Bennett   ♃ ♓ 1

The politically correct ego-testicle world view:
A man's point of view on all issues.   *Adelaida del Castillo*   ♂ ♏ 10

An Englishman thinks he is moral when he is only uncomfortable.
                    George Bernard Shaw   ☽ ♈ 9

Anger is pain aged.   *David Viscott*   ♂ ♑ 12

The physical world exists for us only in terms of relationships.
                    R. Davenport   ♄ ♎ 1

It is only shallow people who do not judge by appearances.
                    Oscar Wilde   ☿ ♎ 1

A man's embittered features are often the petrified
bewilderment of a boy.   *Kafka*   ♄ ♓ 1

To say "I love you" one must know first how to say "I."

Ayn Rand ☉ ♌ 1

**When a personality is in full balance,
you cannot see where it ends and the soul begins.
That is a whole human being.**

Gary Zukov ♆ 1

Fear for one's daily bread destroys one's character.

Kafka ♄ ♍ 1

W.B. Yeats said of Mme. Blavatsky that she was
"the most living person alive." [She was a Leo!]

W.B. Yeats ☉ ♌ 1

The end of man is an action, not a thought, though
it were the noblest.

Carlyle ♂ ♏ 9

Why doesn't infantry mean "the trappings of infants?"

Donald C. Black ♂ ♍ 5

A "geographic" is the futility of trying to get rid of problems
by changing the location in which they were inflicted on me.

Laurens Van der Post ♄ ♓ 1

Nothing is more beautiful than cheerfulness in an old face. *Richter* ♀ ♑ 1

The outer life is proof of the inner pudding. *D.H.* ♀ 1

If the present tries to sit in judgement of the past
it will lose the future. *Winston Churchill* ♄ ♒ 1

Poor little men! Poor little strutting peacocks!
They spread out their tails as conquerors almost
as soon as they are able to walk. *Jean Anouilh* ♂ ♌ 1

The art of living is more like wrestling than dancing.

Marcus Aurelius ♂ ♎ 5

Never wear a hat that has more character than you do.

Michael Harris ♀ 1

Arnold Schwarzenegger looks like a condom full of walnuts.

Clive James ♂ ♏ 1

I rely on my personality for birth control. *Liz Winston* ♄ ♏ 1

It is good to collect things, but it is better to go on walks.

Anatole France ♂ ♋ 2

Call off the search. There is no next. This is it! *Anon* ♄ ♏ 1

When we look into the mirror we see the mask.
What is hidden behind the mask? *Diane Mariechild* ♀ 1

The heights by great men reached and kept
were not attained by sudden flight,
But they, while their companions slept,
were toiling upward in the night. *Longfellow* ♂ ♋ 4

People who know how to act are never preachers. *Emerson* ♂ ♌ 9

It takes a kind of shabby arrogance to survive in our time,
and a fairly romantic nature to want to. *Edgard Friedenberg* ♄ ♓ 1

Why not seize the pleasure at once? How often is happiness
destroyed by preparation, foolish preparation? *Jane Austen* ♀ ♉ 1

Women and men in the crowd meet and mingle,
yet with itself every soul standeth single. *Alice Cary* ☉ ♒ 1

If I have become very spiritual then there is no past. *K.N. Rao* ♅ 1

Babies and yogis have no future. *Baba Hari Dass* ♄ ♒ 1

The telling question of a person's life is whether or not he is
connected to the infinite. *Carl Jung* ☿ ♓ 1

Every hero becomes a bore at last. *Emerson* ♂ ♑ 3

Praise God in the temple of the present. *Psalm 1* ♃ ♐ 1

We aren't afraid that violence will scare our teenagers;
we're afraid that violence <u>won't</u> scare them. *Anon* ♂ ♏ 5

To respond to bullies by asking them how they feel is a
learned response; i.e., a graduate school response. *Dennis Prager* ♂ ♋ 9

Let every man first become himself that which
he teaches others to be. <u>*Gems From the East*</u> *(Blavatsky)* ☉ ♐ 1

To fight aloud is very brave,
But gallanter, I know,
Who charge within the bosom
The cavalry of woe.   *Emerson*   ♂ ♐ 12

That man is not truly brave who is afraid either to seem
or to be, when it suits him, a coward.   *Edgar Allan Poe*   ♂ ♓

We cannot afford to accumulate a deficit in the books
of human fortitude.   *Franklin D. Roosevelt*   ♄ ♈ 3

It takes far less courage to kill yourself than it takes
to make yourself wake up one more time. It's harder
to stay where you are than get out. (Waking up is
involuntary, getting up is gutsy!)   *Judith Rossner*   ♂ ♏ 12

Walk it, <u>then</u> talk it.
                                                      David Hayward   ☉ ♐ 1

I would define true courage to be a perfect sensibility
of the measure of danger, and a mental willingness
to endure it.   *William Tecumseh Sherman*   ♂ ♑ 3

Wherever you go, there you are. (Book title)   *Jon Kabat-Zinn*   ♂ ♐ 1

The enemy say Americans are good at a long shot,
but cannot stand the cold iron. I call upon you instantly
to give a lie to the slander. (Address to U.S. Infantry before
defeat of British forces at Chippawa, Canada, July 5, 1814.)
                                                  Gen. Winfield Scott   ♂ ♏ 7

Judge a man by his questions rather than by his answers.
                                                      Voltaire   ♃ ♊ 1

Drop the cry of I;
Here's why:
When I comes on,
Folks yawn;
What's more, they snore.
I get by
by dropping I.   *Willard Espy*   ♄ ♌ 1

Everything that has anything to do with the cult
of personality has always been painful to me.   *Einstein*   ♄ ♌ 1

I wonder why men can get serious at all. They have
this delicate long thing hanging outside their bodies,
which goes up and down by its own will ... if I were a man
I would always be laughing at myself.   *Yoko Ono*   ♂ ♏ 1

Why torture yourself when life will do it for you?   *Laura Walker*   ♄ ♏ 1

**Some mornings it just doesn't seem worth it
to gnaw through the leather straps.**
                                                          Emo Philips   ♄ ♏ 1

Now is a gift -- that's why they call it the present.   *Anon*   ♀ 1

Go away!   *Florence King*   ♂ ♒ 7

The one true thought you can hold about the past is:
it is not here. Healing can only take place in the present.
                                                      A Course in Miracles   ♄ ♍ 1

The present moment is never a new beginning because
we keep it from becoming one.   *Jon Kabat-Zinn*   ♄ ♒ 1

The word made flesh.   *The Bible*   ♃ ♊ 1

We do not attach ourselves lastingly to anything
that has not cost us care, labor or longing.   *Honoré de Balzac*   ♄ ♋ 1

Character consists of what you do on the third and fourth tries.
                                                        James Michener   ♃ ♑ 1

Life happens too fast for you to ever think about it.
If you could just persuade people of this, but they insist
on amassing information.   *Kurt Vonnegut*   ♅ 1

It doesn't matter how slowly you go so long as you do not stop.
                                                          Confucious   ♄ ♈

A face unclouded by thought. (On Norma Shearer.)
                                                        Lillian Hellman   ☿ ♓ 1

Toward the end of her life she looked like a hungry insect
magnified a million times -- a praying mantis that had
forgotten how to pray.   *Quentin Crisp*   ♄ ♏ 1

A character who, if he did not exist, could not
be imagined. (On Oscar Levant.) *S.N. Behrman* ♆ 1

Cruelty is a mystery, and the waste of pain. *Annie Dillard* ♂ ♏ 12

You can't strengthen the weak by weakening the strong.
Attributed to Abraham Lincoln ♂ ♓ 10

Blessed is the man who, having nothing to say,
abstains from giving wordy evidence of the fact. *George Eliot* ♄ ♈ 9

The people who make no roads are ruled out from intellectual
participation in the world's brotherhood. *Margaret Fairless Barber* ♂ ♊ 11

Where is the life we've lost in the living? *T.S. Eliot* ♆ 1

Everyone has had at least one out-of-body experience: birth.
Hester Mundis ☽ ♓ 1

There's no time like the present to start thinking about tomorrow.
Hester Mundis ☿ ♒ 1

After the massacre
They pacified their conscience
by telling jokes. *W.H. Auden* ♂ ♊ 8

What does the blonde say when you blow in her ear?
"Thanks for the refill." *Anon* ♃ ♊ 1

Middle age is when a narrow waist and a broad mind
begin to change places. *Glenn Dorenbush* ♃ ♊ 1

Personal things is all I care about. *Kathleen Fraser* ☽ ♌ 1

Life shrinks or expands in proportion to one's courage.
Anais Nin ♂ ♈ 1

There is no such thing as bravery; only degrees of fear.
John Wainwright ♄ ♈ 1

You don't learn to hold your own in the world
by standing on guard, but by attacking, and getting
well hammered yourself. *George Bernard Shaw* ♄ ♈ 1

Never let your head hang down. Never give up and sit down
and grieve. Find another way. And don't pray when it rains
if you don't pray when the sun shines.   *Satchel Paige*   ♄ ♈ 9

Courage is fear holding on a minute longer.   *George Patton*   ♄ ♈ 1

Substance is not "stance" enough: you must also heed
circumstance. The wrong manner turns everything sour,
even justice and reason. The right one makes up for
everything: it turns a "no" golden, sweetens truth,
and makes even old age look pretty.   *Baltasar Gracian*   ♀ ♑ 1

Great emergencies and crises show us how much greater
our vital resources are than we had supposed.   *William James*   ♂ ♌ 2

Razors are the scrapes of bath.   *M. Rose Pierce*   ♂ ♋ 1

Debriefing is letting it all hang out.   *M. Rose Pierce*   ♂ ♍

I like a man who talks me to death, provided he is amusing;
t saves so much trouble.   *Mary Shelley*   ♂ ♊ 8

We can live ourselves into right thinking, but we cannot
think ourselves into right living.   *Chuck C.*   ♊ 1

Be the future you now.   *Bashar*   ♅ 1

        For we cannot tarry here,
            We must march my darlings, we must bear
                the brunt of danger,
            We the youthful sinewy races, all the rest on
                us depend, Pioneers! O Pioneers!   *Walt Whitman*   ♂ ♒ 1

Some men are so macho they'll get you pregnant
just to kill a rabbit.   *Maureen Murphy*   ♂ ♏ 6

Men grow tired of sleep, love, singing and dancing
sooner than of war.   *Homer*   ♂ ♈ 7

The basic fact about human existence is not that it is a tragedy,
but that it is a bore.   *H.L. Mencken*   ♄ ♊ 1

We are all strong enough to bear the misfortunes of others.
          Duc de la Rochefoucald   ♂ ♎ 12
          ♄ ♎ 1

I once saw a woman on an elevator carrying a book of mine.
She held the book backwards so I could see myself peering over
her elbow. I found looking at myself very disconcerting.
And when she had left the elevator I had a terrible feeling
that she was taking my face away with her, leaving me nothing
to shave in the morning.   *John Cheever*   ☿ ≈ 1

Joseph Campbell was interested in the active participation
and experience of life more than finding out its meaning.
                                        David Steindl-Rast   ☉ ♈ 6

Action minus integrity is an abuse of power.
                                        David Hayward   ♂ ♑ 1

Trying to define yourself is like trying to bite your own teeth.
                                        Alan Watts   ☿ ♑ 1

I'm extraordinarily patient provided I get my own way in the end.
                                        Margaret Thatcher   ♄ ♌ 1

Personal growth -- SEE TUMOR.   *Rick Bayan*   ♃ ♏ 1

My advice to those who are about to begin, in earnest,
the journey of life, is to take their heart in one hand
and a club in the other.   *Josh Billings*   ♂ ♌ 1

Self reliance is the perfection of reliance on God.   *Emerson*   ♃ ♑ 1

For he who lives more lives than one,
More deaths than one must die.   *Oscar Wilde*   ♃ ♏ 1

Why do blondes have TGIF written on their shoes?
        Toes go in first.   *Anon*   ♀ ♓ 1

If she gets one more face-lift, her ears are going to meet. *Anon*   ☿ ♎ 1

I daily reclaim the lines of doing that run across my forehead.
They are the signatures of coping.   *D.H.*   ☽ ♑ 1
                                                                  ♂ ♊ 6

It is better to face the flaw than pace the floor. *Jonathan Murro*   ♄ ♍ 1

Keep your power just in the day that you are living
on the Earth, and not on how to maneuver tomorrow.
                                        Gary Zukov   ♇ ♏ 1

Rather than a soul in a body, become a body in a soul.

Gary Zukov   ♆ 1

Action: the last resource of those who know not how to dream.

Oscar Wilde   ♄ ♈ 12

She got her good looks from her father. He's a plastic surgeon.

Groucho Marx   ♆ ♌ 1

Admiration is our polite recognition of another's resemblance
to ourselves.   *Ambrose Bierce*   ☿ ♎ 1

Discipline is the background of character.   *John Locke*   ♄ 1

Chop your own wood and it warms you twice.   *Thoreau*   ♄ 1

He has all the charisma of gravel. (On Bill Bradley)

Dave Barry   ♄ 1

Such an active lass. So outdoorsy. She loves nature
in spite of what it did to her. (On Princess Anne)   *Bette Midler*   ♄ ♉ 1

He looks and talks like he just fell off Edgar Bergen's lap.
(On Gerald Ford)   *David Steinberg*   ♄ ♊ 1

With his punk hairdo wound in spines like darts,
he presented a most jaculiferously hirsute visage.   *D.H.*   ♂ ♒ 1

Don't become a cloud because you failed to become a star.

Robert Savage   ♆ ♑ 1

**Men wear their hair in three ways:
parted, unparted, and departed.**

Robert Savage   ♂ ♒ 1

Autobiography is an unrivaled vehicle for telling
the truth about other people.   *Philip Guedalla*   ☿ ♎ 1

I don't think most Westerners, even around here (L.A.),
take karma seriously. Therefore they don't need to address
the consequences, i.e. the power, of their actions. So the dots
<u>don't</u> get connected and the illusion of Separation continues;
the belief that Terrestrial and Celestial are separate.   *D.H.*   ⛢ 1

Some astrologers are expert Physiognomists: ascendant obsessives.

D.H. ♅ ♏ 1

Humility is no substitute for a good personality.

Fran Lebowitz ☽ ♓ 1

Habit is a great deadener. *Samuel Beckett* ♄ ♏ 1

I hold that I am not responsible for the meaningfulness
or meaninglessness of life, but that I am responsible for
what I do with my own unique life. *Hermann Hesse* ♄ ♒ 1
♁ 1

Keep your broken arm inside your sleeve. *Chinese Proverb* ♂ ♓ 6

A man wrapped up in himself makes a very small package.

Robert Savage ♄ ♌ 1

Every conflict that has not been suffered to the end
and resolved will recur. *Hermann Hesse* ♂ ♏

Never contend with a man who has nothing to lose.

Baltasar Gracian ♂ ♎ 12

Go after a man's weakness, and never, ever, threaten
unless you're going to follow through, because if you don't,
the next time you won't be taken seriously. *Roy M. Cohn* ♂ ♎ 12

SECOND HOUSE

The House of Possessions
'my stuff'

the sphere or prosperity
possessions of all kinds
resources
sense of values
earned income
money
sources of income

VENUS

Influence:
appreciation
desire
values
sensuality
pleasure
attraction
food

Examples:
performers
artists
cooks
agriculturists
collectors

TAURUS

patient
grounded
practical
consistent
sensuous

stubborn
indulgent
lustful
lethargic
possessive

Life purpose to:
acquire
shelter
enjoy
sustain
build

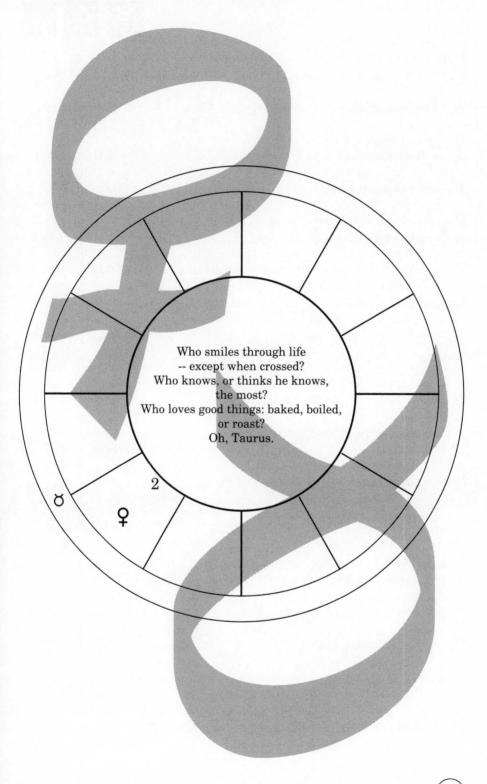

Who smiles through life
-- except when crossed?
Who knows, or thinks he knows,
the most?
Who loves good things: baked, boiled,
or roast?
Oh, Taurus.

If you live according to nature you will never be poor;
if according to opinion you'll never be rich.   *Seneca the Younger*   ☿ ☉ 2

We've exchanged being for having.   *Laurens Van der Post*   ☉ 2

The present moment is never intolerable;
see the flowers not the weeds.   *D.H.*   ☿ ☉ 1

The lust for comfort murders the passion of the soul.   *Gibran*   ♀ ♏ 2

Desires as fierce as hunger -- one by one they all grow still
-- like old hawks in the sun.   *Loren Eiseley*   ♄ ♏ 2

The measure of my tithing is the measure of my fear.   *D.H.*   ♄ ♍ 2

Bart Simpson says Grace:
    "Dear God, we paid for all this stuff ourselves,
    so thanks for nothing."   *Matt Groening*   ♄ ☉ 9

The impassable chasm between get and give.   *Paul Brunton*   ♄ ♌ 2

Narcissism is the handmaiden of materialism.   *D.H.*   ♀ ♌ 2

Money doesn't talk, it swears.
                                Bob Dylan   ♂ ♊ 2

Life's a shit sandwich; the more bread, the better.
                                Jonathan Winters   ♇ ♍ 2

Whoring and hoarding both involve holding.   *D.H.*   ♄ ♏ 2

If one has $100 he has more than Jesus, Buddha and St. Francis
combined when they lived in the world.   *Jonathan Murro*   ♄ ♓ 2

Millionaires don't hire astrologers, billionaires do.   *J.P. Morgan*   ♃ ♒ 2

If you value your time, tithe it.   *D.H.*   ♄ ♍ 2

Affluence is my ability to access the abundance of the universe.
                                Anon   ♃ ☉ 12

Money is something you've got to make in case you don't die.
                                Max Asnas   ♇ 2

Make money and the whole world will conspire to call you a
gentleman. *Mark Twain*   ♃ ♉ 10

Money is human happiness in the abstract. *Schopenhauer*   ☽ ♓ 2

Money isn't everything but it's a long way ahead of
what comes next. *Edmond Stockdale*   ♃ ♉ 1

Pleasure for an hour, a bottle of wine;
pleasure for a year, marriage; pleasure for a lifetime, a garden.
Chinese Saying   ♄ ♉ 4

Nowadays the family who buys together cries together. *Anon*   ♄ ♋ 2

We must like what we have when we don't have what we like.
Roger de Bussy-Rabutin   ♄ ♉ 2

To be able to use leisure intelligently will be the last product
of an intelligent civilization. *George Bernard Shaw*   ♃ ♉ 9

There are two things to aim at in life:
first, to get what you want, and after that to enjoy it.
Logan Pearsall Smith   ♃ ♉ 11

> **To really enjoy the better things in life,**
> **one must first have enjoyed the things**
> **they are better than.**
> *Oscar Homolka*   ♃ ♉ 2

If you resolve to give up smoking, drinking, and loving,
you don't actually live longer, it just seems longer. *Clement Freud*   ♄ ♉ 6

ECOCIDE: The Fall of the Wild. Devaluation of Planet Worth.
Creating the nozone layer. Go waste, young man.
M. Rose Pierce   ♄ ♏ 2

The expression of gratitude is a powerful force that generates
more of what we've already received. *Deepak Chopra*   ♃ ♉ 2

Every excess causes a defect; every defect an excess.
Every sweet has its sour; every evil its good. If riches increase,
they are increased that use them. If the gatherer gathers
too much, Nature takes out of the man what she puts
into his chest; swells the estate, but kills the owner. *Emerson*   ♇ ♎ 2

Strengthening the weak by weakening the strong is Robin Hoodism.	*Anon*	♄ ♈ 2	
Delayed gratification.	*Anon*	♄ ♉ 5	
Money not only changes hands, it changes people.	*Anon*	☿ ♉ 11	
I am at two with nature.	*Woody Allen*	♊ 2	
The man is richest whose pleasures are cheapest.	*Thoreau*	♄ ♉ 2	
Sensuality is the voice of young men and old nations.	*W.E.H. Lecky (1869)*	♀ ♉ 10	
Money talks right up to the doors of hell.	*Fr. Malachi Martin*	☿ ♏ 2	
If we did not see it with our own eyes, could we never imagine the extraordinary disproportion created between men by a larger or smaller degree of wealth?	*La Bruyère (1688)*	♄ ♒ 2	
When I think of all the sorrow and the barrenness that has been wrought in my life by want of a few more pounds per annum than I was able to earn, I stand aghast at money's significance.	*George Gissing*	♃ ♉ 12	
Those who have some means think that the most important thing in the world is love. The poor know that it is money.	*Gerald Brenan*	☉ ♉ 12	
I sit and worry about money who very soon will have to die.	*Peter Porter*	♄ ♏ 2	
One must be poor to know the luxury of giving.	*George Eliot*	♀ ♌ 12	
Palm Beach County, Florida, has the largest number of Rolls Royces in the nation -- one for every 13,000 citizens.	*Lucius Beebe*	♃ ♉ 3	
Eighty percent of today's millionaires are first generation millionaires.	*Govt. Statistic*	♃ ♉ 4	
It's hard to pull yourself up by the bootstraps when you're wearing top-siders.	*Howard Ogden*	♄ ♓ 2	

Individuals no longer exist. They have liquidated themselves
in their demand for comfort.   *Kafka*   ♅ ♏ 2

Desire has no memory.   *Anon*   ♀ ♋ 2

What's the use of money if you have to earn it?   *George B. Shaw*   ♄ ♉ 6

You can have anything you want if you give up the belief
that you don't have it.   *Robert Anthony*   ♄ ♉ 9

> **No man divulges his revenue,**
> **or at least which way it comes in:**
> **but everyone publishes his acquisitions.**
>   *Montaigne (1580)*   ♃ ♏ 2

The value of the universe contrives to throw itself into every point.
                                                        Emerson   ♃ ♉ 12

The only reason in the world to have money, is to tell
any S.O.B. in the world to go to hell.   *Humphrey Bogart*   ♇ 2
                                                                                  ☿ ♈ 2

Give all thou canst; high heaven rejects the lore of
nicely-calculated less or more.   *Wordsworth*   ♃ ♌ 2

Where there is too much, something is missing.   *Leo Rosten*   ♃ ♉ 12

Luxury is more deadly than any foe.   *Juvenal*   ♀ ♏ 2

After death, entering into the spiritual plane, you have all the
abundance you could possibly need. You think and you create.
The wonders of the universe are there for your making,
for your enjoying.   *Li Sung*   ♃ ♏ 2

If every pebble became a priceless ruby, then pebble and ruby
would become equal in value.   *Gems From the East* (Blavatsky)   ♀ ♑ 2

Money brings you food but not appetite, medicine but not health,
acquaintances but not friends, servants but not faithfulness,
days of joy but not peace or happiness.   *Henrik Ibsen*   ♄ ♉ 2

Superstition, idolatry, and hypocrisy have ample wages,
but truth goes a-begging.   *Martin Luther*   ♄ ♐ 2

Money never goes to jail.   *Anon*   ♃ ♉ 12

Each person is born with one possession which out values all others -- his last breath. *Mark Twain* ☿ ♏ 2

It's easy to be independent when you've got money. But to be independent when you haven't -- that's the Lord's test. *Mahalia Jackson* ♃ ♒ 2

We shall never solve the paradox of want in the midst of plenty by doing away with plenty. *Ogden Mills* ♄ ♉ 2

Money isn't everything, but lack of money isn't anything. *Franklin P. Adams (F.P.A.)* ♄ ♉ 2

A change of fortune hurts a wise man no more than a change of the moon. *Ben Franklin* ☽ ♐ 2

Money, which represents the prose of life, and which is hardly spoken of in parlors without an apology, is, in its effects and laws, as beautiful as roses. *Emerson* ♀ ♊ 2

Each dollar is a soldier that does your bidding. *Vincent Astor* ♀ ♈ 2

It is not easy to determine the nature of music, or why anyone should have a knowledge of it. *Aristotle* ♀ ♏ 12

He that is of the opinion money will do everything, may well be suspected of doing anything for money. *Ben Franklin* ♆ 2

Music, the greatest good that mortals know, and all of heaven we have below. *Joseph Addison* ♃ ♓ 2

The oldest, truest, most beautiful organ of music, the origin to which alone our music owes its being, is the human voice.
Richard Wagner ♄ ♉ 3

No good opera plot can be sensible, for people do not sing when they are feeling sensible. *W.H. Auden* ♄ ♉ 5

In the end it all depends on a libretto. A libretto, a libretto and the opera is made! *Giuseppe Verdi* ♀ ♊ 5

"My sons are mine; this wealth is mine:" with such thoughts is a fool tormented. He himself does not belong to himself, much less sons and wealth. *Gems From the East (Blavatsky)* ♇ 2 ☿ ♌ 2

It is extraordinary how music sends one back into memories of the past -- and it is the same with smells.   *George Sand*   ♀ ♓ 4

One flower is beautiful, a surfeit of flowers is vulgar.   *Einstein*   ♃ ♉

They had so much money that when they cashed a check the bank bounced.   *Anon*   ♃ ♉ 2

"Bless me," he (Socrates) said, looking around the market where all an Athenian wanted lay piled in glowing profusion, "What a lot of things there are a man can do without."
Edith Hamilton   ♄ ♉ 2

I will never abdicate. I shall always want everything. To accept my life I must prefer it.   *Marie Lenéru*   ☉ 2

Some people are more turned on by money than they are by love ... in one respect they're alike. They're both wonderful as long as they last.   *Abigail van Buren*   ♀ 5

There's a certain Buddhistic calm that comes from having ... money in the bank.   *Tom Robbins*   ♃ ♋ 2

Nature is not anthropomorphic.   *Lao Tzu*   ♄ ♌ 2

Wind moving through grass so that the grass quivers. This moves me with an emotion I don't even understand.
Katherine Mansfield   ♀ ♉ 12
                                                                   ☿ ♉ 12

Every individual is an expression of the whole realm of nature, a unique action of the total universe.   *Alan Watts*   ♃ ♉ 1

Venus is high maintenance: love, money, friends, art, fashion -- the gardens of desire.   *D.H.*   ♀ ♎ 2

Nothing is a stronger force for conservation than the profit motive.
Richard Ebeling   ♄ ♉ 2

Most men would be willing to earn their money honestly if it didn't take so long.   *Anon*   ♄ ♏ 2

There is nothing useless in nature; not even uselessness itself.
Montaigne   ♉ 12

Nature has neither kernel nor shell; she is everything at once.

Goethe | ♃ ♉ 12

Whether you like it or not, whether you know it or not,
secretly all nature seeks God and works toward him.

Meister Eckhart | ♃ ♉ 12

I believe in God, only I spell it Nature. *Frank Lloyd Wright* | ☿ ♉ 9

The world is not to be put in order, the world is order incarnate.
It is for us to put ourselves in unison with this order.

Henry Miller | ♃ ♉ 10

My father considered a walk among the mountains
as the equivalent of churchgoing. *Aldous Huxley* | ☉ ♉ 9

What I know of the divine science and Holy Scripture
I learnt in woods and fields. *Saint Bernard* | ☿ ♉ 9

Speak to the earth, and it shall teach thee. *Job 12:8* | ☿ ♉ 9

Earth, with her thousand voices, praises God. *Coleridge* | ♃ ♉ 3

Your day is one of leisure in which you search for pleasure.
You're bored when you're adored; you're blasé. *Song, Anon* | ♄ ♉ 1

Leisure is the time for doing something useful. *Ben Franklin* | ♀ ♑ 6

If artists and poets are unhappy, it is after all because happiness
does not interest them. *Santayana* | ♀ ♋ 12

**Rembrandt painted about 700 paintings --
of these, 3,000 are in existence.**

William Bode | ♀ ♏ 12

A rich man's joke is always funny. *Thomas E. Brown* | ♂ ♉ 3

Money is not the most important thing in the world. Love is.
Fortunately, I love money. *Jackie Mason* | ♀ ♉ 2

Attachment is the biggest obstacle. I, me, mine is the biggest
obstacle. "Mine" is the most dangerous obstacle because if you
put it around you, it explodes ... it becomes a battlefield filled
with mines. Renounce the mines. *Swami Satchitananda*

♂ ♉ 2
♀ ♌ 1
♄ ♈ 2

The easiest way for your children to learn about money
is for you not to have any.   *Katharine Whitehorn*   ♄ ♉ 5

When it comes to money, everybody is of the same religion.
                                                Voltaire   ♀ ♐ 2

Be vulgar in nothing. Certainly not in your taste. What a wise
person it was who did not want his things to please the many!
The discreet never gorge themselves on vulgar applause.
Some people are such puffed-up chameleons of popularity
that they enjoy the breath of the crowd more than the
gentle breezes of Apollo.   *Baltasar Gracian*   ♄ ♒ 2

A poor person who is unhappy is in a better position than a rich
person who is unhappy. Because the poor person has hope.
He thinks money would help.   *Jean Kerr*   ♃ ♉ 12

For if I am so rich, if I have so much,
If they see me surrounded by every luxury,
It is because of my noble lineage
That builds castles on my pillow.   *Juana de Barbourou*   ♅ ♌ 2

He's like a blister -- doesn't show up until all the work is done.
                                                Anon   ♄ ♉ 6

We had the laziest rooster. He never crowed. He'd wait for the
rooster next door to crow, and he'd just nod.   *Anon*   ☿ ♉ 1

An economist is a man who wears a watch chain with a Phi Beta
Kappa key at one end and no watch at the other.   *Harry Truman*   ♄ ♉

Capitalism is the only system that can be defended
and validated by reason.   *Ayn Rand*   ♃ ♑ 2

Wealth by which some people think to get a reputation,
does but expose the more their weaknesses and follies.   *Anon*   ♄ ♌ 2

Normally he was the happiest of men. He asked so little of life
that its frugal bounty amazed and delighted him.
                                                Margery Allingham   ♃ ♉

He's been on his back so long, he hasn't seen his shadow in years.
                                                Anon   ♄ ♉ 12

A sperm bank is only a place whose come has time.   *Anon*   ♄ ♏ 2

♉ ♀ 2

With the great part of rich people, the chief employment
of riches consists in the parade of riches. *Adam Smith* ♃ ♉ 10
♀ ♌ 10

The other day he retired form his job, and nobody knew. *Anon* ♄ ♉ 6

Earth's crammed with heaven,
And every common bush afire with God;
But only he who sees, takes off his shoes --
The rest sit around it and pluck blackberries ...
Elizabeth Barrett Browning ♃ ♓ 2

If poverty causes crime, then affluence causes virtue.
Dennis Prager ☿ ♉ 2

Basic values aren't innate, they're passed down ...
what really needs to be said, needs to be said over
and over again, generation to generation,
otherwise a generation misses it
and they don't get it because it's lost.
Joseph Campbell ♃ ♋ 2

There is no way to prosperity -- prosperity is the way. *Icus* ♃ ♐ 2

Seek not, my soul, the life of the immortals; but enjoy to the full
the resources that are within thy reach. *Pindar* ♃ ♉ 1
♉ 3

Don't wish for what's not yours. If you are poor you may
have taken a vow of poverty in the past (a past life) which will
give you only necessities in the midst of wealth around you.
Ann Ree Colton ☋ ♓ 2

Our values are mirrored back to us by how we use our time,
who we associate with and why. *D.H.* ♄ ♎ 2

I prayed for it all. I just didn't think it would cost me everything.
Heather Hayward ♃ ♏ 2

Great spenders are bad lenders. *Ben Franklin* ♉ 8

He doesn't even walk in his sleep. He hitchhikes. *Anon* ☿ ♉ 12

Go ahead, trust yourself if you think you need a new outfit for
every day of the week every week of the year. Spontaneity is
actually the Tao principle of action. Called wu-wei in Chinese, it
becomes whoo-whee! In Bloomingdale's pretty fast. *Hester Mundis* ♂ ♉ 9

When people say: "She's got everything," I've only got one answer: "I haven't had tomorrow."   *Elizabeth Taylor*   ♄ 2

A collectible is an addictive substance that demands a staggering portion of our discretionary income, so that we might die with a complete set of vintage Pez dispensers and $180.00 in the bank.
                                                    Rick Bayan   ☽ ♉ 8

Oh roses for the flush of youth,
And laurel for the perfect prime;
But pluck an ivy branch for me
Grown old before my time.   *Christina Rossetti*   ♄ ♉

Whatever you can lose, you should reckon of no account.
                                                    Publilius Syrus   ♆ 2

Everything in Nature contains all the powers of Nature.
Everything is made of one hidden stuff.   *Emerson*   ♃ ♉ 12

Any man who has to ask about the annual upkeep of a yacht can't afford one.   *J.P. Morgan*   ♄ ♓ 2

There are a lot of men in this world who started at the bottom
-- and stayed there.   *Anon*   ♂ ♑ 2
                                                                ♂ ♉ 12

Nothing makes a woman's clothes go out of style faster than her husband's raise in salary.   *Anon*   ☽ ♉ 7

Contentment is when your earning power equals your yearning power.   *Anon*   ♃ ♉ 1

Sell your cleverness and buy bewilderment; cleverness is mere opinion; bewilderment is intuition.   *Rumi*   ♆ ♊ 2

Jet Set - gypsies with money; a cosmopolitan clique of traveling hedonists who cultivate glamour at the expense of character.
The high-school in-crowd on a global scale.   *Rick Bayan*   ♀ ♐ 5

The biggest lie on the planet: "When I get what I want
I will be happy."   *Robert Anthony*   ☿ ♓ 2

Affluence detaches. It removes you from the old and eternal, it gets you out of the rain. Affluence and technology detach absolutely.   *Peggy Noonan*   ☿ ♒ 2

Only that which does not teach, does not cry out,
does not persuade, does not condescend, does not explain,
is irresistible. *W.B. Yeats* | ♄ 2

Earth is the Garden of Desire and the Hothouse of Ego. *D.H.* | ♀ ♏ 1

You've no idea what it costs to keep the old man in poverty.
Lord Mountbatten | ♃ ♉ 12

One reason it's so hard to save money is that our neighbors
are always buying something we can't afford. *Anon* | ♉ 3

It's true that money talks, but in these days a dollar doesn't
have enough cents to say anything worthwhile. *Anon* | ☿ 2

We're all born brave, trusting and greedy, and most of us
remain greedy. *Mignon McLaughlin* | ♃ ♉ 1

Finance is the art of passing currency from hand to hand
until it finally disappears. *Robert Sarnoff* | ♆ ♊ 2

Fernando Valenzuela now makes one million dollars a year.
Three years ago Valenzuela's alarm clock was a rooster.
Tommy Lasorda | ♄ ♉ 6

He who dies with the most toys dies anyway. *Anon* | ♇ 2

A work ill done must be done twice. [The 2nd House rules the
second occurrence of something.] *Howell* | ♄ ♍ 2

I am wearing an interesting fragrance; you are overdoing it;
she stinks. *Sydney J. Harris* | ☿ ♉ 1

**The admirable firmness in ourselves is detestable
stubbornness in others.**
Laurence J. Peter | ♉ 7

I take advantage of "great facilities;" you live beyond your means;
he is wildly in debt. *Sydney J. Harris* | ☉ ♉ 7

The lilacs are flowering, sweet and sublime,
     with perfume that goes to the head;
And lovers meander in prose and rhyme,
     trying to say, for the thousandth time,
     what's easier done than said. *Piet Hein* | ☿ ♉ 5

Laziness is nothing more than the habit of resting
before you get tired.   *Jules Renard*   ♄ ♉ 6

A minute in the mouth, two hours in the stomach,
and forever on your hips.   *Anon*   ♀ ♋ 1

Workers of the world, relax.   *Anon*   ☽ ♉ 6

Many speak the truth when they say they despise riches,
but they mean the riches possessed by other men.   *Charles Colton*   ♄ ♉ 7

One man's trash is another man's treasure.   *Anon*   ♏ 2

The rich man has his ice in the summer and the poor man
gets his in the winter.   *Scottish Proverb*   ♄ ♉

As for the trumpet: I'll probably be putting plumbing on my face
'til I take a dirt nap.   *D.H.*   ♀ ♏ 1

> **S**mell was the first of our senses, and it was so
> **successful that in time the small lamp of olfactory**
> **tissue atop the nerve cord grew into a brain.**
> **Our cerebral hemispheres were originally**
> **buds from the olfactory stalks.**
> **We think because we <u>smelled</u>.**
>   *Diane Ackerman*   ♃ ♉ 3

3

THIRD HOUSE

The House of Environment
'how I think'

the sphere of communication
mental interests
letters and books
perception and speech
early education
short journeys
siblings

MERCURY

Influence:
exchange
observation
communication
information
thoughts / ideas
reason

Examples:
messengers / clerks
public relations
advertisers
translators
retailers
writers

GEMINI

versatile
quick-witted
inquisitive
curious
logical

inconsistent
superficial
highly-strung
fickle
gossipy

Life purpose to:
communicate
learn
observe
imitate
experiment

Who's fond of life and jest and pleasure:
Who vacillates and changes ever?
Who loves attention without measure?
Why, Gemini.

3

☿

♊

What's between the ears is sexier than what's between the legs. *D.H.*	☿ ♈ 8
Conversation is 90% talking and 10% listening. *Anon*	☿ ♌ 1
The test of a voracious mind is its veracity. *D.H.*	♃ ♏ 3
My mind is my garden, my thoughts are my seeds; I will harvest either flowers or weeds. *Anon*	☿ ♉ 6
The power men possess to annoy me I give them by a weak curiosity. *Emerson*	♄ ♊ 12
Communication intensified becomes communion. *Anon*	♃ ♊ 12
Rumors spreading like a stain. *W.H. Auden*	♃ ♊ 11
"**I**f" is a very safe word; it speculates rather than commits. Its comfort is convenience, not commitment. *D.H.*	☿ ♋ 5
The meaning doesn't matter if it's only idle chatter. *W.S. Gilbert*	☽ ♊ 12
With a 70% functional illiteracy rate among teenagers, we have woefully failed to nourish our most cherished resource. *D.H.*	♄ ♌ 3 ♄ ♋ 2
If other people are going to talk, conversation simply becomes impossible. *Whistler*	♄ ♊ 7
Egotists are always confusing conceit with conversation. *Anon*	☿ ♌ 1
Garbage in, garbage out. *Anon*	♇ 3
It is when man is tossed about mentally or can center his thoughts on nothing in particular that disharmony, and diseased conditions are produced in his body. *H.P. Blavatsky*	☿ ♓ 6
Jargon is local parlance. *Anon*	☿ 3
Before one can go beyond the intellect one must have an intellect. *T.S. Eliot*	♃ ♐ 3
Strategic misrepresentation misinforms while it disinforms. *D.H.*	♄ ♏ 3

To always ask why this word was used and not another
remains the way in which I read everything (which is the reason
I read so slowly).   *Dennis Prager* | ♍ 3

Saturn's rings are comprised of lost airline luggage.
                                                      Mark Russell | ♄ ♐ 3

The original three R's were "reading, reckoning, and rhetoric"
-- a triad known to alarmingly few pedagogues.   *Donald C. Black* | 3

The threat of obliteration produces obliterature.   *James Thurber* | ♀ 3

Don't program yourself to reinforce your current limits.
                                                      Charles Tart | ♄ ♊ 1

If a man say, "I love God," and hateth his brother, he is a liar.
                                                      I John 4:20 | ♄ ♊ 9

Hands that heal are holier than lips that pray.   *Sai Baba* | ☿ ♍ 9

The tongue is the flower of the heart.   *Chinese Medicine* | ♀ ♌ 3

A double minded man is unstable in all his ways.   *The Bible* | ♆ 3

Mind over mattress.   *Stephen Covey* | ♀ ♊ 8

Reading is to the mind what exercise is to the body.
                                                  Sir Richard Steele | ☿ ♊ 6

Most trade books have a shelf life somewhere between milk
and yogurt.   *Anon* | ♄ ♋ 3

In the little gap between thoughts is the window,
the transformational vortex, where I and cosmic mind
communicate.   *Deepak Chopra* | ♆ 3

Where is the knowledge we have lost in information?
                                                      T.S. Eliot | ♆ ♒ 3

nobody, not even the rain, has such small hands.
                                                     e.e. cummings | ♄ ♋ 3

Words are like leaves and where they most abound,
much fruit of sense beneath is rarely found.   *Pope* | ♃ ♍ 3

By writing and speaking about events gone by we can
communicate to some extent with the past. To do this
regularly and intelligently is to expand our being in time.

Robert Grudin ♃ ♑ 3

Youth sees an endless hourglass; age hears the grains running out.

D.H. ♄ ♊ 8

A gossip talks to you about others, a bore talks about himself,
and a brilliant conversationalist talks to you about yourself. *Anon*

☿ ♊ 7

Conversation is a contest in which the first person
to draw a breath is declared the listener.

Anon ☿ 3

A proverb is a short sentence distilled from long experience.

Cervantes ♄ ♓ 3

Yes, in America you have the right of free speech -- provided,
of course, you're dumb enough to actually try it. *Anon*

♅ ♑ 3

You teach best what you most need to learn. *Richard Bach*

♇ ♐ 3

Nothing learned is new. We are simply re-cognizing and
accessing a forgotten reality. Re-membering is re-joining. *D.H.*

♄ ♒ 3

The most potent weapon in the hands of the oppressor
is the mind of the oppressed. *Steve Biko*

♏ 3

Answers without action are like cars without gas. *D.H.*

♄ ♈ 3

A fool is his own informer. *Yiddish Proverb*

♄ ♊ 7

Terms threatened with extinction: "Husband" and "Wife."
They are too exclusive; one should say "domestic partner," or
"significant other," lest we offend someone (or something)
who is gay, Lesbian, Bisexual, Transgendered, or
gender-confused. *Cartoon*

♄ ♊ 7

The known is a greater threat than the unknown
because of its rigid, locked in, patterns from the past.

Deepak Chopra ☿ ♑ 12

As a society we've neglected our homework, and the chickens of
illiteracy and ignorance have come home to roost. *D.H.*

♄ ♊ 4

The greatest problem in communication is the illusion
that it's been achieved.   *Anon* | ♄ ♓ 3

There are two types of minds: circumspect and circumcised.   *D.H.* | ♄ ♏ 3

To see with, not through the eye, is to believe a lie.   *Blake* | ♀ ♐ 3

There's a great affinity between wit and oxygen; with the oxygen
in these crowded parlors my wit always departs. [Oxygen is
ruled by ☉, Oxygen deficiency is ♇.]   *Emerson* | ☉ ♓ 3 / ♇ 3

In American schools you can display a cross in urine but not
a cross by itself.   *William Bennett* | ♄ ♐ 3

Many a man fails to become a thinker for the sole reason
that his memory is too good.   *Nietzsche* | ☽ ♊ 9

Most people don't think, they simply rearrange their prejudices.
                                                     Robert Anthony | ♄ ♊ 11

The ancestor to every action is a thought ... to think is to act.
                                                          Emerson | ♂ ♊ 4

Bernard Shaw conducted a series of extramarital affairs
exclusively by mail.   *Anon* | ♅ ♎ 3

You should be grateful for the weeds you have in your mind,
because eventually they will enrich your garden. Pulling out
the mind-weeds gives nourishment to the plant.   *Shunryu Suzuki* | ♄ ♏ 3

If you could make little fishes talk, they would talk like whales.
                                                  Oliver Goldsmith | ♃ ♓ 3

In the beginning was the Word and the Word was with God,
and the Word was God.   *John 1:1* | ♃ ♊ 1

Let thy speech be short, comprehending much in few words.
                                                    Ecclesiasticus | ♄ 3

Letter-writing is the only device for combining solitude with
good company.   *Lord Byron* | ♄ ♊ 12

Political oratory is an art in which nothing you say reveals
the fact that you're saying nothing.   *Anon* | ♄ ♊ 10 / ☿ ♓ 10

I've yet to hear a man ask for advice on how to combine
marriage and a career.   *Gloria Steinem*   ☿ ♑ 7

Politicians are nattering nabobs of nebulous non-sequitors.   *D.H.*   ♄ ♓ 3

I was the kid next door's imaginary friend.   *Emo Philips*   ☉ ♓ 3

Swearing destroys man's greatest invention -- language. It is an
insult to the soul and a murderous offense against grace.   *Kafka*   ♂ ♊ 9

There are no bloodless fairy stories.   *Kafka*   ☿ ♓ 8

Cognitive dissonance is the psychological term for a divided
mind, or, a mind whose local space is bifurcated -- producing
a "house divided."   *D.H.*   ♅ 3

A book is a mirror: if an ass peers into it you can't expect
an apostle to look out.   *C.G. Lichtenberg*   ☉ ♊ 1

Observing the mistakes of others is an easier learning experience
than benefitting from your own, though both are necessary.
    Baltasar Gracian   ☿ ♎ 12

Language must not be used as a means but must be experienced,
suffered. Language is an eternal mistress.   *Kafka*   ☿ ♏ 5

The blood jet is poetry, there is no stopping it.   *Sylvia Plath*   ♃ ♓ 3

The poet is the caretaker of the soul.   *Erica Jong*   ☿ ♓ 4

The finest poetry was first experience.   *Emerson*   ☽ ♓ 3

The kingdom of thought is a proud aristocracy.   *Emerson*   ☉ ♊ 10

It is a luxury to be understood.   *Emerson*   ♀ ♊ 9

Attention is the greatest wisdom.   *Zen Saying*   ☿ ♐ 1

When one eye is fixed on your destination, there is only
one eye to find the way.   *Zen Saying*   ☿ ♐ 1

The nearest helping hand is at the end of your arm.   *Anon*   ♊ 1

The most profound function of memory is the reflex of identity.

Robert Grudin | ☉ 3

Draw your own conclusions, or, confusions. *Anon* | ☿ ♓ 1

Better to write for yourself and have no public than write
for the public and have no self. *Cyril Connolly* | ☉ ♊ 10

No man, for any considerable period, can wear one face to
himself, and another to the multitude, without finally
getting bewildered as to which may be the true.

Nathaniel Hawthorne | ♄ ♊ 1

To be outspoken is easy when you do not wait to speak
the complete truth. *Rabindranath Tagore* | ♂ ♊ 9

**It's the mark of an educated mind to be able to
entertain a thought without accepting it.**

Aristotle | ♃ 3

We write autobiographies not as an art form, but in order
to mine them further for detail that will serve us in ANY art
form we choose. We want access to our lives as material.

Julia Cameron | ☽ ♌ 3

Even without formally writing on your life, the mere act of
jotting notes will begin to connect the dots of a fragmented self.

Julia Cameron | ☽ ♈ 3

We must capture our personal and idiosyncratic language
so that we may speak about our personal and idiosyncratic LIFE.

Peter London | ☽ ♌ 3

Ultimately, literature is nothing but carpentry. With both
you are working with reality, a material just as hard as wood.

Gabriel Garcia Marquez | ♄ 3

The imagination needs noodling -- long, inefficient, happy
idling, dawdling and puttering. These busy people who are
always briskly doing something and as busy as walking mice,
they have little, sharp, staccato ideas ... but they have no
slow, big ideas. *Barbara Ueland* | ♆ 3

If I wrote something true and good that nobody cared to read,
it would do ME a great deal of good. *Barbara Ueland* | ♃ ♊ 1

The mind eats too, through the senses. We need to be
particularly discriminating in what we read and what we
go to see for entertainment, for we become in part
what our senses take in. *Eknath Easwaran*   ☿ ♍ 1

The worst thing about new books is that they keep us
from reading the old ones.   *Joseph Joubert*   ♅ ♑ 3

We cannot spend the day in explanation. Expect me not
to show cause why I seek or why I exclude company.   *Emerson*   ♄ ♊ 11

What else does a country boy do when he's in trouble
but buy a truck?   *Bryce*   ♄ ♊ 4

Wisdom resteth in the heart of him that hath understanding,
but that which is in the mouth of fools is made known.   *Anon*   ♃ 3

The heart of a fool is in his mouth, but the mouth
of a wise man is in his heart.   *Ben Franklin*   ☿ ♌ 9

No one speaks of us in our presence as he does when
we are gone. Society is based on mutual hypocrisy.   *Pascal*   ♄ ♊ 7

Finally, one just has to shut up, sit down, and write.
Natalie Goldberg   ♄ ♊ 3

When we write from experience we harvest our lives.
Bonni Goldberg   ☽ ♊ 6

**then laugh, leaning back in my arms, for life's not a
paragraph and death I think is no parenthesis.**
e.e. cummings   ♀ ♌ 3

Thinking is like loving and dying. Each of us must do it for himself.
Josiah Royce   ☿ ♏ 5

When words lose their meaning physical force takes over.
W.H. Auden (1973)   ♀ 3

Some writers confuse authenticity, which they ought always
to aim at, with originality, which they should never bother about.
W.H. Auden   ☉ ♒ 3

Do you hunt your own truffles or do you hire a pig?
(Conversational icebreaker.)   *Jean McClatchy*   ☿ ♈ 6

Your own words are the bricks and mortar of the dreams
you want to realize. Your words are the greatest power you have.
The words you choose and use establish the life you experience.
Sonia Choquette — ☉ ♊ 1

A narrow stomach may be filled to its satisfaction,
but a narrow mind will never be satisfied, not even with all
the riches in the world. *Gems from the East (Blavatsky)* — ♄ ♋ 3

He who neglects his duty to his conscience, will neglect to pay
his debt to his neighbor. *Gems from the East (Blavatsky)* — ♄ ♏ 3

A bore is a man who, when you ask him how he is, tells you.
Bert Leston Taylor — ♄ ♈ 3

He's the kind of a bore who's here today and here tomorrow.
Binnie Barnes — ♄ ♊ 1

My mind can never know my body, although it has become
quite friendly with my leg. *Descartes* — ♄ ♊ 1

Some treat all their opinions as principles. *Herbert Agar* — ♃ ♊ 1

Outside of a dog, books are man's best friend. Inside of a dog,
it's too dark to read. *Anon* — ♊ 6 / ☿ ♍ 12

Wit makes its own welcome, and levels all distinctions. *Emerson* — ☿ ♐ 1

**Acronyms are adored by Gemini: "OPATRESOL" is
openness, patience, receptivity and solitude.**
David Hayward — ♄ ♍ 3

Psychiatry is the study of the Id by the odd. *Anon* — ☿ ♒ 12

Conservatives know that some human beings,
as Albert Jay Nock stressed in his heuristic lectures at the
University of Virginia, are educable, others only trainable.
William F. Buckley — ♍ 3

Education, n. That which discloses to the wise and disguises from
the foolish their lack of understanding. *Ambrose Bierce* — ♃ ♓ 3

Internal gossip is the chatter of the monkey mind.
[Monkeys are ☿♊.] *D.H.* — ♊ 12

Language is the archives of history ... language is fossil poetry.

Emerson   ♄ ♊ 3

Plagiarizing from one is stealing, from many is research.   *Anon*   ♂ ♒ 3

I have read your book and much like it.   *Moses Hadas*   ♃♺ ♊

The covers of this book are too far apart.   *Ambrose Bierce*   ♄ ♊ 3
   ♄ ♒ 3

I'm a deeply superficial person.   *Andy Warhol*   ♏ 3

People generally quarrel because they cannot argue.

G.K. Chesterton   ♄ ♈ 3

To me, Poe's prose is unreadable -- like Jane Austen's.
No, there is a difference. I could read his prose on a salary,
but not Jane's.   *Mark Twain*   ♄ ♊ 2

Shelley should not be read but inhaled through a gas pipe.

Lionel Trilling   ☿ ♏ 12

Keats is a miserable creature, hungering after sweets
which he can't get; going about saying, "I'm so hungry;
I should so like something pleasant!"   *Thomas Carlyle*   ♀ ♏ 3
   ☿ ♉ 12

You speak of Lord Byron and me. There is this great
difference between us. He describes what he sees,
I describe what I imagine. Mine is the hardest task.

John Keats   ☿ ♓ 3

He seems to me the most vulgar-minded genius that ever
produced a great effect in literature. (On Lord Byron.)

George Eliot   ♅ ♏ 3

Henry James would have been vastly improved as a novelist
by a few whiffs from the Chicago stockyards.   *H.L. Mencken*   ♇ 3

**My books are water; those of the great geniuses
are wine. Everybody drinks water.**

Mark Twain   ☽ ♊ 10

I prefer dead writers because you don't run into them at parties.

Fran Lebowitz   ☿ ♏ 5

Perhaps "alive" is scarcely the word one would apply to the "luminary" of the Lake District. Wordsworth drew his first orderly and deliberate breath in 1770, and continued the alternative processes of inhalation and exhalation until 1850.

Ezra Pound

☽	♑	3
♄	♊	12

Wordsworth is so often flat and heavy, partly because his moral sense has no theatrical elements; it is an obedience, a discipline which he has not created.

W.B. Yeats

♄ ♊ 5

If this man (William Faulkner) is a good writer, shrimps whistle Dixie. [The Moon rules shrimp.]

Calder Willingham

☽ ♊ 5

On the other side of the poem there is a path as thin as a hairline, and someone lost in time is treading the path barefoot, without a sound.

Rokhl Korn

♄ ♓ 3

Samuel Beckett commenting on meaning in one of his plays: "Don't look for meaning in the words. Listen to the silences."

Samuel Beckett

♄ ♊ 5

Write solid sentences and you can even spare punctuation.

Emerson

♄ ♊ 3

All crime is local (within a local jurisdiction). The Federal government does not belong in it except to give federal politicians and bureaucrats more power.

Harry Browne

♄ ♏ 3

I felt a terrible torment in the man. He always kept his eyes down. We tried to carry on a conversation but he would never participate. Finally he lifted his eyes once to a direct question from me, and the look in his eyes was so terrible, so sad, that I began to cry. [Faulkner, born 9-25-1897, had ♀℞☌♆℞ in ♊.]

Tennessee Williams on William Faulkner

♆℞	☌	
♀℞	♊	1

My joy is to convey the urgency of beauty.

D.H.

♂ ♎ 3

One <u>sees</u> intelligence far more than one hears it. People do not always say transcendental things, but if they are <u>capable</u> of saying them, it is always visible.

Marie Lenéru

☿ ♓ 1

That pestilent cosmetic, rhetoric.

T.H. Huxley

♀ ♏ 3

Thinking is what gets you caught from behind.

O.J. Simpson

♄ ♊ 12

The decay in linguistic and symbolic literacy impairs our
ability to understand, as well as convey, life's experiences.   *D.H.*   ♄ ♓ 3

It was hard to communicate with you. You were always
communicating with yourself. The line was busy.   *Jean Kerr*   ☿ ♌ 7

Books in all their variety are often the means by which
civilization may be carried triumphantly forward.
                                        Winston Churchill   ♃ ♒ 3

A great deal of intelligence can be invested in ignorance
when the need for illusion is deep.   *Saul Bellow*   ☽ ♓ 3/9

Using words to describe magic is like using a screwdriver
to cut roast beef.   *Tom Robbins*   ♂ ♓ 3

A bore came over to me at a party the other day and said,
"I passed by your house the other day." I said, "Thank you."   *Anon*   ♄ ♊ 4

If a man talks dirty to a woman it's sexual harassment.
If a woman talks dirty to a man it's $2.98 a minute.   *Michael Levine*   ♀ ♏ 3
                                                                                ☿ ♏ 2

Most works of art, like most wines, ought to be consumed
in the district of their fabrication.   *Rebecca West*   ♀ ♓ 3

        Your job itself
is "the sound of one hand clapping;"
No use using
Both hands.

        Had you done a good job
clapping with two hands,
No need then to hear
The sound of one.   *Japanese Zen Saying*   ♄ ♊ 6

Don't worry about people stealing your ideas. If your ideas
are any good, you'll have to ram them down people's throats.   ☿ ♏ 2
                                        Howard Aiken   ♂ ♉ 3

Don't express your ideas too clearly. Most people think little
of what they understand, and venerate what they do not.
To be valued, things must be difficult: if they can't understand   ☿ ♓ 11
you, people will think more highly of you.   *Baltasar Gracian*   ♆ ♍ 3

One cannot review a bad book without showing off.   *W.H. Auden*   ☉ ♍ 3

A fool's mouth is his destruction, his lips the snare of the soul.

Proverbs 18:1 ☿ ♏ 12

Winds make weather; weather
Is what nasty people are
Nasty about and the nice
Show a common joy in observing. *W.H. Auden* 3

Breath is the connecting link between body and soul
and the hub in the wheel of yoga. *B.K.S. Iyengar* ☿ ♓ 1

Selective hearing guards the door to selective remembering,
and both are fear-based. *D.H.* ♄ ♋ 3

Oh dear me -- it's too late to do anything but ACCEPT you
and LOVE you -- but when you were quite a little boy
somebody ought to have said "hush" just once! (In a letter
to George Bernard Shaw 1912.) *Mrs. Patrick Campbell* ♄ ♊ 5

Cognitive skills will be rewarded as never before. It will be
more important to think clearly, as ideas will become a form
of wealth. *James Davidson, Lord Rees-Mogg* ☿ ♒ 2

Clear thinking requires courage rather than intelligence.

Thomas Szasz ♂ ♊

If you don't listen to yourself, you won't hear what others say.

Thomas Szasz ☉ ♎ 3

Journalism is the last resource of the educated
poor who could not be artists and would not be
teachers.

Henry Adams ♄ ♊ 2

If you can't convince them, confuse them. *Anon* ♆ ♊ 11

Thinking is the talking of the soul with itself. *Plato* ♆ 3

One stops being a child when one realizes that telling one's
trouble does not make it better. *Cesare Pavese* ☽ ♌ 3

♄ ♋ 3

4

FOURTH HOUSE

**The House of Home
and Parents**
'where I come from'

*the sphere of heredity
base of operations
psychological roots
beginning and end of life
domestic affairs
parents' attitudes
private life*

MOON

Influence:
*instincts
emotional needs
subconscious
breast / stomach / womb
public opinion
routines
females and babies*

Examples:
*writers
diplomats
mothers
cooks*

CANCER

*responsive
sensitive
sentimental
tenacious
shrewd*

*touchy
pessimistic
defensive
insecure
fearful
moody*

Life purpose to:
*nurture
provide
preserve
earn
absorb*

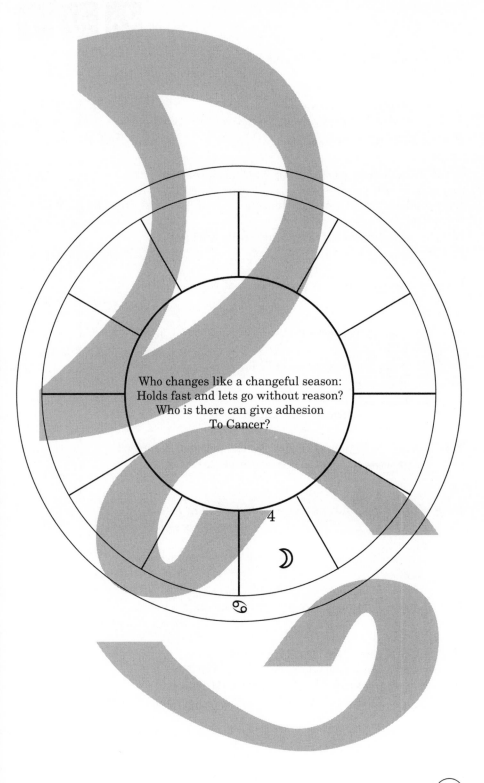

Who changes like a changeful season:
Holds fast and lets go without reason?
Who is there can give adhesion
To Cancer?

4

☽

♋

What the mother sings to the cradle goes all the way to the coffin.
Henry Ward Beecher   ☽ ♏ 5

A healthy family is a joyous karma.   *D.H.*   ☍ ♍ 4

Problems like relatives standing.   *W.H. Auden*   ♄ 4

When the American people give up freedom for security
they deserve neither. [Uranus was in Capricorn from
1988 to 1996,a time of great governmental growth.]   *Ben Franklin*   ♅ ♑ 4

Hope is the feeling you have that the feeling you have
isn't permanent.   *Jean Kerr*   ♃ ♋

If you feel neglected by your family, think of Whistler's father.
Anon   ♄ ♌ 4

S.N.A.G. = a sensitive new-age guy.   *Anon*   ♂ ♋ 11

Women are like tea bags; you never know how strong
they are until they get into hot water.   *Anon*   ☽ ♈

Contentment -- the smother of invention.   *Anon*   ♄ ♒ 4

What we call the beginning is often the end and to make an end
is to make a beginning. The end is where we start from.
T.S. Eliot   ♂ ♏ 4

If we want things to stay as they are, things will have to change.
Giuseppe Tomasi de Lampedusa   ☽ ♑

Intimacy is a willingness to let the other enter into the chaos
that is ours.   *Urban T. Holmes*   ☽ ♓ 7

The folktale is the primer of the picture language of the soul.
Joseph Campbell   ☿ ♋ 4

Ours is a continent where waves from all directions
have sloshed against each other and broken. The land itself,
furthermore, has given forth a mythology of its own.
Joseph Campbell   ♄ ♓ 4

Personal liberty and private property rights have never
been so insecure in America. *Richard Ebeling* | ♅ ♋ 1

Greeting is the beginning of farewell. *Zen Saying* | ♀ ♈ 4

Trust is the thrust of faith. *D.H.* | ☽ ♈ 9

Sympathy is the principal tool for the advancement of decadence.
Nietzsche | ☽ ♏ 10

Sympathy preserves what is ripe for extinction. *Nietzsche* | ☽ ♑ 8

If a man owns land, the land owns him. *Emerson* | ♄ ♉ 4

A man's home is his wife's castle. [Castles are ☉♌.]
Alexander Chase | ☉ ♎ 4

The surroundings householders crave are glorified autobiographies.
T.H. Robsjohn-Gibbings | ☉ ♊ 4

Home is the place where, when you have to go there,
they have to take you in.
Robert Frost | ☽ ♎ 4

The truth is that the home is the only place of liberty,
the only spot on earth where a man can alter arrangements
suddenly, make an experiment or indulge in a whim.
G.K. Chesterton | ♃ ♒ 4

The fellow that owns his own home is always just coming out
of a hardware store. *Kin Hubbard* | ♂ ♋ 1

An old soul is simply a very slow learner. *Dr. Peebles* | ♄ ♊ 4

God could not be everywhere, therefore he made mothers.
Jewish Proverb | ☽ ♋ 9

A modest man is usually admired -- if people ever hear of him.
E.W. Howe | ☽ ♈ 12

This is the reason that mothers are more devoted to their
children than fathers: it is that they suffer more in giving them
birth and are more certain that they are their own. *Aristotle* | ☽ ♏ 5

Blessed are those among women, and blessed is the fruit
of thy womb. *Luke 1:42* — ♃ ♋ 5

I know that a woman is a dish for the gods, if the Devil dress
her not. [6th House is "one's manner of dress" as well as food;
hence, the use of Virgo.] *Shakespeare* — ☽ ♍ 9

Alas! You three on me, threefold distress'd,
Pour all your tears. I am your sorrow's nurse,
and I will pamper it with lamentation. *Shakespeare, Richard III* — ☽ ♍ 12

Children may tear up a house, but they never break up a home.
Anon — ♄ ♋ 5

Can you remember when the family meals were thought out
instead of thawed out? *Anon* — ☿ ♋ 6

In today's world of inflation a big spender is any man
who supports a wife and kids. *Anon* — ♃ ♋ 2

One of life's major mistakes is being the last member of the
family to get the flu -- after all the sympathy has run out. *Anon* — ☽ ♓ 6

Celibate I sit and see
Women figures round my cell.
Women figures on the wall
Point their little breasts at me;
I must wait for a woman's smile
Not in the sun but in the dark. *Dylan Thomas* — ♄ ♋ 12

Life is either a daring adventure or nothing. Security
does not exist in nature, nor do the children of men
as a whole experience it. Avoiding danger is no safer
in the long run than exposure. *Helen Keller* — ♂ ♋ 5

> **T**he moon peered through (rain clouds) as if
> **she were an old woman opening a drawer**
> **to find something lost in the bottom of it -- me.**
> *Alice Howell* — ☽ ♓ 12

With the sacred marriage we return to where we started and
know that place for the first time; know that everything we are
and think and do springs from the Divine Ground and falls back
into the Divine Essence. *Andrew Harvey, Anne Baring* — ♆ ♎ 4

It wasn't until life on earth became too dangerous
that man began to fly to the moon.   *Anon*   ☽ ≈ 9

The number associated with the moon (besides 13)
in many cultures is nine. Nine (3x3) is the number
of months of gestation.   *Alice Howell*   ♄ ⊚

Excessive sorrow laughs. Excessive joy weeps.   *William Blake* ♃ ⊚ 5

She was not a woman likely to settle for equality
when sex gave her an advantage.   *Anthony Delano*   ☽ ≈ 8

Women who set a low value on themselves
make life hard for all women.   *Nellie McClung*   ♄ ⊚ 2

The Moon meets Saturn in the image of the egg. The process
involved in the shell (Calcium is ruled by Saturn) is one
of protection through limitation. This is its positive purpose.
However, if the shell is not sacrificed at the right moment,
the unhatched new life would succumb as if in a tomb.
                                                 Alice Howell   ♄ ⊚ 8

Unhappiness equals image minus reality.   *Dennis Prager* ♄ ⊚ 12

It's ironic that women are increasingly handling their issues
with men in a paternal way by going to Big Daddy government
through litigation.   *Dennis Prager* ☽ ♑ 7

On some days it's hard to figure out how a species
that controls 97% of the money and all the pussy
can be downtrodden.   *Larry King* ☽ ♏ 2

A woman's desire for revenge outlasts all her other emotions.
                                                Cyril Connolly ☽ ♏ 7

That staying home to be a full-time parent needs to be defended
is a sad statement of our times.   *Dennis Prager* ♄ ⊚ 4

America is a large, friendly dog in a very small room.
Every time it wags its tail, it knocks over a chair. *Arnold Toynbee* ♃ ⊚ 6

He is a first rate collector who can upon all occasions,
collect his wits.   *George D. Prentice* ☽ ♊ 1

When a woman behaves like a man,
why doesn't she behave like a nice man?   *Edith Evans*   ☽ ♈ 1

Most mothers are instinctive philosophers.
                                        Harriet Beecher Stowe   ☽ ♋ 9

if there are any heavens my mother will (all by herself) have one.
                                        e.e. cummings   ♅ 4

The American way is to acculturate not multiculturate.
                                        Dennis Prager   ♋ 11

What is a weed? A plant whose virtues
have not yet been discovered.   *Emerson*   ☽ ♏ 6

Soul loss is regarded as the gravest diagnosis in shamanism,
being seen as a cause of illness and death. Yet it is not referred
to at all in modern Western medical books.   *Jeanne Achterberg*   ♄ ♏ 4

Cancers arpeggiate their emotions; the rest of us tend
to augment them by chromatics.   *D.H.*   ♃ ♋ 5

We live in an age when we ache for advice and all we get is:
"How do you feel about it?"   *Dennis Prager*   ♄ ♋ 9

Follow the moon to be in the receptive flow of the quality of the day.
                                        Ann Ree Colton   ☽ ♋ 6

Sometimes a scream is better than a thesis.   *Emerson*   ☽ ♈ 9

The lighthouse in a sea of absurdity. [The moon rules lighthouses.]
                                        Nietzsche on Victor Hugo   ☽ ♊ 12

Poets have been remarkably silent on the subject of cheese.
                                        G.K. Chesterton   ♄ ♋ 3

Frustrate a Frenchman, he will drink himself to death;
an Irishman, he will die of angry hypertension;
a Dane, he will shoot himself;
an American, he will get drunk, shoot you, then establish
a million dollar aid program for your relatives.
Then he will die of an ulcer.   *Stanley Rudin*   ♄ ♋ 8

We do not attach ourselves lastingly to anything that has not
cost us care, labor or longing.   *Honoré de Balzac*   ♄ ♏ 4

He who rejects change is the architect of decay. The only
human institution which rejects progress is the cemetery.
Harold Wilson | ☽ ♑ 11

Where do all the women who have watched so carefully
over the lives of their beloved ones get the heroism to send
them to face the cannon? (August 27, 1914)
Käthe Kollwitz (1867-1945) | ♂ ♋ 8

The two women gazed out of the slumped and sagging bodies
that had accumulated around them. *Nadine Gordimer* | ♄ ♋ 1

When you leave New York, you are astonished at how clean
the rest of the world is. Clean is not enough. *Fran Lebowitz* | ☽ ♍ 10

Man is a history-making creature who can neither
repeat his past nor leave it behind; at every moment
he adds to and thereby modifies everything that had
previously happened to him. *W.H. Auden* | ☉ ♑ 4

Incest is relatively boring. *Anon* | ☽ ♏ 12

Above all I dislike family quarrels and when they happen
among my relations nothing gives me more pain. *Ben Franklin* | ♄ ♋ 3

Women give men the very gold of their lives. But then
they invariably want it back in small change. *Oscar Wilde* | ☽ ♌ 2

The history of women is the history of the worst form
of tyranny the world has ever known. The tyranny
of the weak over the strong. It is the only tyranny that lasts.
Oscar Wilde | ☽ ♈ 4

A woman will flirt with anybody in the world
as long as other people are looking on. *Oscar Wilde* | ☽ ♎ 5

Women have a wonderful instinct about things.
They can discover everything except the obvious.
Oscar Wilde | ☽ ♓ 12

No woman should ever be quite accurate about her age.
It looks so calculating. *Oscar Wilde* | ♄ ♋

Emerson is the caretaker of my roots as a New Englander. *D.H.* | ♄ ♋ 4
| ♃ ♊ 4

A clear stream follows
Its own way without
growing into a river. *Japanese Zen Saying* | ♃ ♋ 1

Whether women are better than men I cannot say
-- but I can say they are certainly no worse. *Golda Meir* | ☽ ♈ 11

People in the East starve for food; in the West,
they are starving for love. *Mother Teresa* | ☽ ♍ 7

Home is where you hang your head. *Anon* | ♄ ♈ 4

For the womb has dreams. It is not as simple as the good earth.
Anais Nin | ☽ ♓ 4

When you are old and grey and full of sleep,
And nodding by the fire, take down this book
And slowly read and dream of the soft look
Your eyes had once, and of their shadows deep. *W.B. Yeats* | ☿ ♓ 4

The mother's heart is the child's schoolroom.
Henry Ward Beecher | ☽ ♌ 3

Before a nation collapses
the families of that nation must go down first. *Jerry Falwell* | ♄ ♋ 10

Cleaning your house while your kids are still
growing
Is like shoveling the walk before it stops
snowing. *Phyllis Diller* | ♄ ♍ 4

Women who miscalculate are called "mothers." *Anon* | ♄ ♋ 3

Discipline is a symbol of caring to a child. He needs guidance.
If there is love, there is no such thing as being too tough
with a child ... if you have never been hated by your child,
you have never been a parent. *Bette Davis* | ♄ ♋ 5

Children aren't happy with nothing to ignore,
And that's what parents were created for. *Ogden Nash* | ♄ ♋ 5

The family is one of nature's masterpieces. *George Santayana* | ♃ ♉ 4

The seen is the changing. The unseen is the unchanging. *Plato* | ☽

Though I have kind invitations enough to visit America,
I could not, even for a couple of months, live in a country
so miserable as to possess no castles.   *John Ruskin*   ♄ ♌ 4

My mother is so proud. I go to a psychologist five times a week
and just talk about her.   *Anon*   ☽ ♌ 8

There is a house whose people sit in darkness;
dust is their food and clay their meat. They are clothed
like birds with wings for coverings; they see no light;
they sit in darkness.   *The Epic of Gilgamesh (c. 2300 B.C.)*   ♄ ♋ 12

Conscience -- the accumulated sediment of ancestral
faintheartedness.   *H.L. Mencken*   ♄ ♋ 12

Be cautious when bestirring the source of things
lest we disavow their creator.   *D.H.*   ♀ ♌ 4

One woman's poise is another woman's poison.   *Katherine Brush*   ☽ ♎ 8

When I can no longer think of the victims of broken homes,
I begin thinking of the victims of intact ones.   *Peter DeVries*   ☿ ♏ 4
                                                                                  ☿ ♋ 12

It doesn't matter what you do in the bedroom
as long as you don't do it in the streets and frighten the horses.
          Mrs. Patrick Campbell   ☿ ♐ 4

Greatness is the willingness to expose one's littleness
and risk embarrassment.   *Thomas Szasz*   ♃ ♋ 1

Boredom is the feeling that everything is a waste of time;
serenity, that nothing is.   *Thomas Szasz*   ♄ ♋ 1

When it becomes more difficult to suffer than change ...
you will change.   *Anon*   ♄ ♋ 12

Families break up when people take hints you don't intend
and miss hints you do intend.   *Robert Frost*   ♅ ♒ 4

In a family argument if it turns out you are right, apologize at once!
          Robert A. Heinlein   ♀ ♋ 3

No worldly success can compensate for failure in the home.
          David O. McKay   ♄ ♋ 12

A sentimentalist is simply one who desires to have the luxury
of an emotion without paying for it. *Oscar Wilde*   ☽ ♓ 2

Everyone is a moon and has a dark side which he never
shows to anybody. *Mark Twain*   ☽ 12

Whenever a man encounters a woman in a mood he doesn't
understand, he wants to know if she is tired.
George Jean Nathan   ☿ ♋ 12

The distance to the moon was once measured in miles,
but now it's in dollars. *Anon*   ♄ ♋ 2

In the past the moon was an inspiration to lovers and poets;
in the future it will be just another airport. *Anon*   ☽ ♒ 9

Intuition is the voice of the non-physical world. *Gary Zukov*   ☽ ♊ 12

Women, as most susceptible, are the best index of the coming hour.
Emerson   ☽ ♐ 1

The most remarkable thing about my mother is that for 30 years
she served the family nothing but leftovers. The original
has never been found. *Calvin Trillin*   ☽ ♍ 12

A tremendous amount of emotional drama propels my
communication always, from the kitchen to the stage. *Noel Tyl*   ☽ ♌ 3

Modesty is the conscience of the body. *Honoré de Balzac*   ☽ 1

Some parents want their children to HAVE IT better,
others want them to DO better. The former are likely
to have incompetent and unhappy children,
the latter, competent and happy ones. *Thomas Szasz*   ♃ ♋ 5

Falsies are delusions of glandeur. *M. Rose Pierce*   ♆ ♋ 1

Be gentle to the otherness you carry,
broken by
        the truth you cannot tell yet.
Mother and be mothered by your burden.
Trust, and learn
to travel with the music. *Sydney Carter*   ☽ ♓

There's no yes in yesterday. (Song lyric) *Artie Butler*   ☽ ♑ 12

Our actions are not determined by abstract insights or considerations; every step we take in life has its source in the primal ground of our being, in our temperament, our race. Afterwards we cast about for a philosophy that conforms with these unconscious motivations. *Hermann Hesse*

♀ ♐ 4

Happiness is a how, not a what; a talent, not an object.
Hermann Hesse

☽ ♌ 5

There was a young man of Khartoum,
The strength of whose balls was his doom.
     So strong was his shootin',
     The third law of Newton
Propelled the poor chap to the moon. *Anon*

♂ ♋ 8

"Praise the child, and you make love to the mother"
-- [and if she's your daughter you go to jail.] *William Cobbett*

♀ ♋ 12

From what I have seen, if you have a parent's love you may or may not turn out okay. But if you have never had a parent's love you will go through life with a parent-shaped hole inside you, and it will most likely, unless you have a very strong soul or very good luck or another power intervenes, leave you thwarted, and disturbed, and possibly dangerous. *Peggy Noonan*

♄ ♋ 5

Babies are such a nice way to start people. *Don Herold*

☽ 1

The unmade bed embraces the world in its natural state: Entropy. Planets spin and race apart, continents sink into the sea, mountains breathe fire and beds go unmade.
Tamara Jones

☽ ♓ 4

The moon like a flower
In heaven's high bower,
With silent delight
sits and smiles on the night. *William Blake*

☽ ♉ 4

We must cut our coat according to our cloth, and adapt ourselves to changing circumstances.
Dean William Inge

☽ ♍ 1

Perhaps the greatest social service that can be rendered by anybody to the country and to mankind is to bring up a family.
George Bernard Shaw

♃ ♋ 11

I don't make a habit of wishing for what I don't have,
but I often wish I had a lighter nature. Dizzy (Gillespie)
has that beautiful gift. I can't say, "Be happy, people."
It's something I can't command. But you have to be
true to your own nature.   *John Coltrane*   ☽ ♋ 1

If nothing changes, nothing changes.   *A.A.*   ♄ ♋ 1

People are to be taken in very small doses.   *Emerson*   ♄ ♋ 11

Humanity is a pigsty where liars, hypocrites
and the obscene in spirit congregate.   *George Moore*   ☽ ♍ 11
                                                                ♄ ♋ 11

Man is the missing link between apes and human beings.
                                                Konrad Lorenz   ♅ ♋ 3

Women should be obscene and not heard.
                                                Groucho Marx   ♀ ♋ 3

The events of childhood do not pass,
but repeat themselves like seasons of the year.   *Eleanor Farjeon*   ☽ ♊ 5

The beauty of the black community has always been
the diverse cultural aspects of its people. Since slavery
began in 1444, African slaves came from different tribes
with different languages, traditions and cultures. We were
forced into one language and one culture but have always
kept some differences. It seems there are elements in
America that still expect us to be predictable and
controllable. I hope they handle disappointment well.
                                                Mason Weaver   ♄ ♒ 4

No woman shall have the legal right to bear a child,
no man shall have the right to become a father without
a permit for parenthood. (Article 4)
No permit for parenthood shall be valid for more than one birth.
(Article 6) [From Planned Parenthood's Outline to Rid the
World of Inferior People, published in a 1934 article in the
AMERICA WEEKLY magazine.]   *Margaret Sanger*   ♄ ♋

All is impermanence; the great threat to ego and sidekick to soul.
                                                D.H.   ☽ ♓ 1

Our feelings are the source of our energy; they provide
the horsepower that makes it possible for us to accomplish
the tasks of living.   *M. Scott Peck*   ☽ ♐ 1

Every crowd has a silver lining.   *P.T. Barnum*   ☽ 2
                                                                           ☽ ♉ 11

How many alcoholics does it take to change a lightbulb?
Change?   *Anon*   ☽ 12
                                                                           ☽ ♑ 12
                                                                           ☽ ♉ 12

LEO

creative
generous
loyal
dignified
dramatic

conceited
vain
arrogant
pretentious
imperious

Life purpose to:
express
radiate
impassion
entertain
impress

SUN

Influence:
life force
ego
identity
fathers
individuality
power

Examples:
figureheads
royalty
managers
governors
chairpersons

FIFTH HOUSE

The House of Creativity
'my fun'

the sphere of self-
expression
entertainment
amusements
speculation
pleasures
artistic creations
romance
love affairs

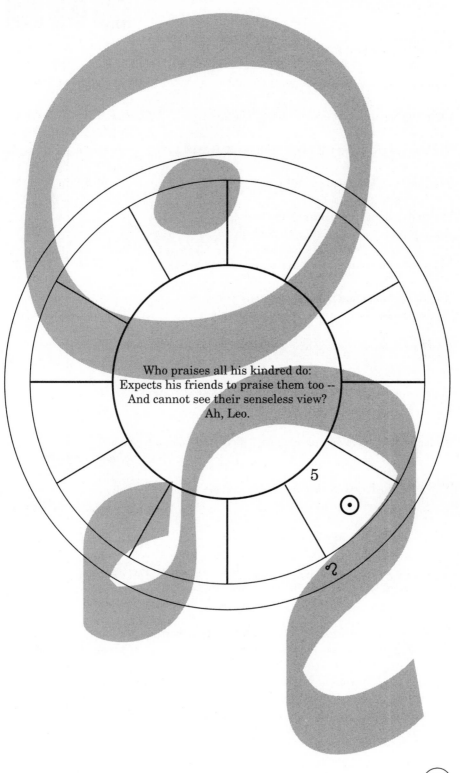

Who praises all his kindred do:
Expects his friends to praise them too --
And cannot see their senseless view?
Ah, Leo.

5

I'm more important than my problems.	*José Ferrer*	☉ ♌ 12
If you would be loved, love and be loveable.	*Ben Franklin*	♀ ♌ 5
One who is capable of love is happy, nothing else.	*Herman Hesse*	☽ ♌ 5
We have art in order not to die of the truth.	*Nietzsche*	♃ ♏ 5
Man refracts love as glass refracts light; he bends it.	*D.H.*	☽ ♒ 5
We find delight in the beauty and happiness of children that makes the heart too big for the body.	*Emerson*	♃ ♌ 1
My success is contingent on the quality of my loving.	*D.H.*	☉ ♑ 5
So, to remember our changing garden, We are linked as children in a circle dancing.	*W.H. Auden*	☽ ♓ 5
Ego based power lasts as long as the thing it is attached to lasts.	*Deepak Chopra*	♄ ♌ 1
Baby: an alimentary canal with a loud voice at one end and no responsibility at the other.	*Anon*	☽ ♊ 5
Teach us to count every passing day til our hearts find wisdom.	*Psalm 90:12*	♄ ♌ 9
The difference between art and life is that art is more bearable.	*Charles Bukowski*	☉ ♎ 5
Opera is to soul as Rap is to sewer.	*D.H.*	♀ ♏ 5
Authentic power is built step by step, choice by choice. It cannot be meditated or prayed into being. It must be earned.	*Gary Zukov*	☉ ♑ 2
Horse sense is something that keeps horses from betting on people.	*Anon*	♀ ♐ 5
Let us not be desirous of vain glory.	*Galatians 5:26*	♄ ♌ 1
The ultimate indignity is to be given a bedpan by a stranger who calls you by your first name.	*Maggie Kuhn*	♄ ♌ 12

The goal is to leave a legacy of love.   *Bernie Seigel* | ☉ ♒ 8

Every act of creation is at first an act of destruction.   *Picasso* | ♇ ♏ 5

The ego needs survival, the soul intimacy.   *Dr. Peebles* | ☉ ♎ 4

Love is not a mere sentiment, it is the ultimate truth
that lies at the very heart of creation.   *Deepak Chopra* | ☉ ♌ 9

Now that my ladder's gone, I must lie down where all ladders
start, in the foul rag and bone shop of the heart.   *W.B. Yeats* | ♄ ♌ 12

Will is power ready for concrete expression: actualized potential.
    Dane Rudhyar | ♂ ♌ 1

If a man is not ready to risk his life, where is his dignity?
    André Malraux | ☉ ♏ 5

**It is only with the heart that one can see rightly;
what is essential is invisible to the eye.**
    St. Exupéry | ☿ ♌ 12

Trumpeters do at one end of the alimentary canal what
the rest of us do in private at the other.   *D.H.* | ♂ ♋ 5
   ☿ ♏ 12

A talent can be cultivated in tranquility;
character, only in the rushing stream of life.   *Goethe* | ☉ ♐ 1

The emotion of love, in spite of the romantics, is not
self-sustaining; it endures only when the lovers love
many things together, and not merely each other.   *Joseph Campbell* | ☿ ♌ 7

To choose what you've chosen, want what you have,
and express it with passionate integrity, opens the heart
to the soul's grace.   *D.H.* | ☊ ♌ 9

I believe that the heavenly powers protect heroes since,
in Plato's view, heroes are born from the love of Gods.
And I know by direct experience that philosophers are
reborn from the love of heroes.   *Ficino (b. 1433)* | ♂ ♌ 9

So many drummers, so little time.   *Anon* | ♄ ♈ 5

So many men, so little time.   *Shirley MacLaine* | ♂ ♑ 5

The heart has its reason of which reason knows nothing.   *Pascal*   ♄ ♐ 5

Two things that I love well turned: phrases and ankles.   *D.H.*   ☿ ♒ 5

Love is a midpoint between notion and motion. It is the
etheric essence we can spray at will and has only one scent
-- that of truth.   *D.H.*   ♀ ♌ 9
♀ = (☿/♂)

Just know your lines and don't bump into the furniture.
Spencer Tracy   ♀ ♊ 5

Life consists of what a man is thinking all day.   *Emerson*   ☉ ♊ 1

The best thing a man can do for his children is love their mother.
Anon   ☉ ♋ 5

Risk or Rust.   *D.H.*   ♄ ♈ 5

I'm sick of talking about me; let's talk about you. What do you
think of me?   *Anon*   ☿ ♌ 1

Character is the ability to follow through on a decision long
after the excitement of the moment has passed.   *Cavett Robit*   ☉ ♑ 6

The raised fist and phallus: two pegs on which to hang the
platitudes of modern narcissism.   *Malcolm Muggeridge*   ♇ ♌ 3

Diogenes struck the father when the son swore.   *Burton*   ♄ ♊ 5

All I have to do is what I want to do -- and exactly what I want is
what I have to do ... three cheers! [Campbell had ☽ ♌ 10th!]
Joseph Campbell   ☽ ♌ 10

When there's anything to steal, I steal.   *Picasso*   ☿ ♏ 5

We can all add our share of love without leaving the room.
Helen Nearing   ♃ ♌ 3

All children are foreigners.   *Emerson*   ♅ 5

His mother should have thrown him away and kept the stork.
(Large flying birds are ♅ ♒.)   *Mae West*   ☽ ♒ 5

Your children are not your children. They are the sons and
daughters of Life's longing for itself. They come through you
but not from you, and though they are with you
yet they belong not to you. *Gibran* ☽ ♒ 5

We may not be able to make the world safe for our children.
But we must at least make our children safe for the world.
William Bennett ☽ ♑ 5

Praise does wonders for the sense of hearing. *Anon* ♃ ♌ 3

He who cannot love must learn to flatter. *Goethe* ♄ ♌ 7

The process is not the product; listen to the concert, not the scales.
Dr. Peebles ♀ ♍ 5

Love is not consolation, it is light. *Simone Weil* ♀ ♌ 9

Man is condemned to life, not to death. *Kafka* ♄ ♌ 8

It is there, nevertheless, this other part of me that wishes
for it all, that wishes that my heart's questions will be,
when all is said and done, my heart's answers. *The Daybook* ♇ ♌ 3

A central purpose serves to integrate and prioritize
all other concerns in one's life. *Ayn Rand* ☉ ♍

Mme. Blavatsky was referred to by a disciple, George Mead,
as "the old Lioness from Russia." [She was a Leo.] *George Mead* ♄ ♌ 9

Love is our vehicle for connecting the third dimension
with those above it as well as below. *D.H.* ☿ ♒ 5

I must complain the cards are ill shuffled, til I have a good hand.
Jonathan Swift ♄ ♏ 5

I am one of those unhappy persons who inspire bores
to the greatest flights of art. *Dame Edith Sitwell* ♄ ♎ 5

For this is the hardest of all; to close the open hand out of love.
Nietzsche ♄ ♌ 3

We only believe we are masters in our own house
because we like to flatter ourselves. *Carl Jung* ♀ ♌ 4

Love is high maintenance.	*D.H.*	♄ ♌ 6
We are shaped and fashioned by what we love.	*Goethe*	☉ ♑ 5
We do not learn by experience, but by our capacity for experience.	*Buddha*	☉ ♐ 1
Creation is on-going and flat tires are part of it. [Tires are ruled by Neptune.]	*Schlemmer & Jenkins*	♄ ♓ 5
"But by the grace of God, go I," should be, "But by the grace of what I created go I."	*Anon*	♃ 5
In this life we cannot do great things. We can only do small things with great love.	*Mother Teresa*	♃ ♌ 6
All art begins and ends with discipline and is first and foremost a craft.	*Archibald MacLeash*	♄ ♍ 5
Self-reliance is the perfection of reliance on God.	*Emerson*	☉ ♍ 9
The whole labor of art is to create the form which will contain the relationship -- turn glimpse into image.	*Archibald MacLeash*	♄ ♎ 5
August is a brass fanfare danced by a pride of lions.	*Marge Piercy*	♂ ♓ 5
...tipsy griffin-prowed gondolas weaved on dizzy rails and The Wall of Death was a spinning rim of ruin.	*Dylan Thomas, <u>Quite Early One Morning</u>*	♃ ♓ 5
The winter of love is a cellar of empty bins, In an orchard soft with rot.	*Edna St. Vincent Millay*	♄ ♏ 5
It doesn't matter who my father was; it matters who I remember he was.	*Anne Sexton*	☽ ♌ 4
It is the child that sees the primordial secret in Nature and it is the child of ourselves we return to. The child within us is simple and daring enough to live the secret.	*Lao-Tzu*	☽ ♏ 5
A child, hearing a list of sins, soon realizes, "If this is all I have to do to go to hell, I'M GOING TO HELL."	*Peter McWilliams*	♄ ♏ 5

Creativity is a drug I can't live without.   *Cecil B. De Mille*   ♌ 12

Let not thy will roar when thy power can but whisper.
Thomas Fuller   ☉ ♓ 3

Egoism is the very essence of a noble soul.   *Nietzsche*   ☉ ♌ 1

There is a vast deal of vital air in loving words.   *Walter Landor*   ☿ ♌ 3

I am certain of nothing but of the holiness of the heart's
affections and the truth of Imagination. What the Imagination
seizes as Beauty must be Truth.   *John Keats*   ♃ ♓ 5

Our disowned gifts become shadow versions of themselves.
Julia Cameron   ♄ ♌ 12

We've gone from majority to minority arrogance.   *Dennis Prager*   ♄ ♌ 11

The notes I handle no better than many pianists. But the
pauses between the notes -- ah, that is where the art resides.
Artur Schnabel   ♄ ♒ 5

Let me have my own way exactly in everything, and a sunnier
and pleasanter creature does not exist.   *Thomas Carlyle*   ☉ ♌ 1

Where there is no risk, the emotional terrain is flat and
unyielding, and, despite all its dimensions, valleys, pinnacles,
and detours, life will seem to have none of its magnificent
geography, only a length.   *Diane Ackerman*   ☽ ♈ 5

Creative people do not run away from non-being, but by
encountering and wrestling with it, force it to produce being.
They knock on silence for an answering music; they pursue
meaninglessness until they can force it to mean.   *Rollo May*   ♇ 5

Art is the indispensable medium for the communication of
a moral idea.   *Ayn Rand*   ☿ ♐ 5

Men at forty
Learn to close softly
The doors to rooms they will not be
Coming back to.   *Donald Justice*   ☉ ♑ 4

I teach my sighs to lengthen into songs.   *Theodore Roethke*   ♄ ♋ 5

Never raise your hand to your children; it leaves your
midsection unprotected.   *Robert Orben*   ♂ ♋ 5

Love is a reciprocity of soul and has a different end and obeys
different laws from marriage. Hence one should not take the
loved one to wife.   *Alessandro Piccolomini*   ♄ ♌ 7

Moved by a passion they do not understand for a goal
they seldom reach, men and women are haunted by the vision
of a distant possibility that refuses to be extinguished.
                                          Nathaniel Branden   ♂ ♓ 5
                                                                  ♇ ♎ 5

Lovers who have nothing to do but love each other are not really
to be envied; love and nothing else very soon is nothing else.
                                          Walter Lippmann   ♄ ♎ 5

To know the secret of life you must first know the secret of death.
To know the secret of death you must first know the secret of love.
Know the secret of love and you will know the secret of life
everlasting.   *Anon*   ☉ ♏ 12

A change of heart is the essence of all other change
and it is brought about by a re-education of the mind.
                                          Emmeline Pethick-Lawrence   ☽ ♌ 3

I think most people are more important than their opinions.
                                          Jorge Luis Borges   ☉ ♌ 3

Honor is a form of recognition that society bestows according to
its codes, whereas dignity can be experienced even by the
isolated individual. (From *Facing The Extreme* -- moral life in
concentration camps.)   *Tzvetan Todorov*   ☉ ♑ 12

The preservation of dignity requires transforming a situation of
constraint into one of freedom; where the constraint is extreme,
such a transformation can amount to choosing to do something
one is forced to do.   *Tzvetan Todorov*   ⚳ ♌ 12

Dignity does not insure survival.   *Tzvetan Todorov*   ⚳ ♌

Big-heartedness is the most essential virtue on the
spiritual journey.   *Matthew Fox*   ♃ ♌ 9

Artists need not only their material but also the strength
to handle it.   *Julia Cameron*   ⚳ 5

I thought perhaps my "real" father might not have really been my father and you know what? It does not matter! I am who I am all by myself! *Anon* ☉ ♌ 4

Life can only be understood backward, but it must be lived forward. *Niels Bohr* ☉ ♈ 4

Since the creative part of us is always childlike no matter what our chronological age, we have no sophisticated defenses that are proof against volleys of disparagement. The very vulnerability and openness that makes us creative makes us able to be wounded, hurt, and misled. *Julia Cameron* ☽ ♓ 5

If you still find yourself stuck, list twenty things that you love and ask yourself which part of you loves them.
Julia Cameron ♄ ♌ 12

Looking back over my own body of work, which includes four full-length plays as well as a dozen screenplays ... I learn that I am interested in love and death, and the fateful combining of the two. *Julia Cameron* ♀ ♏ 5

To paint is to love again, and to love is to live to the fullest. *Henry Miller* ♀ ♌ 5

The reason there are so many Jewish violinists is that our fingers are circumcised, which gives us very good dexterity. *Itzak Perlman* ☿ ♏ 5

Anytime you transcend the usual superficial way of connecting with others and share from the heart, you can have a "real moment." And whenever you're sharing love you're living your purpose. *Barbara de Angelis* ☽ ♌ 1
☊ ♌

Hold the elevator until you have finished your conversation. *Charles Dane* ♃ ♌ 3

Children are wonderful, they are the pearls of creation -- only puppies are better. [Pearls are ruled by the moon.] *Tchaikovsky* ☽ ♌ 6

The hour of God and mankind's greatest ordeal is now here. Everything depends on whether we can abandon our pride before it is too late. (Said just before he died.) *Father Bede Griffiths* ♇ ♌
♄ ♌

The object of art is to give life shape. *Jean Anouilh* | ☉ ♑ 5

Every real teacher is myself in disguise. *Richard Bach* | ☉ ♓ 9

No time to marry, no time to settle down;
I'm a young woman, and I ain't done
runnin' around. *Bessie Smith* | ♀ ♏ 5
♄ ♎ 5
☽ ♊ 5

Football combines the two worst things about American life.
It is violence punctuated by committee meetings. *George Will* | ♂ ♒ 5

Courtship is pulling the woo over her eyes. *M. Rose Pierce* | ♀ ♓ 5

An artist does not fake reality -- he stylizes it. *Ayn Rand* | ♄ ♓ 5

Know your best quality, your outstanding gift. Cultivate it
and nurture all the rest. All people could have achieved
eminence in something if only they had known what they
excelled at. Identify your king of attributes and apply it in
double strength. *Baltasar Gracian* | ♃ ♌ 1

Don Juan is a grope addict. A dally slave. A lasshopper.
A Big Dame Hunter who will settle for any game. *M. Rose Pierce* | ♂ ♏ 5

Great loves too must be endured. *Coco Chanel* | ♄ ♌ 5

my father moved thru theys of we,
singing each new leaf out of each tree
(and every child was sure that spring
danced when she heard my father sing) *e.e. cummings* | ☉ ♌ 5
☽ ♓ 5

Better to be driven out from among men
than to be disliked by children. *Richard Henry Dana* | ♄ ♒ 5

What maintains one vice would bring up two children. *Ben Franklin* | ♄ ♏ 5

The Americans are certainly hero-worshipers, and always
take their heroes from the criminal classes. *Oscar Wilde* | ♃ ♌ 12

I have roses on my piano.
But I prefer having two lips on my organ. *Anon* | ♀ ♏ 5

Joy: "**I** have to be super-careful to avoid getting pregnant."
Joyce: "But your husband just had a vasectomy."
Joy: "That's why I have to be so careful."   *Anon*   ♄ ♍ 5
                                                                          ♀ ♌ 12

What's the difference between anxiety and panic?
Anxiety is the first time you can't do it a second time;
panic is the second time you can't do it the first time.   *Anon*   ♄ ♍ 5

(On Beethoven): **F**or me too dramatic and too personal.   *Einstein*   ♃ ♌ 1

Wherever I go and wherever I stay
There's always a picture of me on display.
On top of the desk, or out in the hall,
Tied round a neck or hung on the wall.   *Einstein*   ☉ ♌ 10

Women and men, they play a strange game,
Asking, beseeching: "Please sign your name."
From the erudite fellow they brook not a quibble,
But firmly insist on a piece of scribble.   *Einstein*   ☿ ♌ 10

Sometimes, surrounded by all this good cheer,
I'm puzzled by some of the things that I hear,
And wonder, my mind for a moment not hazy,
If I and not they could really be crazy.   *Einstein*   ☿ ♓ 5

The man who would learn the human mind ...
[should] put away his academic gown ... and wander
with the human heart through the world.   *Carl Jung*   ♃ ♌ 10

Among those I like or admire, I can find no
common denominator, but among those whom
I love, I can: all of them make me laugh.
                                                          W.H. Auden   ♀ ♌ 11

We cannot permit love to run riot; we must build fences
around it, as we do around pigs.   *Edgar Watson Howe*   ♇ ♌ 6

Of all the clever people round me here
I most delight in me --
Mine is the only voice I care to hear,
And mine is the only face I care to see.   *Roy Campbell* ☉ ♌ 1

Recently they held a Reincarnation Ball. You came as you were.
                                                              Anon   ♋/♍ 5
                                                                          ♀ ♐ 5

If you ever feel like having a kid, go to a restaurant
and sit next to one.   *Anon*   ♄ ♌ 6

The soul's mission is to break through the envelope of
unknowing and leave evidence that God has been here
-- a legacy of love.   *D.H.*   ♃ ♓ 5
                                                                 ♀ ♌ 12

Christ was crucified for saying "the Kingdom is within you."
                                    Joseph Campbell   ♀ ♌ 9

We spend most our time in one of two ways -- making money or
spending it. Only when we gamble can we do both at once,
the proportion varying with our luck.   *Thomas Szasz*   ♄ ♉ 5

Be a lamp unto yourself. (The Buddha's last words.)   *Buddha* ☉ ♒ 1

We are theotropic beings who grow toward God.
                    Rabbi Zalman Schacter-Shalomi   ☉ ♉ 9

Where does self-confidence end and conceit begin?
Where dusk ends and night begins. In each case,
an indistinct boundary demarcates a distinction
as clear as that between white and black.   *Thomas Szasz*   ♆ 5

Wives and children have killed more artists than the cholera.
                                            Nietzsche   ♀ ♌ 4

July is the month when mothers are again reminded
why school-teachers need long summer vacations.   *Anon*   ☽ ♌ 3

The sonatas of Mozart are unique: they are too easy
for children, and too difficult for artists. *Artur Schnabel*   ♅ 5
                                                                 ♃ ♓ 5

Good musicians execute their music, but bad ones murder it.
                                            Anon   ☿ ♍ 5

Go for your own gold, not the world's, which by comparison is only tin.
                                            D.H.   ☉ ♌ 10

The mistake we make is not going for happiness first.
                                    Deepak Chopra   ☽ ♌ 1
                                                                 ♄ ♌ 1

Love is an exploding cigar we willingly smoke.
[Neptune rules cigars.]   *Lynda Barry*   ♂ ♓ 5

A lover without indiscretion is no lover at all.   *Thomas Hardy*   ♂ ♎ 5

Excepting suicide, the most serious decision in life should be
to have a child; however, not to have a child, if one is capable of
having children, should perhaps be an even more serious decision.
                                                 Thomas Szasz   ♄ ♊ 5

I like young girls. Their stories are shorter.   *Tom McGuane*   ♄ ♎ 5

**What's the difference between a soprano
and the PLO? You can negotiate with the PLO.**
                                                      Anon   ♂ ♎ 5

Why do bagpipers walk when they play?
To get away from the sound.   *Anon*   ♂ ♎ 5

In the act of loving someone you arm them against you.   *Anon*   ♂ ♎ 5

There was a young fellow of Keating
Whose pride took a terrible beating.
    That happens to males
    When they learn the details
Of their wives' extramarital cheating.   *Anon*   ♀ ♌ 7

Although it is hard for a son to compete with a successful
father, it may be even harder for him to compete with an
unsuccessful one. This is because most young men find the
prospect of their own failure easier to bear than the prospect
of being instruments of their fathers' humiliation.
                                                 Thomas Szasz   ♃ ♌ 12

♍ ☿ 6

VIRGO

efficient
discriminating
meticulous
precise
industrious

critical
worrying
petty
narrow
puritanical

Life purpose to:
analyze
research
specialize
correct
purify

MERCURY

Influence:
craftsmanship
evaluation
service
precision / detail
intellectualism
discernment

Examples:
healers
critics
health / safety
accountants
researchers

SIXTH HOUSE

**The House of Work
and Health**
'daily grind'

the sphere of self-
adjustment
daily work
capacity to serve
food and diet
sickness and health
exercise

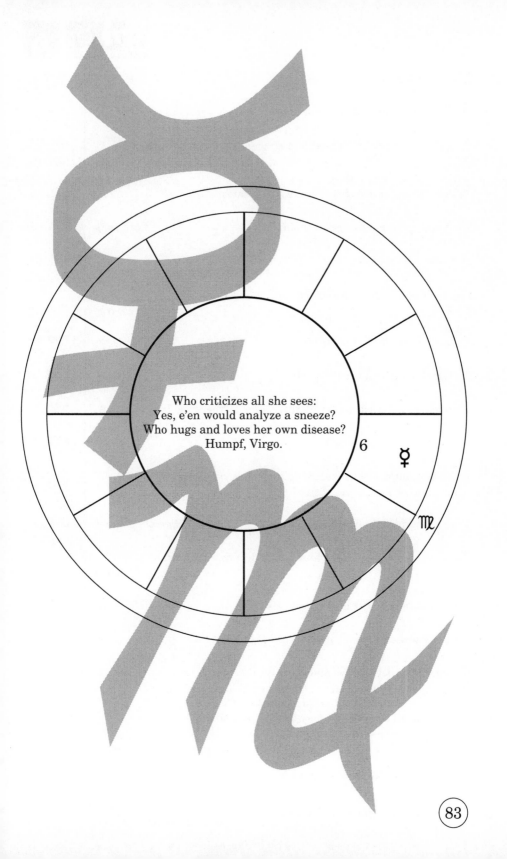

Who criticizes all she sees:
Yes, e'en would analyze a sneeze?
Who hugs and loves her own disease?
Humpf, Virgo.

6

☿

♍

You don't have to be sick to get better.　　　　　　*Anon*　| ♃ ♍ 6

To know and not to do is not to know.　　　*Leo Buscaglia*　| ♂ ♐ 6

Youth thinks nothing of health, and age thinks of nothing but.
　　　　　　　　　　　　　　　　　Anon　| ♄ ♊ 6

Where the gotta dues become the gutter dues.　　　*D.H.*　| ♄ ♏ 6

Don't cure symptoms, follow them.　　　　*Carl Jung*　| ☿ ♏ 6

A horse is an oatsmobile.　　　　　　　　*Anon*　| ☿ ♐ 6

Zip your pants up, turn your hat around and get a job.
　　　　　　　　　　　　　　　P.J. O'Rourke　| ♂ ♏ 6

A joyful heart is good medicine.　　　　*Proverbs*　| ☽ ♌ 6

Patience is applied timelessness.　　　　　*Anon*　| ♄ ♍ 12

Perfection, Procrastination, Paralyzation ... "the three P's."　*A.A.*　| ♄ ♍ 6

Healing hands heal hearts.　　　　　　　*Anon*　| ☿ ♍ 5

Turn stumbling blocks into stepping stones, obstacles into
opportunities, and get on with it!　　　　　*D.H.*　| ♂ ♑ 6

If you would live in health, be old early.　*Spanish Proverb*　| ♂ ♑ 6

How many times has the water you're drinking been drunk before?
　　　　　　　　　　　　　　　　　Anon　| ♄ ♋ 6

Not crack or pot, just food -- quite a lot.　*Heather Hayward*　| ♃ ♋ 6

Life is a sexually transmitted terminal disease.　　*Anon*　| ☉ ♏ 6

Joseph Campbell always made a point that meat eating
was our heritage as hunters. A vegetarian he described as
"someone who had never heard a carrot or a tomato scream",
feeling that the distinction between the animal and vegetable
orders of life was artificial. "Life feeds on life," he would say.
　　　　　　　　　　　　　　　　Larsen　| ♇ ♍ 4

Sacred cows make great hamburger.　　*Robert Reisner*　| ♃ ♋ 6

The definition of a vegetarian is a person who doesn't like
his food to run away.   *Joseph Campbell*   ♂ ♍ 3

Joseph Campbell averaged ten-and-a-half hours of reading
and writing four days a week for 35 years. The other three
days were dedicated to teaching at Sarah Lawrence.
[He had four planets in 6th house.]   *Larsen*   ♃ ♐ 6

Virgo meditates to transcend the daily crush of virus,
bacteria, and other microbial menaces.   *D.H.*   ♆ ♍ 12

We must all realize that the behavior is just behavior,
unskilled behavior. What used to be called sin is now
"unskilled behavior."   *Jean Houston*   ♄ ♍ 1

There are people who so arrange their lives as to only feed
themselves on side dishes.   *Ortegy y Gassett*   ♄ ♋ 6

Gluttony is not a secret vice.   *Orson Welles*   ♃ ♋ 6

Stress is the perception of threat.   *Deepak Chopra*   ☽ ♈ 6

Good medicine increases the number of sick people
by keeping them alive.   *Dr. Willard Gaylin*   ♃ ♍ 6

We must practice (being conscious) in a way that removes
the barrier between practice and non-practice.   *Thich Nhat Hanh*   ♄ ♓ 6

If you think health care is expensive now, wait until it's free.
                                        P.J. O'Rourke   ♃ ♍ 2

God has no need of your service; give it to man.
                                        Sai Baba   ♃ ♍ 11

Hands that help are holier than lips that pray.   *Sai Baba*   ♃ ♍ 3

Duty without love is deplorable; duty with love is good;
love without duty is divine.   *Sai Baba*   ♃ ♍ 5

Having your cake and eating it too is the best clue to the divine.
                                        Joseph Campbell   ♀ ♍ 9

The first wealth is health.   *Emerson*   ♃ ♍ 2

Perfect health is a contradiction in terms. *Larry Dossey* | ♅ ♊ 6

James Joyce's Refrigerator [cartoon]
1. Call bank
2. Dry cleaner
3. Forge in the smithy of my soul the uncreated conscience of my race
4. Call mom
Anon | ♄ ♍ 6

May my physical skills be used in Godly works. *D.H.* | ♃ ♍ 1

Work is a release from the longings of our dreams,
which often only blind and flatter us to death. *Kafka* | ♆ ♍ 8

Be first a good animal. *Emerson* | ♍ 1

My husband thinks that health food is anything he eats
before the expiration date. *Rita Rudner* | ♄ ♍ 7

Ever notice that fifteen minutes into a Jerry Lewis telethon you
start rooting for the disease? *Jim Sherbert* | ♅ ♍ 8

Preserving health by too severe a rule is a worrisome malady.
Duc de La Rochefoucauld (1613-1680) | ♄ ♍ 12

The entire economy of the western world is built on things
that cause cancer. *Anon* | ♃ ♍ 6

If there's anything I hate it is the high maintenance details of
physical survival. *D.H.* | ♄ ♍ 1

We're going to push through health care reform regardless
of the views of the American people. *David Rockefeller* | ♄ ♒ 6

We are involved in a life that passes understanding
and our highest business is our daily life. *John Cage* | ♃ ♍ 3

Love is a behavior, not a feeling. *Anon* | ♂ ♌ 6

The devil's in the details. *Anon* | ☿ 6

Prove all things and hold fast to that which is good. *St. Paul* | ♄ ♍ 9

Quit worrying about your health. It'll go away. *Robert Orben* | ☽ ♓ 6

For me, hard work represents the supreme luxury of life.

Albert Greenfield   ♄ ♂ 6

Someone else's need is not a claim on your life -- you have a
fundamental right to live that does not have to be validated
by service to others. (Ayn Rand described this as the right
to live for your own sake.)   *Sheldon Richman*   ☉ ♒ 6

In two decades I've lost a total of 789 pounds. I should be
hanging from a charm bracelet.   *Erma Bombeck*   ♄ ♍ 5

Jung 101 teaches there are two roots to psychological disease
-- the gods we forget and the gods we overdo.   *Dana Gerhardt*   ♄ ♍ 9

The relative value of health and wealth depends on
which one you've lost.   *Anon*   ♄ ♂ 6

To be stupid, selfish, and have good health are three
requirements for happiness, though if stupidity is lacking,
all is lost.   *Gustave Flaubert*   ♄ ♍ 1

The highest reward for a person's toil is not what they get
from it, but what they become by it.   *John Ruskin*   ♃ ♏ 6

Careful attention paid to anything is a window into the universe.

Anon   ♃ ♍ 12

You don't realize what life is all about until you have found
yourself lying on the edge of a great abscess. [Jupiter rules
abscesses.]   *Samuel Goldwyn*   ♃ 6

You already have the precious mixture that will make
you well. Use it.   *Rumi*   ♀ ♍ 6

Salutagenics is the salutary, beneficial side of health;
the study of the promotion of wellness.   *Dr. Paul Pearsall*   ♃ ♍ 6

**Every complex problem has a simple solution
-- and it's usually wrong.**

H.L. Mencken   ♄ ♍

I've just heard about his illness. Let's hope it's nothing trivial.

Anon   ☿ ♏ 6

I'm on a seafood diet. I see food and I eat it.   *Anon*   ☿ ♋ 6

Health nuts are going to feel stupid someday,
lying in hospitals dying of nothing. *Redd Foxx* ♆ ♍ 12

The Son of Man came not to be ministered unto, but to minister.
Matthew 20:28 ♍

Total freedom from error is what none of us will allow to our
neighbors; however, we may be inclined to flirt a little with
such spotless perfection ourselves. *Charles Caleb Colton* ♍ 3

Virgo will find something to DO about other people's problems.
Grant Lewi ♂ ♍ 11

We shall never have friends, if we expect to find them without fault.
Thomas Fuller ♄ ♒ 6

Could everything be done twice everything would be done better.
German Proverb ♃ ♍

In small proportions we just beauties see,
And in short measures life may perfect be. *Ben Jonson* ♄ ♍ 6

Perfection has one grave defect: it is apt to be dull.
Somerset Maugham ♄ ♍ 8

**In anything at all, perfection is finally attained not
when there is no longer anything to add, but when
there is no longer anything to take away.**
St. Exupéry ♄ ♍ 5

There is tragedy in perfection, because the universe in which
perfection arises is itself imperfect. *Santayana* ♆ 6

The indefatigable pursuit of an unattainable Perfection,
even though it consist in nothing more than the pounding of an old
piano, alone gives a meaning to our life on this unavailing star.
Logan Pearsall Smith ♄ ♍ 5

It is through art, and through art only, that we can realize
our perfection. *Oscar Wilde* ♀ ♍ 5

Judgment is not upon all occasions required, but discretion
always is. *Lord Chesterfield* ♄ ♍ 9

Nobody, as long as he moves about among the chaotic currents
of life, is without trouble.   *Carl Jung*   ♄ ♓ 6

The only reason I would take up jogging is so I could hear
heavy breathing again.   *Erma Bombeck*   ☿ ♏ 6

Health is infinite and expansive in mode, and reaches out
to be filled with the fullness of the world; whereas disease
is finite and reductive in mode, and endeavors to reduce the
world to itself.   *Oliver Sacks*   ♍ 6

Optimistic lies have such immense therapeutic value
that a doctor who cannot tell them convincingly has mistaken
his profession.   *George Bernard Shaw*   ♃ ♓ 6

It takes a wise doctor to know when not to prescribe.
                                           Baltasar Gracian   ♄ ♍ 9

THE IRISH PIG

'Twas an evening in November,
And I very well remember
I was walking down the street in drunken pride.
But my knees were all aflutter,
So I landed in the gutter,
And a pig came up and lay down by my side.

Yes, I lay there in the gutter,
Thinking thoughts I could not utter,
When a colleen passing by did softly say,
"Ye can tell a man that boozes
By the company he chooses" --
At that the pig got up and walked away.   *Anon*   ♆ 6

I wonder why ye can always read a doctor's bill
an' ye niver can read his purscription?   *Finley Peter Dunne*   ☿ ♍ 2

No one is more liable to make mistakes than the man
who acts only on reflection.   *Vauvenargues*   ♄ ♍ 1

Nothing will ever be attempted, if all possible objects
must be overcome.   *Dr. Johnson*   ♄ ♍ 1

The most perfect technique is that which is not noticed at all.
                                               Pablo Casals   ♓ 6

It was no more use arguing with him than it would have been
trying to staunch the flow of saliva dribbling from the jaws of
Pavlov's dogs when they heard the dinner bell.   *Rebecca West*   ♄ ♊ 6

I see a household cat in my despairing,
Who makes no noise and knows how to behave.
Her needs are few -- a scratch will start her purring.
A scrap to eat and whispered words: "Be brave!"
(Quoted from a Russian prison camp mid-1980's.)   *Omar Khayyám*   ♃ ♍ 12

There are two kinds of statistics, the kind you look at
and the kind you make up.   *Rex Stout*   ☿ ♍ 5

The worst disease in the world is the plague of vengeance.
                                             Dr. Karl Menninger   ♀ 6

Purge me with hyssop, and I shall be clean: wash me,
and I shall be whiter than snow. [The moon rules hyssop,
cleaning, wash, and white.]   *Psalm 51:7*   ☽ ♏ 6

If a man has nothing to eat, fasting is the most intelligent thing
he can do.   *Hermann Hesse*   ♄ ♍ 3

Nothing can cure the soul but the senses, just as nothing
can cure the senses but the soul.   *Oscar Wilde*   ♃ ♉ 6

What do you give a sick guru? Transcendental medication.
                                             Hester Mundis   ♆ ♍ 9

Sow your oats where you please -- just don't expect them
to come up as bran muffins.   *Hester Mundis*   ♂ ♏ 6

How much wood would a woodchuck chuck if a woodchuck could
chuck wood?   *Hester Mundis*   ♂ ♑ 6

Always think twice about something you can do only once.
                                             Hester Mundis   ♄ ♍ 1

My favorite animal is steak.   *Fran Lebowitz*   ♀ ♏ 6

Cats are a waste of fur.   *Rita Rudner*   ♀ ♍ 6

Other dogs look at French poodles and wonder if
they are members of a weird religious cult.   *Rita Rudner*   ♆ ♐ 6

My dog is worried about the economy because Alpo is up
to .99 cents a can. That's almost $7.00 in dog money.

Joe Weinstein   ♄ ♍ 2

**Britain plans to stop the breeding of pit bulls.
It's hard enough to put a muzzle on a pit bull
-- lots of luck with those condoms.**

Jay Leno   ♄ ♏ 6

I don't jog. It makes the ice jump right out of my glass.

Martin Mull   ♂ ♓ 6

I spilled some spot remover on my dog -- now he's gone.

Steven Wright   ♆ 6

The sin that is the hardest to atone for is habit. That is the
biggest obstacle to reaching new levels, as one rabbi put it.
When in an habitual state we hear the routine rather than the
challenge that comes at this moment.

Rabbi Zalman Schachter-Shalomi   ☿ ♐ 6

To fall into a habit is to begin to cease to be.

Miguel de Unamuno   ♄ ♍ 12

Opportunities are usually disguised as hard work,
so most people don't recognize them.   *Ann Landers*   ♃ ♑ 6

A decision is what a man makes when he can't find anybody
to serve on a committee.   *Fletcher Knebel*   ♄ ♍ 11

Massage is the joy of necks, and meeting need by kneading meat.

M. Rose Pierce   ♂ ♍ 1

For a pig, the sty's the limit.   *M. Rose Pierce*   ♄ ♍ 6

Job -- From hire to infirmity.   *M. Rose Pierce*   ♄ ♍ 6

Swiss doctors, in the journal *Neurology*, describe a new disorder
they call "Gourmand Syndrome." It is a food obsession linked to
brain injuries. That explains the ease with which some people
pay $4.25 for a cup of coffee and steamed milk.   *Mark Wheeler*   ♄ ♊ 6

I bought some powdered water; now I don't know what to add.

Steven Wright   ♆ 6

When you consider how indifferent Americans are to the quality
and cooking of the food they put into their insides, it cannot but
strike you as peculiar that they should take such pride in the
mechanical appliances they use for its excretion.

W. Somerset Maugham | ♀ ♌ 6

A critic is a man who knows the way but can't drive the car.

Kenneth Tynan | ♄ ♍ 3

Dogs look up to us, cats look down on us, pigs see us eye to eye.

Winston Churchill | ☿ 6

Hoping is to trying as doing is to done. *D.H.* | ♂ 6

Student to Zen Master: "How can I get enlightened?"
Master: "Did you have your lunch?"
Student: "Yes."
Master: "Then wash your bowl." *Zen Story* | ♇ ♐ 6

There's a new Japanese-Jewish restaurant in town.
It's called So-Sumi. *Anon* | ♎ 6

The great happiness of life, I find, after all, to consist
in the regular discharge of some mechanical duty. *Johann Schiller* | ♂ ♑ 6

Rabbits of the world -- stop! *Anon* | ♄ ♐ 6

The barking of a dog does not disturb the man on a camel.

Egyptian Proverb | ☽ ♓ 6

He who plays with cats must bear the scratches. *Persian Proverb* | ♂ ♍ 5

It's all process, not perfection. Yet in the process lies the perfection.

D.H. | ♃ ♍ 1

People in offices have a heightened affect; they move their faces
all day to register reactions and responses. Smiles, frowns,
laughter, the furrowed brow. Your face gets tired and you
age quicker. *Peggy Noonan* | ♄ ♈ 6

A fork is an instrument used chiefly for the purpose of
putting dead animals into the mouth. *Ambrose Bierce* | ♂ ♍ 6

Kitty heaven is mousy hell. *Anon* | ♇ 6

There is not the least use preaching to anyone
unless you chance to catch them ill.   *Sydney Smith* | ☿ ♐ 6

Some 49% of women put on their panties first, and a third
add the bra while 16% put on their hose next, 19% start with
the bra, 15% wear their hose <u>under</u> their panties, and 22%
can't recall.   *Bernice Kanner* | ☽ ♍ 11

Exercise is bunk. If you are healthy, you don't need it;
if you are sick, you shouldn't take it.   *Henry Ford* | ♄ ♍ 6

Mingle occasional pleasures with your care
that you with courage any task may bear.   *Cato* | ♀ ♈ 6

The quizzical expression of the monkey at the zoo comes from
his wondering whether he is his brother's keeper, or his
keeper's brother.   *Evan Esar* | ♊ 6

Why can't somebody give us a list of things that everybody
thinks and nobody says, and another list of things that
everybody says and nobody thinks?   *Oliver Wendell Holmes* | ♍ 3

Venereal disease is insidious,
And the end results truly are hideous,
    So the pure and ethereal
    Try to shun the venereal,
Though they're NOT really all that fastidious.   *Anon* | ♆ 6

ON ELEPHANTIASIS

I view with no end of compassion
Any fellow bedecked in this fashion.
    Such a horribly odd piece
    Would call for a codpiece,
And sitting down slow to save mashin'!   *Anon* | ♄ ♐ 6

**I have gained and lost the same ten pounds
so many times over and over again my cellulite
must have déjà vu.**
    Jane Wagner | ♄ ♍ 6

Herpes: A permanent case of the cooties, rendering the victim
untouchable except by fellow sufferers, who must then spend
their lives searching for each other like fireflies in the twilight.
    Rick Bayan | ♀ ♎ 6

♍ ☿ 6

The Dodo never had a chance. He seems to have been
invented for the purpose of becoming extinct and that
was all he was good for.   *Will Cuppy*   ♄ ♍ 8

A door is what a dog is perpetually on the wrong side of.
                                                                Ogden Nash   ♄ ♍ 6

The best thing about animals is that they don't talk much.
                                                                Thornton Wilder ♃ ♍ 3

Man's unique reward ... is that while animals survive
by adjusting themselves to their background, man survives
by adjusting his background to himself.   *Ayn Rand*   ☉ ♒ 6
                                                                                   ☉ ♍ 3

You must do the things you think you cannot do.
                                                                Eleanor Roosevelt ♄ ♐ 6

I'm like an ant that's gotten into the granary, ludicrously
happy, and trying to lug out a grain that's way too big.   *Rumi*   ♃ ♍ 1

The rooster of lust, the peacocks of wanting to be famous,
the crow of ownership, and the duck of urgency, kill them
and revive them in another form, changed and harmless.
                                                                Rumi   ♀ 6

> **There's hidden sweetness in the stomach's
> emptiness ... The fog clears, and new energy
> makes you run up the steps in front of you ...
> When you're full of food and drink, an ugly
> metal statue sits where your spirit should.
> When you fast, good habits gather like friends
> who want to help.**
>   *Rumi*   ♄ ♍ 11
>   ☽ ♍ 1

I think there's something incredibly sexy about a woman
wearing her boyfriend's t-shirt and underwear.   *Calvin Klein*   ☽ ♈ 6

When in doubt wear red.   *Bill Blass*   ♂ ♎ 6

> **T**o obsessions for possessions
> Amid 'the ten-thousand things'
> We've added pills and powders
> For carcass tinkerings   *D.H.*   ♃ ♍ 2
>   ♀ 6

(94) virgo - mercury - sixth house

A super Virgo who has a million asteroids in their chart
and does the seventh harmonic of the composite re-located
semi-arc.   *Maritha Pottenger*

♃ ♍ 3

♀ 6

☿ ♏ 12

So much perfection argues rottenness somewhere.   *Beatrice Webb*

SEVENTH HOUSE

The House of Partnerships
'what they show me'

the sphere of relationships
interaction
contacts
close relationships
business partners
cooperation
open adversaries
legal contracts

VENUS

Influence:
democracy
luxury
fashion
relationships
persuasion
harmony

Examples:
arbitrators
advocates
designers
musicians
decorators

LIBRA

sociable
fair
diplomatic
considerate
refined

indecisive
lethargic
self-indulgent
narcissistic
ambivalent

Life purpose to:
balance
relate
cooperate
blend
mediate

Who puts you off with promise gay,
And keeps you waiting half the day?
Who compromises all the way?
Sweet Libra.

7   ♀

♎

I'm glad I got married before I knew I was supposed to have a meaningful relationship.   *Joy Hayward*   ☿ ♏ 7

Men replace relationships; women mourn them.   *Anon*   ♎ 5

Politics doesn't make strange bedfellows -- marriage does.   *Groucho Marx*   ♅ 7

An appeaser feeds the crocodile hoping it will eat him last.   *Winston Churchill*   ♀ ♏ 6

George Bernard Shaw has no enemies but is intensely disliked by his friends.   *Oscar Wilde*   ♄ ♎ 11

The surest cure for vanity is loneliness.   *Thomas Wolfe*   ♀ ♍ 12

Peace is the reconciling of the co-existence of opposites.   *Deepak Chopra*   ♀ ♈ 7

Why can't the leprechaun lady have a baby? Her husband has shamrocks.   *Anon*   ♆ ♑ 7

To be consistent with political correctness we should outlaw Valentine's Day as sexual harassment. Also, by expressing a preference for one person, or species, we are showing a disinclination towards another. This is preferential harassment.   *DH.*   ♄ ♑ 7

If the trumpet give an uncertain sound, who shall prepare himself for the battle?   *1st Corinthians 14:8*   ♄ ♎ 7
                    ♂ ♓ 7

The meeting of two personalities is like the contact of two chemical substances; if there is any reaction, both are transformed.
                    Carl Jung   ♆ ♏ 7

My husband doesn't want me to think for myself; he expects me to think for him.   *Joy Hayward*   ♄ ♊ 7

Some of us are becoming the men we wanted to marry.   *Gloria Steinem*   ♂ ♒ 7

Excellence is no flatterer and does not comfort the mediocre.   *D.H.*   ♄ ♎ 9

Art is the apotheosis of solitude. *Samuel Beckett* | ♀ ♓ 9

The one who loves the least controls the relationship.
Robert Anthony | ♄ ♒ 7

We are here on this Earth to do good to others;
what others are here for I don't know. *W.H. Auden* | ♃ ♍ 7
♃ ♎ 11

Marriage is stirring the oatmeal. *Robert Johnson* | ☽ ♍ 7

A jazz musician is a juggler who uses harmonies
instead of oranges. [Oranges are ruled by ☉.] *Benny Green* | ☉ ♎ 5

A wise woman will always let her husband have her way.
Richard B. Sheridan | ♃ ♋ 7

The hardest job kids face today is learning good manners
without seeing any. *Fred Astaire* | ♄ ♎ 5

Dorothy Parker was unhappily married three times,
twice to the same man. *Anon* | ♄ ♎ 12

Attila the Hun dies from a nosebleed on wedding night in 453.
Anon | ♂ ♏ 7

**Every time I look at you I get a fierce desire
to be lonesome.**
Oscar Levant | ♄ ♎ 12

Eighty-two year old Leo Tolstoy flees from wife,
dies in railway station of exposure in 1910. *Anon* | ♄ ♏ 7
♂ ♎ 8

The war between the sexes is the only one in which both sides
regularly sleep with the enemy. *Quentin Crisp* | ♀ ♏ 12
♇ 7

No married man is genuinely happy if he has to drink
worse whisky than he used to drink when he was single.
H.L. Mencken | ♄ ♓ 7

Marriage is like a very long meal with the dessert at the beginning.
Toulouse Lautrec | ♄ ♋ 7

A woman usually respects her father, but her view of her husband is mingled with contempt, for she is of course privy to the transparent devices by which she snared him.

H.L. Mencken | ♄ ♓ 7

We study ourselves three weeks, we love each other three months, we squabble three years, we tolerate each other thirty years, and then the children start all over again.

Hippolyte Taine | ♄ ♎ 5

> **I** never married because I have three pets that answer the same purpose as a husband. I have a dog that growls every morning, a parrot that swears all afternoon, and a cat that comes home at midnight.

Marie Corelli | ♄ ♎ 6

At 64 years the difference between monotony and monogamy blurs.

Anon | ♄ ♓ 7

Seldom, or perhaps never, does a marriage develop into an individual relationship smoothly and without crises; there is no coming to consciousness without pain.

Carl Jung | ♀ ♍ 7
♄ ♏ 7

The way to hold a husband is to keep him a little jealous; the way to lose him is to keep him a little more jealous.

H.L. Mencken | ♀ ♏ 7

Any marriage, happy or unhappy is infinitely more interesting and significant than any romance, however passionate.

W.H. Auden | ☿ ♎ 5

No matter how happily a woman may be married, it always pleases her to discover that there is a nice man who wishes she were not.

H.L. Mencken | ♀ ♎ 5

One of the best hearing aids a man can have is an attentive wife.

Groucho Marx | ♂ ♎ 3

A woman is not a whole woman without the experience of marriage. In the case of a bad marriage, you win if you lose. Of the two alternatives -- bad marriage or none -- I believe bad marriage would be better. It is a bitter experience and a high price to pay for fulfillment, but it is the better alternative.

Fanny Hurst | ♄ ♋ 7

A rich widow weeps with one eye and signals with the other.

Portugese Proverb ☽ ♎ 8

Conrad Hilton was very generous to me in the divorce settlement. He gave me 5,000 Gideon Bibles. *Zsa Zsa Gabor* ♃ ♎ 8

It destroys one's nerves to be amiable to the same human being every day. *Benjamin Disraeli* ♅ ♎ 6

The only thing that holds a marriage together is the husband being big enough to step back and see where the wife was wrong.

Archie Bunker ♃ ♈ 7
♂ ♎ 3

There's nothing like living together for blinding people to each other.

Ivy Compton-Burnett ☿ ♓ 7

When a man opens the car door for his wife, it's either a new car or a new wife. *Prince Philip* ♅ ♊ 7

A cling-clung relationship may offer a lot of security, but who wants to be married to a roll of flypaper?

Anne Wilson Schaef ☽ ♋ 7

Marriage is putting one's hand into a bag of snakes on the chance of drawing out an eel. *Leonardo da Vinci* ☿ ♏ 7

When people do as they please, they usually imitate each other.

Eric Hoffer ♀ ♊ 7

Marriage is a word that should be pronounced "mirage."

Herbert Spencer ♆ 7
☿ ♓ 7

Americans are so enamoured of equality they would rather be equal in slavery than unequal in freedom. *De Tocqueville* ♄ ♎ 12

Love is blind and marriage heals it. *Lichtenberg* ♀ ♓ 7

LICKSPITTLE -- a parasite who kisses the person he flatters on all four cheeks. *Anon* ♀ ♏ 1

Venus is to Neptune what glamour is to enchantment -- a carrot on a stick. *D.H.* ♀ ♓

I never allowed myself to be the important one in a relationship.

Anon | ♄ ♌ 7

In married life, three is company and two is none. *Oscar Wilde* | ♄ ♎ 11

Both marriage and death ought to be welcome: the one
promises happiness, doubtless the other assures it. *Mark Twain* | ♎ 8

Love seems the swiftest, but it is the slowest of all growths.
No man or woman really knows what perfect love is until they
have been married a quarter of a century. *Mark Twain* | ♄ ♎ 7

Marriage is popular because it combines the maximum of
temptation with the maximum of opportunity.

George Bernard Shaw | ♃ ♏ 7

A good marriage is that in which each appoints the other
guardian of his solitude. *Rainer Maria Rilke* | ♂ ♎ 12

Envy is ignorance; imitation is suicide. *Emerson* | ♄ ♏ 7

When seen in the perspective of half-a-dozen years or more,
the best of our fashions strike us as grotesque, if not unsightly.

Thorstein Veblen, 1899 | ♄ ♎

When my arms have rapt you 'round
I press my heart upon the loveliness that
Has long faded from the world. *W. B. Yeats* | ♀ ♌ 10

He couldn't swing if he were hanging from a rope. *Anon* | ♀ ♏ 5

Death does not end relationship, but advances it. *Fred Buechner* | ♇ ♎ 3/
7/11

The secret of a long and happy marriage: "You have to
remember those three little words -- I was wrong." *Charlton Heston* | ♄ ♊ 7

I haven't committed a crime. What I did was fail to comply
with the law. *David Dinkins (N.Y. City Mayor)* | ♄ ♓ 7

Where there is marriage without love, there will be love
without marriage. *Ben Franklin* | ♄ ♌ 7

Life is not so short but that there is always time enough
for courtesy. *Emerson* | ♀ ♑ 1

Art is a jealous mistress. *Emerson*	♀ ♏ 5
I don't think any modern artist -- Cézanne, Matisse, Picasso and the rest -- has been as great as the great of the past -- Rubens or Velasquez or Rembrandt. *Willem de Kooning*	♃ ♎ 4
If you're an artist the problem is to make a picture work whether you are happy or not. *Willem de Kooning*	♀ ♋ 5
My wife gives good headache. *Rodney Dangerfield*	♄ ♈ 7
Mr. Right is now a guy who hasn't been laid in fifteen years. *Elaine Boosler*	♄ ♏ 7
Diplomacy is the art of letting someone else have your way. *Anon*	♀ ♏ 7
Man and woman are two locked caskets, of which each contains the key to the other. *Isak Dinesen*	♄ ♏ 7
I married beneath me -- all women do. *Nancy Astor*	♃ ♋ 7
I do give and bequeath to Mary Davis the sum of five shillings, which is sufficient to enable her to get drunk for the last time at my expense. (Excerpt from a will, 1788.) *David Davis*	♀ ♓ 8
It should be a very happy marriage -- they are both so much in love with <u>him</u>. *Irene Thomas*	♂ ♌ 7
I like him and his wife. He is so ladylike, and she is such a perfect gentleman. *Sydney Smith*	♅ ♎ 7
The most happy marriage I can picture or imagine to myself would be the union of a deaf man and a blind woman. *Samuel Taylor Coleridge*	♄ ♊ 7
Her lustful loins are never stilled: By just one man she's unfulfilled. She'll spread her legs to all the men But, ever hungry, won't say "when." Thus married women love to stray And wish their husbands' lives away. Since none a woman's lust can sate I don't commend the marriage state. *Anon, c. 1225-50*	☽ ♏ 7

Bigamy is having one husband too many. Monogamy is the same.

Erica Jong | ♄ 7

Here lies my wife; here let her lie!
Now she's at rest, and so am I. (Epitaph for his wife.)

John Dryden | ☿ ♎ 8

Marriage is a sort of friendship recognized by the police.

Robert Louis Stevenson | ♄ ♎ 11

**It was very good of God to let Carlyle and Mrs.
Carlyle marry one another and so make only
two people miserable instead of four.**

Samuel Butler | ♄ ♎ 9

Brigands demand your money or your life; women require both.

Samuel Butler | ☽ ♏

Form without meaning is not a hand but an empty glove
filled with air.   *Hans Roethel on Kandinsky* | ♄ ♎ 3

If you want to make enemies, try to change something.

Woodrow Wilson | ☽ ♒ 7

The worst sin toward our fellow creatures is not to hate them,
but be indifferent to them; that's the essence of inhumanity.

George Bernard Shaw | ♄ ♒ 7

Eighty percent of married men cheat in America.
The rest cheat in Europe.   *Jackie Mason* | ♀ ♏ 9

Good taste and humor are a contradiction in terms,
like a chaste whore.   *Malcolm Muggeridge* | ♀ ♏ 5

The Talmud says, that when a wedding procession
and a funeral procession meet at a crossroads,
the wedding procession has the right of way.   *Eda Leshan* | ♀ ♏ 11

In c. 700 the Chinese invented the brassiere.   *Anon* | ☽ ♎ 11

Co-dependents buy my-fault insurance.   *Anon* | ☽ ♎ 8

I don't very much enjoy looking at paintings in general.
I know too much about them. I take them apart. *Georgia O'Keefe* | ♀ ♍ 7

Flattery is so necessary that we flatter one another just to be
flattered in return.   *Marjorie Bowen* | ♀ 11
| ♀ 7

Vanity is as ill at ease under indifference, as tenderness
is under the love which it cannot return.   *George Eliot* | ♄ ♋ 7

There was a time when only the dead could smile.
(1935-1940 Soviet Russia.)   *Anna Akhmatova* | ♀ ♑ 8

Hell is -- other people!   *Jean Paul Sartre* | ♀ 7/11

Art enables us to find ourselves and lose ourselves at the same time.
                                                        Thomas Merton | ♀ ♌ 12

I compose as a sow piddles.   *Mozart* | ♀ ♏ 6

How many husbands have I had? You mean apart from my own?
                                                        Zsa Zsa Gabor | ♀ ♏ 5

A man in love is incomplete until he's married. Then he's finished.
                                                        Zsa Zsa Gabor | ♄ ♎ 5

It seems likely that many of the young who don't wait for others
to call them artists, but simply announce that they are, don't
have the patience to make art.   *Pauline Kael (1968)* | ♄ ♎ 3

Being divorced is like being hit by a Mack truck. If you live
through it, you start looking very carefully to the right
and to the left.   *Jean Kerr* | ♂ ♊ 7

I'm tired of all this nonsense about beauty being only skin-deep.
That's deep enough. What do you want -- an adorable pancreas?
[Pancreas is ruled by Moon/Venus.]   *Jean Kerr* | ♀ ♋

Works of art are of an infinite loneliness.   *Rilke* | ♀ ♋ 12

The object of art is to give life shape.   *Jean Anouilh* | ♀ ♑ 1

Painting is a faith, and it imposes the duty to disregard
public opinion.   *Van Gogh* | ♀ ♐ 10

He owes his success to his first wife,
and his second wife to his success.   *Anon* | ♄ ♑ 7/8

Art is I, science is we. — Claude Bernard — ♀ ♒

There are some mothers of five children, particularly some
of the black mothers I have seen down South, who are great
yogis and know more about common courtesy than some of the
people whose books we read -- because that is what it is all about,
common courtesy. — Stephen Levine — ☽ ♎ 11

No marriage can be judged truly successful unless
husband and wife are each other's best critics. — Scott Peck — ♍ 7

A wholesome sexual relationship changes with marriage
because all of a sudden you're sleeping with a relative.
[Relatives by marriage are 9th House.] — Andrew Ward — ♇ ♎ 9

Courtship is to marriage, as a very witty prologue
to a very dull play. — William Congreve — ☿ ♎ 5

Platonic love is love from the neck up. — Thyra Samter Winslow — ♀ ♊ 1

How many loved your moments of glad grace,
And loved your beauty with love false or true,
But one man loved the pilgrim soul in you,
And loved the sorrows of your changing face. — W.B. Yeats — ♀ ♓ 1

The reason grandparents and grandchildren get along so well
is that they have a common enemy. — Sam Levenson — ☽ ♎ 9

Were that my afternoon self would match my morning self.
That I could be in the world but not _of_ it all day. The illusion
of separation grows as the sun descends. — D.H. — ☉ ♒ 7

Every woman is entitled to a middle husband she can forget.
— Adela Rogers-St. John — ☿ ♎ 8

I'm going to be assertive ... if that's ok with you!
— Robert Anthony — ♂ ♎

My Dear One is mine as mirrors are lonely,
As the poor and sad are real to the good king,
And the high green hill sits always by the sea. — W.H. Auden — ☽ ♎ 12

Georgie Porgie puddin' and pie kissed the girls and made them
seek legal representation in a class action sexual harassment
law suit. — Anon — ♇ ♒ 7

Dependency is slavery by mutual agreement.   *Robert Anthony*   ☽ ♎ 12

All unhappiness is caused by comparison.   *Anon*   ♄ ♎ 1

The more I accuse myself, the more I have a right to judge you.
Albert Camus   ♀ 7

If men knew how women pass the time when they're alone,
they'd never marry.   *O. Henry*   ♂ ♎ 7

Love is not the opposite of hate. Being whole, love has no opposites.
Deepak Chopra   ♂ ♎ 5

Not to decide, is to decide.   *Robert Anthony*   ♄ ♎ 3

A host is like a general: it takes a mishap to reveal his genius.
Horace   ☽ ♒ 7

Do not do unto others as you would that they should do unto you.
Their tastes may not be the same.   *George Bernard Shaw*   ☿ ♒ 7

Said the wife of the great intellectual:
"My problem is quite frankly sexual.
When for hubby I pant
he just quotes Will Durant,
And remains, in the sack, ineffectual."   *Anon*   ♀ ♐ 7
♄ ♏ 7

Meet me half-way, you need the exercise.   *Robert Anthony*   ♂ ♎ 6

Would you still have married me if my father
had not given me a million dollars?
Of course darling, I would have married you
no matter who gave you a million dollars.   *Anon*   ♎ 8

With my wife there's a place where the rubber doesn't reach
the road. With me the tire often runs on its rims ... a curious
polarity of primal energy.   *D.H.*   ♅ ♎ 7

I hate careless flattery, the kind that exhausts you
in your effort to believe it.   *Wilson Mizner*   ♀ ♓ 1
♆ ♎ 1

One man's folly is another man's wife.   *Helen Rowland*
[One man's Molly is another man's folly.]   *[D.H.]*   ☿ ♏ 7

My wife is one of the least present people I know.
The advantage of this to me is that it allows much privacy.   *D.H.*   ♏ 7

Vanity is the last disease.   *George Moore*   ♀ ♍ 8

The music at a wedding procession always reminds me
of the music of soldiers going into battle.   *Heinrich Heine*   ♂ ♓ 7

If I return people's greetings, I do so only to give them
their greetings back.   *Karl Kraus*   ♄ ♊ 7

If you and your partner always agree, one of you is unnecessary!
[and lying.]   *Anon*   ♄ ♎

Never despise fashion. It's what we have instead of God.
                                Malcolm Bradbury   ♄ ♎ 9

We live in an age when the prison inmates are suing
because their mashed potatoes are lumpy.   *Anon*   ♆ ♎ 6

A woman who takes her husband about with her everywhere
is like a cat that goes on playing with a mouse long after she's
killed it.   *Saki*   ☽ ♏ 7
                                                          ♀ ♎ 6

No him, no me. (On Louis Armstrong)   *Dizzy Gillespie*   ♄ ♎ 5

We are the people our parents warned us about.   *Anon*   ♄ ♎ 4

An amateur is an artist who supports himself with outside jobs
which enable him to paint. A professional is someone whose
wife works to enable him to paint.   *Ben Shahn*   ♄ ♎ 5

Beauty is unbearable, drives us to despair, offering us
for a minute the glimpse of an eternity that we should like
to stretch out over the whole of time.   *Albert Camus*   ♄ ♎ 12

There is nothing worse than solitude, growing old without
a shoulder to lean on. Marry, marry -- even if he's fat and boring.
                                Coco Chanel   ♄ ♎ 12

Once it was power that created style. But now high styles
come from low places, from people who have no power ... who are
marginal, who carve out worlds for themselves in the nether
depths, in tainted "undergrounds."   *Tom Wolfe (1965)*   ♀ ♎ 12

Just because you're paranoid doesn't mean they aren't after you.

Alan Arkin, Catch 22 | ♆ ♏ 7

**I am continually fascinated at the difficulty
intelligent people have in distinguishing what is
controversial from what is merely offensive. (1976)**

Nora Ephron | ☿ ♎ 11

All diplomacy is a continuation of war by other means.

Chou En-Lai | ♀ ♈ 7
♂ ♎ 12

Sometimes I forget, completely forget,
What companionship is.
Unconscious and insane, I spill sad energy everywhere,
My story gets told in various ways: a romance, a dirty joke,
a war, a vacancy. *Rumi* | ☽ ♎ 12

If your wife wants to learn how to drive, don't stand in her way.

Sam Levinson | ♂ ♊ 7
♆ 7

Never get married in the morning, 'cause you may never know
who you'll meet that night. *Paul Hornung* | ♄ ♎ 11

Visit, that ye be not visited. *Don Herold* | ♀ ♋ 12

The person you call an enemy is an exaggerated aspect
of your own shadow self. *Deepak Chopra* | ♎ 12

I'll love you, dear, I'll love you
Till China and Africa meet,
And the river jumps over the mountain
And the salmon sing in the street,
I'll love you till the ocean
Is folded and hung up to dry
And the seven stars go squawking
Like geese about the sky. *W.H. Auden* | ♌ 7

EIGHTH HOUSE

The House of Regeneration
'their stuff'

*the sphere of renewal and
release
other people's possessions
death and legacies
insurance
financial obligations
research
restoration
occult
sexual energy
Kundalini energy*

PLUTO

Influence:
*compulsions
control
extremes
regeneration
transformation
taboos*

Examples:
*detectives
psychoanalysts
explorers
strategists
spin doctors
morticians
gangsters
prostitutes*

SCORPIO

*decisive
powerful
strong-willed
passionate
deep*

*controlling
jealous
vindictive
destructive
subversive*

Life purpose to:
*transform
purge
challenge
penetrate
investigate*

Who keeps an arrow in his bow,
And if you prod, he lets it go?
A fervent friend, a subtle foe --
Scorpio.

8

Recognize what is before you and what is hidden will be revealed.

St. Thomas   ☿ ♏ 1

Then there was the big-game hunter who fashioned a wallet
from the skin of an elephant's penis. When you rub the wallet,
it turns into a suitcase. [Elephants are ruled by ♃.]   *Anon*   ♃ ♏ 2

The recognition of spirit at work is the touchstone of my awakening.

D.H.   ☿ ♏ 1

Mystery is the only addiction I wholeheartedly recommend.

Scott Peck   ♃ ♏ 12

On death: Do you grieve when a light bulb burns out?
It's the light, the energy behind, not the bulb that counts.

Joseph Campbell   ☉ ♒ 8

Bread results from the death of wheat.   *Joseph Campbell*   ♍ 8

We are fertilized by mysterious circumstances.   *Saint Exupéry*   ☽ ♏ 12

The whiter the lace the blacker the leather.   *Heather Hayward*   ♀ ♏ 1

Know thyself, halo to hemorrhoids.   *Anon*   ♃ ♏ 1

**What the caterpillar calls the end of the world,
the master calls a butterfly.**

Richard Bach   ♃ ♏ 8

Victimhood is the neighborhood of spiritual vagrants.   *D.H.*   ♇ ♐ 3

Sex is a means of coming to an end.   *Anon*   ♇ ♏ 4

I cling to my prejudices; they're the testicles of the mind.

Eric Hoffer   ♇ ♏ 3

To practice death is to practice freedom. A man who has
learned how to die has unlearned how to be a slave.   *Montaigne*   ♇ ♐ 12

Where Sturm and Drang meets sperm and bang.   *D.H.*   ♄ ♏ 12

Death -- the impartial friend.   *Mark Twain*   ♇ 11

Every seed destroys its container.   *Anon*   ☽ ♏ 8

When you touch mortality, what used to be tragedies are
mere inconvenience. *Jack Klugman* | ♄ ♏ 6

Women in conversation deep sea dive, men snorkel.
Heather Hayward | ☿ 3
| ☽ ♏ 3

If the rich could hire other people to die for them, the poor
could make a wonderful living. *Yiddish Proverb* | ♀ ♏ 12

Death is the soul's triumph and the ego's defeat. *D.H.* | ♃ ♏ 1

All situations are primarily neutral; "don't paint legs on snakes."
D.H. / Chinese Saying | ☿ ♏ 12
| ♀ ♏ 12

Leaving sex to the feminists is like leaving the dog at the
taxidermists while on vacations. [Taxidermy is ruled by ♄.]
Camille Paglia | ♄ ♏ 6

Conflatulations -- breaking wind over good fortune. *Jack Hitt* | ☿ ♏ 2

Flatulence is the sincerest form of flattery. *D.H.* | ♇ 7

He who dies before he dies does not die when he dies.
Tibetan Book of the Dead | ☉ ♏ 8

That day which you fear as the end of all things is the birthday
of your eternity. *Seneca* | ☉ ♏ 4

You need a license to sell pretzels, but any schmuck can make
a child. *Dennis Prager's Dad* | ♃ ♏ 5

From maim to miracle. *Anon* | ♂ ♒
| ♇ ♐

Life does not accommodate you, it shatters you, and that's what
it's supposed to do. *Florida S. Maxwell* | ☉ ♒ 8

The grand Mulah of the Church of Cosmic Proctology. *Anon* | ♇ ♐

Pluto comes through after the battle and bayonets the wounded.
Anon Mythology | ♇ 7
| ♂ ♏ 7

♏ ♇ 8

All life bears the smear and smudge of death -- the great illusionist.

D.H. — ♄ ♓ 8

A gross of pathologists.

Anon — ♄ ♏ 11

Now there ain't no chorus 'ere to give
nor there ain't no band to play;
an' I wish I was dead 'fore I done what I did,
or seen what I see'd that day!

Kipling — ♇ 7 / ♂ ♏ 7

An obscene fern call -- is talking dirty to plants.

Anon — ☿ ♉ 8

2,800,000 babies die each year of diarrhea -- who's wearing brown ribbons?

P.J. O'Rourke — ☽ ♍ 8

Growing up is growing in.

Anne Wilson-Schaef — ♃ ♏ 8

The shadow is our share of the imperfection of human nature.

Carl Jung — ♇ ♍ 12

Passion punches no timeclock.

Anon — ♄ ♏ 6

Life begets life. Energy creates energy. It is by spending oneself that one becomes rich.

Sarah Bernhardt — ♃ ♉ 8

He who lives on hope dies farting.

Ben Franklin — ♃ ♏ 8

I want death to find me planting my cabbages.

Montaigne — ☽ ♍ 8

My death will be my wedding with eternity.

Rumi — ♀ ♏ 12

Does God comprehend our vanity when dressed in wrinkles is how we'll meet?

Heather Hayward — ♄ ♎ 8 / ♀ ♏ 9

Everything that deceives may be said to enchant.

Plato — ♀ ♏ 12 / ♇ 12

Our president should worry less about same sex marriage and more about same marriage sex.

Anon (1995) — ☉ ♏ 7

Repressed negative emotions may result in insurrection rather than resurrection.

Sam Keen — ☽ ♏ 12

What doesn't kill us makes us stronger.   *Nietzsche*   ♄ ♏ 1

As far as sex, women need a reason; men need a location.   *Anon*   ☿ ♏ 3

Sin is the fuel for virtue's fire.   *Hazrat I. Khan*   ☿ ♐ 9

A clear conscience is a constant Christmas.   *Ben Franklin*   ☿ ♐

Joseph Campbell's last wish: "Death is the greatest adventure
of them all, and I just ask God one thing, and that is to be totally
aware when I walk into the next fabulous realm." (According to
his wife, who was present, he was aware at death.)   *(Larsen)*   ♃ ♐ 8

Venus cunningly raised the price of her goods by making
pimping illegal.   *Montaigne*   ♄ ♏ 9

A prostitute is a woman who does for a living what other women
do for pleasure.   *Anon*   ♀ ♏ 10

One of the hardest and most beneficial kicks of life comes from
the decaying foot of death. (From a letter at 19 years old.)
                                         Dylan Thomas   ♄ ♓ 8

If I could drop dead right now I'd be the happiest man alive.
                                        Samuel Goldwyn   ♃ ♏ 1

It's all good when it's all wood.   *D.H.*   ♃ ♏ 8

Four and fifty years
I've hung the sky with stars.
Now I leap through --
What shattering!
(Japanese Zen Master -- written, or spoken, at his death in 1253.)
                                              Dogen   ♅ 8
                                                         ♄ ♒ 8

Life is a state of becoming, and death is merely a part of the process.
                              Jane Roberts (Seth Speaks)   ☉ ♏ 8

The end is where we start from.   *T.S. Eliot*   ♂ ♏ 4

Sadly I have come to realize that a great many so-called
liberals aren't liberal -- they will defend to the death your right
to agree with them.   *Ronald Reagan*   ☿ ♎ 3

I met a girl at a party and found out sex is for two.
[Hands are 3rd House.]   *Wayne B.*   ♀ ♏ 3

The false God changes suffering into violence,
The true God changes violence into suffering.   *Simone Weil*   ♀ ♐ 12

Whitewatergate: If this were sex it would be incest.   *Gil Gross*   ♄ ♏ 4

Life and death, ice and water.   *Zen Saying*   ♏

Shame is the social side of guilt.   *John Grier*   ☽ ♏ 11

We've defined deviancy down.   *Daniel Moynihan* ☿ ♏ 11

We see life not as it is but as we are ... "Thru a glass darkly."
                                                         Eknath Easwaran ☽ ♏ 1

When misinformation becomes disinformation,
decadence becomes decay.   *D.H.*   ♇ 3
                                                                         ♄ ♏ 3

Pheromones are the essential aroma of erotica.   *D.H.*   ♀ ♏ 5

Do you smoke after sex? I don't know, I never looked. *Anon*   ♂ ♏ 3

Thanatology -- the science of death.   *Anon*   ♇ ♏ 9

People born in the U.S. after 1993 will pay an effective tax rate
over their lifetime of 84%!   *Anon*   ♅♆ ♑ 8

Death is the signature of life.   *Emil Brunner* ♇ ♏ 3
                                                                         ♊ 8

Condoms are tubesteak wrappers.   *M. Rose Pierce* ♂ ♏ 6

Does reincarnation rob death of its gift of freedom from time?
                                                         D.H.   ♄ ♒ 8

To think of and prepare for death, is not a surrender
-- it's a victory over fear.   *Paul Wilhelm Von Teppler (1911)*   ♃ ♏ 12

The birth of a man is the birth of his sorrow.
His thirst for survival keeps him   ♄ ♏ 12
        chained to the morrow.   *D.H.*   ♄ ♏ 2

In Vietnam we had what we called "the Minuet:" a star-shaped ambush of snipers. *Craig Roberts*	♂ ♏ 5
And this last blessing most, That the closer I move to death, one man through his sundered bulks, The louder the sun blooms and the tusked ramshackling sea exults .... and my shining men no more alone as I sail out to die. *Dylan Thomas*	☉ ♓ 8
Nothing in his life became him like the leaving it. *Shakespeare, <u>Macbeth</u>*	♀ ♌ 8 ♇ ♌
A solemn funeral is inconceivable to the Chinese mind. *Lin Yutang*	♃ ♏ 5
Mausoleum, N: the final and funniest folly of the rich. *Ambrose Bierce*	♇ ♌ 4
The art of living well and the art of dying well are one. *Epicurus*	♀ ♏
Men read maps better than women because only men can understand the concept of an inch equaling a hundred miles. *Roseanne*	♄ ♏ 3
The panhandler tells the taxpayer his first gift wasn't big enough. *D.H.*	♄ ♏ 7 ♄ ♓ 8
It is a moral crime to give money to support your own destroyers. *Ayn Rand*	♇ ♐ 8
Suicide is egotism raised to the point of absurdity. *Kafka*	♇ ♌ 1
Saving is a very fine thing. Especially when your parents have done it for you. *Winston Churchill*	☽ ♉ 8
She was born with an entire silver dinner service in her mouth. *Clive James (on Grace Kelly)*	☽ ♊ 8
Desires are insatiable; when old desires are satisfied new ones take their place. *Timothy Miller*	♏ 2

Our heart's final wish is that we do not die unaware, like a hapless dog beside a road, but that we die at home, home in all that is, home in a mystifying cosmos that, in its own way, plunges toward an autumn beyond imagining.   *The Daybook*   ☉ ♏ 4

Nothing sticks so fast in the mind as a groundless sense of guilt, because, since it has no real foundation, one cannot eliminate it by any form of repentance or redemption.   *Kafka*   ♀ 12

The real rub is the reconciliation of spirit functioning in the physical world. The Illusion of Separation (I.O.S.) is the shadow-boxing trickster. My job is dealing with the I.O.S., not the I.R.S.   *D.H.*   ♀ 12
♆ ♒

Everyone is weaving, thread by thread, around themselves, as a spider does his web, a karmic destiny.   *Blavatsky*   ♀ 5

While we cannot will ourselves to grace, we can by will open ourselves to its miraculous coming.   *Scott Peck*   ♀ ♐ 5

If heterosexuals are homophobic are homosexuals vaginaphobic?   *Dennis Prager*   ♄ ♒ 8
♅ ♏

Karma predestines nothing or no one, creates nothing, nor does it design. Man plans and creates causes, karmic law adjusts the effects. Karma is an act of universal harmony tending ever to resume its original position, like a bough, which, bent down too forcibly, rebounds with corresponding vigor.   *Blavatsky*   ♀ ♏ 8

The root of men's guilt is that they prefer the evil which lies so temptingly close at hand to the moral values which seem so difficult to attain.   *Kafka*   ♀ ♐ 1/3

Reincarnation -- the lost chord of Christianity.   *William Q. Judge*   ♀ ♓ 9

Reincarnation -- the circle of necessity.   *Blavatsky*   ☉ ♑ 8

There is nothing more dangerous for man in the bush than regular habits.   *Laurens van der Post*   ♂ ♏ 6

True inner work becomes outer work.   *D.H.*   ♄ ♏ 1

Neither death nor life hinder our progress.   *Sogyal Rinpoche*   ♀ 11
♅ ♏ 1

Let a man in a garret but burn with enough intensity
and he will set fire to the world.   *Saint Exupéry (1939)*   ♂ ♏ 12
                                                                      ♀ ♌ 10

Death has to be waiting at the end of the ride before you truly see
the earth, and feel your heart, and love the world.   *Jean Anouila*   ♀ ♐ 10

We never know we go when we are going
We jest and shut the Door
Fate -- following -- behind us bolts it --
and we accost no more.   *Emily Dickinson*   ♄ ♏ 1

A hooker told me she'd do anything I wanted for fifty bucks I said,
"Paint my house."   *Henny Youngman*   ♀ ♏ 4

Evil dwells in moist places.   *Sister Mary Olivia*   ♀ ♏ 12

If a pit bull romances your leg, fake an orgasm.   *Hut Landom*   ♆ ♏ 6

I tried phone sex and it gave me an ear infection.   *Richard Lewis*   ☿ ♏ 6

We all worry about the population explosion,
but not at the right time.   *Arthur Hoppe*   ♄ ♏ 5

Masturbation is the thinking man's television.
                                             Christopher Hampton   ☿ ♒ 8

I finally found my wife's G-spot. A neighbor lady had it.
                                                  Jim Sherbert   ♀ ♏ 3

Today when you get the clap, it's a relief.   *Brad Garrett*   ☽ ♏ 6

If God doesn't destroy Hollywood Blvd., he owes Sodom and
Gomorrah an apology.   *Jay Leno*   ♀ 10

If meat is murder are eggs rape?   *P.J. O'Rourke*   ☽ ♏ 8

**Guilt is to Freudianism what original sin is to
fundamentalism: a lynch-pin of negativity.**
                                                 David Hayward   ♀ 9

Resentment is fermented anger. Arrogance is fermented egotism.
                                                       Anon   ♄ ♏ 1

The discipline of desire is the background of character.

John Locke ♂ ♏ 1

The original intention was to come here to "paradise," to learn balance between the physical and spiritual. We've become attached, due in part to the <u>unique</u> density of Earth, to pleasures and desires largely physical. Thus we keep coming back instead of moving on to other experiences. Earth is the only planet that has created a "bottleneck" of souls refusing to move on in their recycling -- i.e., reincarnating.   *The Only Planet of Choice* ♄ ♉ 8

People ought to start dead, then they would be honest so much earlier.

Mark Twain ♂ ♏ 9

(On suicide): The question is whether it's the way out or the way in.

Emerson ☿ ♐ 12

The thought of suicide is a great source of comfort: with it a calm passage is to be made across many a night.   *Nietzsche* ☽ ♏ 12

The soul of man does violence to itself first of all.   *Marcus Aurelius* ♀ 1

Fornication is the fodder of foppish fools.   *D.H.* ♀ ♏ 3

The figures out on the lawn playing croquet have changed.
They are not playing croquet anymore and there's somebody
with a gun in the bushes.   *Archibald MacLeash (1974)* ♂ ♏ 4

Is death like a comma in a long sentence? Or, is it the other way
around: physicality is the comma?   *D.H.* ☿ ♏ 1

> Yet when the danger's near
> We manage to appear
> As insensible to fear
> As anybody here.   *Gilbert & Sullivan* ♆ ♏ 1

I'm always seeking background to fill out the message ... how did
Albioni live in order to have composed his soulful Andante?   *D.H.* ☿ ♏ 4

Rolla Primarda was struck by lighting in 1949 while standing on
the same spot upon which both his father (20 years earlier) and his
grandfather (50 years earlier) had been killed in identical fashion.
[Uranus was in Cancer in 1949.]   *Anon* ♅ ♋ 8

Never forget we walk on hell gazing at flowers.   *Issa* ♀ ♏ 1

The world is full of double beds
  and sweet young things with maidenheads.
This being so, there's no excuse,
  For sodomy or self-abuse. *Hilaire Belloc*   ♀ ♏ 10

Outside of the killings, Washington has one of the lowest crime
rates in the country. *Mayor Marion Barry*   ♀ 10

In America now (1996) there are 9,000 street gangs with 400,000
members. *News Media*   ♄ ♏ 10

To be who I was before I was. *Sufi Saying*   ☉ ♏ 4

Our society is increasingly populated by well-understood barbarians.
  Dennis Prager   ☿ ♏ 11

Gratitude is the key for me. If I drop, or misplace it, I'm locked out
of life's positive flow and trapped in my closet with no flashlight.
  D.H.   ♃ ♏ 12

To be purified is to will one thing. *Sören Kierkegaard*   ♀ 5

Oral sex is like being attacked by a giant snail. *Germaine Greer*   ♂ ♏ 1

The advantage of masturbation over intercourse is that it's
less competitive. *Robert Byrne*   ♏ 7

I don't mind sleeping on an empty stomach provided it isn't my own.
  Philip J. Simborg   ☽ ♏ 12
    ☽ ♏ 7

It is a gentleman's first duty to remember in the morning
who it was he took to bed with him. *Dorothy Sayers*   ♄ ♏ 1

**We are healed of our suffering only by experiencing
it to the full.**
  Marcel Proust   ♀ 12

Privacy differs from secrecy. It has little to do with hiding
something and far more to do with protecting something
-- ourselves. What our privacy protects is not our dignity;
that is inviolably ours as a soul. What our privacy protects is
our Creative Child. *Julia Cameron*   ☽ ♏ 12

There is nothing so boring as depravity. *Ayn Rand*   ♄ ♏ 3

The mystics believe the ideal man shall walk himself to a
"right death."   *Bruce Chatwin* | ♂ ♓ 8

The ground of the soul is dark.   *Meister Eckhart* | ♄ ♏ 4

Life is not a problem to be solved, but a mystery to be lived.
                                                      Thomas Merton | ♆ ♏ 1

Compassion Terrorism: "A rat dies in a medical experiment in
Canada and I can't eat my breakfast."
                                          Inspired by Dr. Paul Pearsall | ♀ 6

Shrapnel is the fragmented manifestation of resentment.
                                                      Deepak Chopra | ♂ ♏

There is no dial tone in the horizontal telephone booth.
                                                   Lagowski & Mumma | ♄ ♏ 3

If you are of the opinion that the contemplation of suicide is
sufficient evidence of a poetic nature, do not forget that actions
speak louder than words.   *Fran Lebowitz* | ♂ ♏ 3

The endurance of darkness is preparation for great light.
                                                 St. John of the Cross | ♃ ♏ 12

The Republicans made me raise taxes.   *Bill Clinton* | ☿ ♓ 8

That man has missed something who has not left a brothel at
sunrise feeling like throwing himself in a river out of pure disgust.
                                                   Gustave Flaubert | ♄ ♏ 1

Guilt is the mafia of the mind.
                                                        Bob Mandel | ♀ 3

Death, you are my indispensable enemy.   *Dan Wakefield* | ♄ ♏ 7

Above us, stars. Beneath us, constellations. Five billion miles
away, a galaxy dies like a snowflake falling on water.   *Ted Kooser* | ♀ ♐ 12

Hell, in short, being a place where you have nothing to do
but amuse yourself, is the paradise of the worthless.
                                               George Bernard Shaw | ♀ 5

To fear love is to fear life, and those who fear life are already
three parts dead.   *Bertrand Russell* | ♄ ♌ 8

Snakes whose length is less than five times the width of the road's yellow line are considered small snakes.

Roger Knutson (from <u>Flattened Fauna</u>)   ♄ ♏ 3

We leave and go onward and onward ... People say that a shot in the back cannot be heard. (Written from a Soviet prison camp where she served three years from 1983 to 1986. Physicist and well-published poet. Immigrated to U.S. after her release from prison.)   *Irina Ratushinskaya*   ♂ ♏ 3

How much longer will those camps stand upon the soil of my country? How can I sleep while they continue to exist?

Irina Ratushinskaya   ♀ 4

Nothing is certain but death and taxes.   *Ben Franklin*   ♄ ♏ 8

Being over seventy is like being engaged in a war. All our friends are going to be gone and we survive amongst the dead and the dying as on a battlefield.   *Muriel Spark*   ♄ ♏ 7

If I had my life to live over again I should form the habit of nightly composing myself to thoughts of death. I would practice, as it were, the remembrance of death. There is no other practice which so intensifies life. Death, when it approaches, ought not to take one by surprise. It should be part of the full expectancy of life.

Muriel Spark   ☽ ♏ 6

Practice random acts of arousal.   *D.H.*   ♃ ♏ 5

Without deliberately cultivated compassion for ourselves, spiritual and creative growth becomes a forced march through the hostile territory of our own judgments.   *Julia Cameron*   ☽ ♏ 12
       ♀ 12

Shut up and say something.   *Anon*   ♄ ♏ 3

Our faith comes in moments; our vice is habitual.   *Emerson*   ♀ ♐ 12

I believe that sex is the most beautiful, natural, and wholesome thing that money can buy.   *Steve Martin*   ♏ 2

Never lie down with a woman who's got more troubles than you.

Nelson Algren   ☽ ♏ 12

I am essential Scorpio: my gaze disembowels then folds back upon itself... the invagination of a curious passion and the decoction of ardor.   *D.H.*   ♏

SAGITTARIUS

optimistic
expansive
far-sighted
generous
adventurous

wasteful
self-righteous
blunt
bigoted
reckless

Life purpose to:
inspire
teach
promote
expand
explore

JUPITER

Influence:
authority
success
ambition
beliefs
wisdom
expansion

Examples:
politicians
actors / entertainers
adventurers
evangelists
executives

NINTH HOUSE

The House of Philosophy
'deep stuff'

the sphere of expansion
inspiration
higher education
moral ideals
distant travel
foreign lands and people
expansion of mental and
spiritual horizons

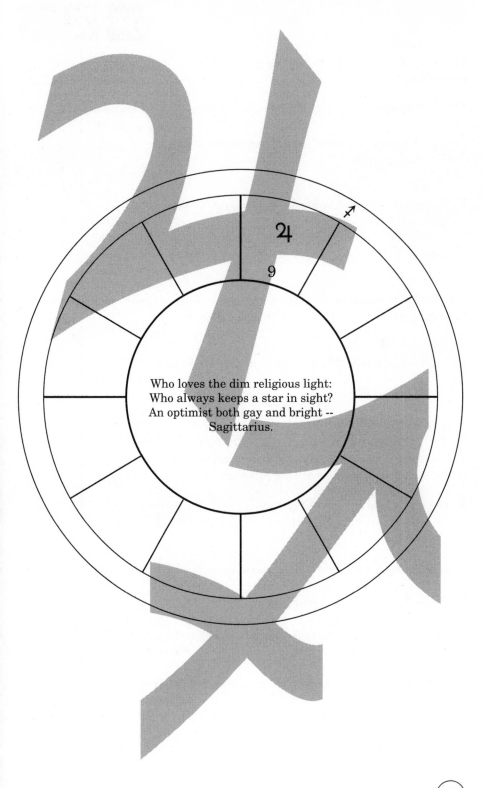

Who loves the dim religious light:
Who always keeps a star in sight?
An optimist both gay and bright --
Sagittarius.

9

Right is right even if no one is doing it. Wrong is wrong even if no one is doing it. *Anon*   ♃ ♐ 9

Wisdom is common sense in an uncommon degree. *Emerson*   ☽ ♒ 9

There's no use talking if you're not going to exaggerate.
Ortega y Gassett   ♃ ♐ 3

Is the time coming again when we choose not between good and bad but bad and worse? *Anon*   ♄ ♒ 9

Those who lack courage will always find a philosophy to justify it. *Albert Camus*   ♄ ♈ 9

Every religion has to renew itself continually in order to rediscover the hidden Mystery to which it is intended to bear witness. *Bede Griffiths*   ☿ ♐ 12

If God lived on Earth, people would break his windows. *Yiddish Proverb*   ☿ ♐ 4
♂ ♋ 9

You'll see it when you believe it. *Wayne Dyer*   ♃ ♐ 1

We can keep from a child all knowledge of earlier myths, but we cannot take from him the need for mythology. *Carl Jung*   ☽ ♐ 5

Everything you're against can be restated in such a way that puts you in favor of something else, thus promoting abundance. *Anon*   ♃ ♊ 2
♆ ♐ 2

Prayer acknowledges universal partnership. *Anon*   ♀ ♓ 9

FILLOSOPHY -- if some is good, more is better. *D.H.*   ♃ ♐ 9

Piety is the recognition that everything is linked to the presence of God in every moment. *Thich Nhat Hanh*   ♃ ♓ 3

In this very breath we take now lies the secret that all great teachers try to tell us. *Peter Mathiessen*   ♃ ♊ 9

A professor is one who talks in someone else's sleep. *W.H. Auden*   ♆ ♐ 7

My heart is nourished on no more than air, since every breath
I draw is answered prayer.   *May Sarton*   ☿ ♌ 9

It is another's fault if he be ungrateful; but it is mine if I do not give.
To find one thankful man I will oblige many who are not.
                                                       Seneca   ♃ ♌ 9

I believe the Torah's greatest moral achievement is its injunction
to love the stranger.   *Dennis Prager*   ♃ ♎ 9

Hope presupposes doubt which is faith in a reality you do not prefer.
                                                       Bashar   ♄ ♐ 9

One of mankind's greatest fears is that of confrontation
with the soul.   *D.H.*   ♄ ♏ 4

Out beyond ideas of right-doing and wrong-doing there is a field:
I'll meet you there.   *Rumi*   ♆ ♎ 9

Condemnation is judgment in its negative form.   *D.H.*   ♄ ♍ 9

On publishing and book pricing -- a phone call from an editor to
an author: "Listen, Mr. Tolstoy, if we're going to hold the price of
your book below $29.95, you'll have to do some judicious pruning
in the "Peace" section and get right into the "War" stuff. Maybe
you could trim that ballroom scene, edit some of Sonya's business,
chop the pre-battle chit chat, and for God's sake get rid of that
peasant and his dog ..."   *Richard Curtis*   ♄ ♉ 9

Non-judgementalism is often just an exchange of moral blank
checks.   *Ayn Rand*   ♃ ♓ 2

I want my judgementalism to hit you upside the head.
                                                       Rush Limbaugh   ♂ ♑ 9

The symbol is the connecting point between man and divinity.
                                                       Carl Jung   ☉ ♓ 9

Belief becomes biology.   *Deepak Chopra*   ☉ 9

Curb your dogma.   *Anon*   ♄ ♏ 9

Prayer is a scanning of the heavens for the chink through which
angels travel and divinity looks on.   *Thomas Moore*   ☿ ♓ 9

He's a hard man who is only just, a sad one who is only wise.

Voltaire   ♄ ♎ 9

Masterpieces are no more than the shipwrecked flotsam of great minds.

Marcel Proust   ♃ ♓ 9

Down the highway of the Milky Way we ride on horses made of stars.

Hilda Conklin   ♆ ♐ 9

Faith is the substance of things hoped for, the evidence of things not seen.

Hebrews 11:1   ♆ 9

The monk and the trespasser have something in common -- both have been arrested by a higher power.

Adapted from Thomas Moore   ♄ 9

It is good that I've been afflicted that I might learn thy statutes.

Psalm 119   ♄ ♓ 9

Prayer as a means to effect a private end is theft and meanness. It suggests dualism in nature and consciousness. As soon as the man is at one with God he will not beg. He will then see prayer in all action.

Emerson   ♄ ♊ 9

My contention is: the less prayer you need the better; life itself should be your prayer.

David Steindl-Rast   ☉ ♑ 9

Paths to enlightenment: The Long Path -- Ego seeks perfection (future). The Short Path -- Soul invokes grace (now).

Paul Brunton   ♃ ♐ 9

Joseph Campbell's female students at Sarah Lawrence College tended to put their hearts before the course.

Anon   ♀ ♌ 9

Experience is to meaning what knowledge is to wisdom.

D.H.   ♄ ♐ 9

Humor is God laughing at itself.

D.H.   ♃ ♊ 9

Enlightenment is a quality of being that does not reproduce ignorance.

D.H.   ♇ ♐ 9

Our beliefs are shaping our lives to a far greater extent than any supposed influence from the unconscious.

Dennis Elwell   ♇ ♐ 12

Pray that everything should happen just as it does.

Epictitus   ♄ ♐ 1

Expansion is simply re-membering the garden that already exists.

Bashar | ♃ ☌ 2

We shall not cease from exploration, and the end of all our exploration will be to arrive where we started and know the place for the first time.

T. S. Eliot | ♀ ♐ 1

Where is the wisdom we have lost in knowledge?

T. S. Eliot | ♀ 9

There is no non-judgment: non-judgment <u>is</u> a judgment, an action.

Dennis Prager | ♄ ♍ 9

The wise make proverbs and fools repeat them.

Disraeli | ☿ ♓ 9

There is no problem that enough acceptance can't overcome.

Anon | ☽ ♓ 9

A maximholic: one addicted to the shorthand of meaning.

D.H. | ♄ ♐ 12

To fear anything is to believe you are separate from God.

Emmet Fox | ♄ ♒ 9

The migrating bird leaves no trace behind and does not need a guide.

Dogen | ♅ ♐

Character is ethics in action.

Anon | ☉ ♐ 1

As the body without the spirit is dead, so faith without works is dead also.

James 2:26 | ♀ ♐ 1

It's one thing to get a lot of knowledge; it's another to relate it to life, which is what literature does. (Campbell said this after receiving a prize for Literature rather than Scholarship.)

Joseph Campbell | ♃ ♐ 1

Once you know the difference between right and wrong, you have lots fewer decisions to make.

Joseph Campbell | ♄ ♐ 9

The true traveler loves something just because it is different.

Aldous Huxley | ♅ ♒ 9

The three levels of the truth: the things you tell yourself, the things you tell other people, and The Truth.

Anon | ☉ ♎ 9

Ambition first sprung from blest abodes,
The glorious fault of Angels and of Gods.   *Pope*   ♃ ♑ 9

He fathers-forth whose beauty is past change: Praise him.
                              Gerald Manley Hopkins   ♄ ♌ 9

The souls of pure teachers are arriving like rays of sunlight.
                                              Rumi   ☉ ♌ 9

He without benefit of scruples, his trouble and poverty soon
quadruples.   *D.H.*   ♄ ♐ 2

The innocent loves justice; everyone else prefers mercy.   *Anon*   ♀ ♐

Every violation of truth is not only a sort of suicide to the liar,
but a stab at the health of human society.   *Emerson*   ♇ ♐ 11

Ethics requires us to abandon the notion that an act is ethical
simply because it is legal.   *Michael Josephson*   ♄ ♐ 9

The tongue is the flower of the heart. Teach it to bloom in God's
time.   *D.H.*   ♀ ♌ 9

Bless all that I'm about that I may be a blessing to all about me.
                                              D.H.   ♃ ♌ 1

Prayer: To open the hearts of the oppressed <u>and</u> the oppressors.
                                              D.H.   ♇ ♌ 9

Never look down to test the ground before taking your next step;
only those who fix their eyes on the far horizon will find the right
road.   *Dag Hammarskjöld*   ♄ ♐ 1

Excitement + integrity are my guidelines to living as a whole idea.
                                              D.H.   ♂ ♑ 9

The Archer sees the mark upon the path of the infinite, and He
bends you with His might that His arrows may go swift and far.
Let your bending in the Archer's hand be for gladness; for even
as He loves the arrow that flies, so He loves also the bow that
is stable.   *Kahlil Gibran, <u>The Prophet</u>*   ☉ ♐ 9

By spiritualizing intellect, experience becomes a conscious
higher progression.   *D.H.*   ♆ ♐ 1

Let wisdom mediate trust and faith.   *D.H.*   ☽ ♐ 9

Our universities don't teach goodness, they teach socio-pathology. *Dennis Prager*   ♀ ♐ 7

Both pain and pleasure are one in the same process of seeing the situation as the guru. *Chogyam Trungpa*   ☿ ♐ 1

Belief in anything is simply a way of labeling the mystery. *Chogyam Trungpa*   ☿ ♓ 9

To mistake the map for the territory
is to mistake the menu for the meal. *Greg Bateson*   ♆ ♐ 6

The knowledge of God is very far from the love of Him. *Pascal*   ♄ ♌ 9

On any given day God may not exist. That is the terrible power of His gift to us. *D.H.*   ♄ 9

Fear is the burden of playing God. *Anon*   ♄ 9

If you want to give God a laugh, tell Him your plans. *Anon*   ♅ 9   ♀ ♐ 11

The only way some people exercise their mind is by jumping to conclusions. *Cullen Hightower*   ♃ ♊ 9   ♂ ♐

We are not seeking answers to problems, but the assurance that no answers are possible. *Ayn Rand*   ♄ ♐ 3

Forgive me, Father, for I know not what I'm doing --
and please don't tell me. *Anon*   ♄ ♌ 9

Knowledge accumulates in universities because the freshmen bring a little in and seniors take none away. *Academic Saying*   ♃ ♐ 9

Where there is no God, all is permitted. *Dostoyevsky*   ♄ ♒ 9

When someone says, "Oh, I can worship God anywhere," the answer is, "Do you?" *James Pike*   ♆ 9

Fundamentalism is a favorite playground of the shadow. *D.H.*   ♄ ♐ 12

Right or wrong is more important than life or death.   *Plato*   ♃ ♐ 8

Do our experiences become more precious with age or is it just that we don't realize when they occur how really beautiful and precious they are? [Joseph Campbell had ♆ ♋ 9.]
Joseph Campbell   ♆ ♋ 9
                                                              ♃ ♑ 4

In the past I put philandery ahead of philosophy but, alas, philosophy revealed the folly of philandery.   *D.H.*   ♀ ♐ 5

Thoughts are things that give us wings.   *Anon*   ♅ 9

There is no moral precept that does not have some inconvenience about it.   *Diderot*   ♅ 9

I want to know the thoughts of God; the rest are details.   *Einstein*   ☉ ♐ 3

Poetry implies the whole truth, philosophy expresses a particle of it.
Thoreau   ♃ ♓ 9

The sensitive mother cooks fish differently for each of her hungry children -- plain and bland for one, rich and spicy for the other. In exactly the same way, the Mother of the Universe reveals various spiritual approaches to the Divine, provided that you experience passionate longing for it.   *Ramakrishna*   ♆ ♍ 9
                                                              ♀ ♐ 6

Some will receive their meal early in the morning, others at noon, still others not until evening. But none will go hungry. Without exception, all living beings will eventually know their own true nature to be the Great Light.   *Ramakrishna*   ♃ ♍ 9
                                                              ☉ 9

We are moving towards a completely religionless time; people as they are now simply cannot be religious any more.
Dietrich Bonhoeffer   ♄♐ 9

If a musician has the desire for spiritual perfection, I think he can perfect himself much more easily and quickly than another person.
Hazrat Inayat Khan   ♃ ♓ 9

There is nothing better than music for the upliftment of the soul.
Hazrat Inayat Khan   ♆ 9

SPIRITOSCLEROSIS: living from the outside in, rather than inside out. i.e., living exogenetically rather than endogenetically. [Scleroses is ruled by Cancer.]   *D.H.*   ♄ ♋ 9

Prayer is primary speech.   *Ulanov*   ♃ ♊ 9

There is no place for prayer to go because it is inherently non-local.
                                    Larry Dossey   ♆ 9
                                                          ♆ ♐ 3

Advice is like snow; the softer it falls, the longer it dwells upon, and the deeper it sinks into, the mind.   *Coleridge*   ♀ ♑ 9

Thank God I'm an atheist.   *Anon*   ♄ ♐ 9

We have sold our birthright for a mess of facts.   *Oscar Wilde*   ♀ ♍ 9

... Faithlessly unto Him
Who is the light of old and air shaped Heaven
Where souls grow wild as horses in the foam ...   *Dylan Thomas*   ♅ ♐ 12

Because human consciousness must involve both pleasure and pain, to strive for pleasure only is to strive for a loss of consciousness.   *Alan Watts*   ♄ ♉ 9

Some people want to recognize God only in some pleasant enlightenment -- and they get pleasure and enlightenment, but not God.   *Meister Eckart*   ♄ ♉ 9

Our knowledge can only be finite, while our ignorance must necessarily be infinite.   *Karl Popper*   ♄ 9

Judge and be prepared to be judged.   *Ayn Rand*   ♄ ♐ 3

The same people who deny values want more laws.
                                    Dennis Prager   ♄ ♐ 7

The more laws, the less justice.   *German Proverb*   ♄ ♎ 9

The dream of destroying evil is only a reflection of the sense of despair which comes from loss of faith.   *Kafka*   ♄ ♏ 9

Faith is imagination that has seasoned.   *The Daybook*   ♄ ♓ 9

There is but one truly serious philosophical problem, and that is suicide. Judging whether life is or is not worth living amounts to answering the fundamental question of philosophy.   *Camus*   ♀ 9

Everything, even lies, advances the truth. Shadows do not blot out the sun.   *Kafka*   ♄ ♌ 9

Without martyrs every movement degenerates into a pressure group of ordinary fortune-hunters. Ideas of a superpersonal value only live by personal sacrifices.   *Kafka*   ♄ ♐ 11
                                                                                   ♄ ♓ 1

Praise God who comes for us again, our lives pulled to their fisted knot, cinched tight with cold, drawn to the heart's constriction.   *William Everson*   ♄ ♌ 9

We have a situation in America today where lawyers subvert justice and teachers subvert education.   *Dennis Prager*   ♀ ♐ 9

What I find most in my whole life is illusion, wanting to be something of which I have formed a concept.   *Thomas Merton*   ♆ 9

Simone Weil once made a note to herself: "As soon as one has arrived at any position, try to find in what sense the contrary is true."   *Doris Grumbach*   ♅ 9

Thirty years of secular extremism has produced a backlash fear of religious extremism.   *Dennis Prager*   ♄ ♏ 9

Fingers pointing toward the sacred need no vocabulary, for they do not preach. Beyond the dialects of all religions they witness to a religious attitude toward life itself.   *Frederick Franck*   ♊ 9

The longest journey is the shortest way to the heart.   *The Daybook*   ♌ 9

Prayer is absolute attention.   *Simone Weil*   ♄ ♊ 9

Knowledge is unable to impress itself on a false personality.   *Mme. Blavatsky*   ♃ ♓ 1

What a cruel God it is who makes it possible for his creatures not to recognize Him.   *Kafka*   ♆ 9

Philosophers are broken down poets.   *Thoreaux*   ♄ ♓ 9

When one prays, he takes the outer life inward. When one
meditates, he takes the inner life outward.   *Ann Ree Colton*   ♆ 9

I will not effect to suffer. Be my life then a long gratitude.   *Emerson*   ♃ ♌ 12

The liver is a secondary heart in its emotional dealings.
                                                     Ann Ree Colton   ♃ ♌ 4

**The new morality is moral relativism:
"shoplifting is ok -- it's a big company."**
                                                     Dennis Prager   ♅ ♑ 9

Prayer is the concrete manifestation of faith. Faith is believing
that the desire for good is always answered.   *Simone Weil*   ♄ ♐ 9

Luck never made a man wise.   *Seneca*   ♄ ♐ 9

All cruel people describe themselves as paragons of frankness.
                                                     Tennessee Williams   ♄ ♏ 9

If you are seeking pleasure more than truth you run the risk of
distorting your perceptions.   *Charles Tart*   ♀ ♓ 9

For us there is only the trying.
The rest is not our business.   *T.S. Eliot*   ♄ ♐ 6

America is becoming a nation of laws rather than one of goodness.
                                                     Solzhenitsyn   ♑ 9

Rather than right or wrong -- "Is it legal?"   *Dennis Prager*   ♄ 9

I wish my house to be a college, open as the air to all to whom I
spiritually belong, and who belong to me.   *Emerson*   ☽ ♐ 4
                                                                      ♒ 9

The devil can quote texts.   *Emerson*   ♇ ♐

God is the supreme holistic concept.   *Paul Davies*   ♆ 9

The wise are always impatient, for he that increases knowledge
increases impatience of folly.   *Baltasar Gracian*   ♂ ♐

If I could find a spot where God is not I might still be an atheist --
definition creates reality.   *D.H.*   ☿ ♏ 9

True integrity must be holistic; you can't compartmentalize truth.

D.H.

♄ ♓ 9

Happiness can be felt only by the soul, not by the intellect,
the belly, the head, or the purse.   *Hermann Hesse*

♃ ♌ 4

Unlived awareness was another characteristic evil of our time,
so full of thinkers who did not do and doers who did not think.

Laurens van der Post

♄ ♈ 9

When a thing is funny, search it carefully for a hidden truth.

George Bernard Shaw

♃ ♐ 12

If wisdom were to vanish suddenly from the universe, no one yet
would suspect himself a fool.   <u>*Gems from the East*</u> *(Blavatsky)*

☿ ♓ 9

Every child comes into this world, into this time, with the
message that God is not yet discouraged by mankind.   *Anon*

☽ ♐ 1

A good is made of the same elements as a good life.

Howard Thurman

♃ ♌ 1

Great men are they who see that spiritual is stronger than any
material force, that thoughts rule the world.   *Emerson*

♂ ♐ 10

If the only prayer you say in your whole life is "Thank you", that
would suffice.   *Meister Eckhart*

♀ ♐ 9

When the gods choose to punish us, they merely answer our prayers.

Oscar Wilde

♄ ♏ 9

It is not self sacrifice to die protecting that which you value:
if the value is great enough you do not care to live without it.

Ayn Rand

♏ 9
♄ ♏ 2

The sad fact is that all too many people all over the world lack
faith in the market economy, which means that they lack faith
in themselves and in others.   *Jacob G. Hornberger*

☽ ♑ 9

I believe we've had fifty years of secret research and development
based on defending ourselves from space. General MacArthur
stated in his final speech, "Our next big war will be in space."
President Reagan stated similarly eight times. Australia has been
a major research and development place for years ...   *Stan Deyo*

♀ ♐

My primary purpose is the projections of an ideal of man as he might be and ought to be. Philosophy is the necessary means to that end. *Ayn Rand*

☉ 9
☉ ♓ 9

Horse sense is the ability to say nay. *Anon*

♄ ♐ 3

We must become spies for God in the world.
Shakespeare, Macbeth

♀ ♐ 10

Grace is the tranquilizer of the soul. *Gary Zukov*

♃ ♓ 6

Gratitude could be the greatest grace. *D.H.*

♃

My epistemology is an endless agnosticism. *Michael Tippett*

♃ ♐ 9

It takes most men five years to recover from a college education, and to learn that poetry is as vital to thinking as knowledge.
Brooks Atkinson

♃ ♓ 9

My wife and I are increasingly grateful for having had the wisdom, though probably not calling it that at the time, to drop out of college when we married in 1960. Just think of all the garbage and muddle-headedness we've not had to unlearn! *D.H.*

♄ ♐ 9
♄ ♎ 9

Everyday people are straying away from the church and going back to God.
Lenny Bruce

♄ ♓ 9

We are shut up in schools and college recitation rooms for ten or fifteen years, and come out at last with a bellyful of words and don't know a thing. *Emerson (☽ ♊ 9)*

♄ ♊ 9

Education is an admirable thing, but nothing worth knowing can be taught. *Oscar Wilde*

♄ 9

The best EDUC8ION should reflect the uniqueness of the individual.
D.H.

♄ ♒ 9

He learned the arts of riding, fencing, gunnery, and how to scale a fortress -- or a nunnery. *Lord Byron*

♂ ♏ 9

A person who publishes a book appears willfully in public with his pants down. *Edna St. Vincent Millay*

☽ ♏ 9

sagittarius - jupiter - ninth house (137)

Trust is Stage II faith; it takes faith to the streets.   *D.H.*   ☽ ♑ 9

The price of justice is eternal publicity.   *Arnold Bennett*   ♀ ♐ 9
                    ♄ ♋ 10

Emerson is a person who lives instinctively on ambrosia -- and
leaves everything indigestible on his plate.   *Nietzsche*   ☽ ♍ 9

A way is only the way when one finds it and follows it oneself.
There is no general prescription for "how one should do it."
                    Carl Jung   ☉ ♐ 1

**Atheist: A man that has no invisible means of
support.**
                    John Buchan   ♄ ♓ 9

No man in a thousand has the strength of mind or goodness
of heart to be an atheist.   *Samuel Taylor Coleridge*   ☉ ♒ 9

Some persons are likeable in spite of their unswerving integrity.
                    Anon   ♃ ♑ 7

If you do not feel pleasantly toward your workman or workwoman,
your kinsman or townsman, you have not dealt justly.   *Emerson*   ♃ ♎ 11

We are too ready to assume that we know, better than the
unbeliever, what ails him.   *Thomas Merton*   ♄ ♐ 7

Fervid atheism is usually a screen for repressed religion.
                    Wilhelm Stekel   ♄ ♏ 9

Some are atheists by neglect; others are so by affectation; they that
think there is no God at some times do not think so at all times.
[Note the author's last name -- Libra connotation.]
                    Benjamin Whichcote   ☿ ♎ 9

We were born believing. A man bears beliefs as a tree bears apples.
[Venus rules apples and apple trees.]   *Emerson*   ♀ ♐ 1

People who think they're generous to a fault usually think
that's their only fault.   *Sydney Harris*   ♃ ♌ 2

The great religions teach salvation as an individual matter.
There are no group discounts in the Ten Commandments.
Christ was not a committee.   *P.J. O'Rourke*   ♄ ♒ 9

Isolation has led me to reflection, reflection to doubt, doubt to
a more sincere and intelligent love of God.   *Marie Lenéru*   ♄ ♐ 12

I tore myself away from the safe comfort of certainties through
my love for truth; and truth rewarded me. [She had Mars
conjoining the moon and ruling the 5th House of risks.]
                                          Simone de Beauvoir   ♃ 5

Everything can be taken from a man but one thing, the last of
human freedoms -- to choose one's attitude in any given set of
circumstances, to choose one's own way. (Writing of life and death
in the concentration camps.)   *Viktor Frankl*   ♄ ♐ 12

Any doctrine that will not bear investigation is not a fit tenant
for the mind of an honest man.   *Robert G. Ingersoll*   ♄ ♏ 9

Religion, like water, may be free, but when they pipe it to you,
you've got to help pay for the piping. And the piper!
                                          Abigail van Buren   ♄ ♉ 9

In university they don't tell you that the greater part of the law
is learning to tolerate fools.   *Doris Lessing*   ♄ ♊ 9

America is waiting for an Attorney General who will enforce
the law -- and a President with the courage to demand that
he do so.   *Phyllis Schlafly (1967)*   ♄ ♌ 9

I don't know. I don't care. And it doesn't make any difference.
                                          Jack Kerouac   ♄ ♓ 9

All that we know is nothing, we are merely crammed wastepaper
baskets, unless we are in touch with that which laughs at all our
knowing.   *D.H. Lawrence*   ♃ ♊ 9

I have a simple philosophy: Fill what's empty. Empty what's full.
Scratch where it itches.   *Alice Roosevelt Longworth*   ♄ ♋ 9

Think enough and you won't know anything.   *Kenneth Patchen*   ♄ ♊ 9

It takes a long time to understand nothing.   *Edward Dahlberg*   ♄ ♓ 9

Work is prayer. Work is also stink. Therefore stink is prayer.
                                          Aldous Huxley   ♄ ♏ 9

Doubt's door is opened by the illusion of separation.   *D.H.*   ♄ ♓ 9

We should take care not to make the intellect our God; it has, of course, powerful muscles, but no personality.   *Albert Einstein*   ♄ ♐ 1

... **A**s Dorothy said to Toto, "I don't think we're in Kansas anymore."
                                                        Frank Baum   ♀ ♐

I keep my ideals, because in spite of everything I still believe people are really good at heart.   *Anne Frank*   ♃ ♌ 9

If you wish to obtain an orthodox understanding of Zen, do not be deceived by others. Inwardly or outwardly, if you encounter any obstacles kill them right away. If you encounter the Buddha, kill him.   *Rinzai*   ♀ 9

God will not have His work manifest by cowards.   *Emerson*   ♂ ♐ 9

When faith meets trust the rubber meets the road: "Oh my God, I'm no longer training -- this <u>is</u> the race!"   *D.H.*   ♂ ♏ 9

A heavy woman walked into a department store and said to the clerk, "I'd like to see a bathing suit in my size." The clerk said, "So would I!"   *Anon*   ♃ ♋ 6

Men will confess to treason, murder, arson, false teeth, or a wig. How many of them will own up to a lack of humor?
                                                  Frank Moore Colby   ♄ ♐ 3

Everything human is pathetic. The secret source of humor itself is not joy but sorrow. There is no humor in heaven.   *Mark Twain*   ♄ ♐ 12

We are witnessing the destruction of the Judaeo Christian tradition. I'm fighting it because I believe what will supersede it will be worse.   *Dennis Prager*   ♀ ♐

Gratitude, like love, works best as a verb.   *D.H.*   ♃ ♎ 5

Enthusiasm is nothing more than faith with a tin can tied to its tail.
                                                        Anon   ♃ ♊ 6

Those who died as heroes in the (concentration) camps were believers for the most part, Christians or Communists. Their faith was obviously of enormous help to them when it came time to die.   *Tzvetan Todorov*   ♄ ♏ 12

A monastery is a consecration camp.   *M. Rose Pierce*   ♐ 12

A Chinese Proverb: "When one dog begins barking at a shadow,
ten thousand make it into a reality" - an epigraph to any
commentary on ideologies.   *E.M. Cioran*   ☿ ♍ 9

                                                    ♃ ♍ 11

♑ **♄** **10**

TENTH HOUSE

The House of Public Standing
'where I'm going'

the sphere of worldly
attainment
profession or career
honor
public standing
social status
fame
attainment

SATURN

Influence:
time
discipline
caution
delays
duty
responsibilities
limitations
restrictions

CAPRICORN

responsible
ambitious
realistic
professional
dependable

pessimistic
depressed
inhibited
cold
avaricious

Examples:
scientists
researchers
instructors
officers
civil servants

Life purpose to:
establish
manage
regulate
commit
provide

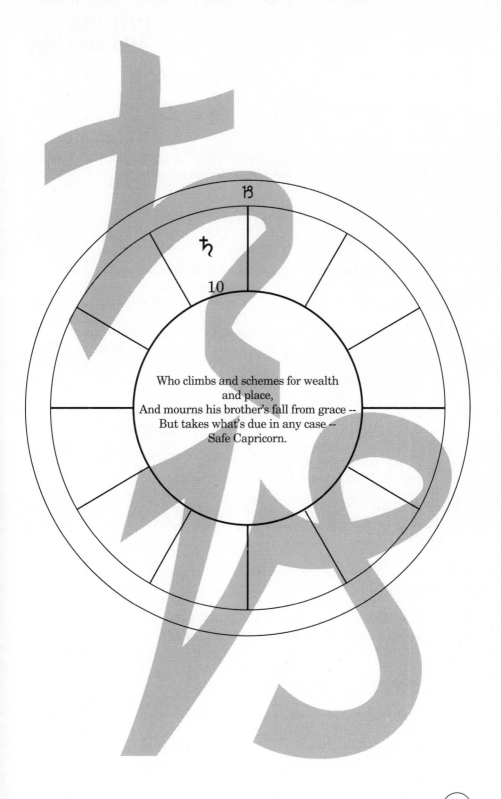

♑

♄

10

Who climbs and schemes for wealth
and place,
And mourns his brother's fall from grace --
But takes what's due in any case --
Safe Capricorn.

Success is just a matter of luck; ask any failure.   *Robert Anthony*   ♃ ♑ 12

Economy is the armchair of old age.   *Yankee Wisdom*   ♄ ♋ 2

Be someone, not something.   *Coco Chanel*   ☉ 10

Time past and time future allow but a little consciousness.
To be conscious is not to be in time.   *T. S. Eliot*   ♄ ♒ 12
                                                              ♄ ♓ 1

Patience is applied timelessness.   *Anon*   ♄ ♓ 6

I hope this does not mean, either the establishment is doomed,
or that I'm doomed to be established. (On receiving honors at
Oxford 1962.)   *W.H. Auden*   ☉ ♑ 12

A negative use of power is not powerlessness, it is acting outside
of one's integrity.   *D.H.*   ♄ ♏ 12

Nature knows no indecencies, man invents them.   *Mark Twain*   ♄ ♏ 5

In politics, if you want anything said ask a man. If you want
anything done, ask a woman.   *Margaret Thatcher*   ☽ ♑ 10

Go beyond your enslavement to time and live fully in this,
the only time you have; the now, the working unit of your life.
      Wayne Dyer   ♃ ♑ 1

Self-control is infinitely more important than self-esteem.
It emphasizes behavior over feelings.   *Dennis Prager*   ☽ ♑ 1

Time that tires of everyone has corroded all the locks and thrown
away the key for fun.   *W.H. Auden*   ♄ ♌ 12

Time that is indifferent in a week to a beautiful physique,
pardons cowardice and conceit, lays its honor at their feet.
      W.H. Auden   ♄ ♑ 1

Angels cannot stand in proximity to doubt.   *Ann Ree Colton*   ♄ ♓ 9

Nanny-staters have an umbilical attachment to government.   *D.H.*   ☽ ♑ 8

Seeking pleasure over truth runs the risk of distorting reality.
      Charles Tart   ♀ ♑ 9
                         ♇ ♑ 9

In headache and in worry vaguely life leaks away and time
will have his fancy tomorrow or today.   *W.H. Auden*   ♄ ♓ 1

Bureaucracy always betrays.   *Simone Weil*   ♀ 10

Political correctness is political cleansing.   *Rush Limbaugh* ♀ 10

Success is relative; it is what we can make of the mess
we have made of things.   *T.S. Eliot*   ♃ ♍ 10
                                                                           ♅ 10

      Fall in love with what you do,
      <u>then</u> what you sell is love.
                                                           Wayne Dyer   ♀ ♌ 10

And the wind shall say: "Here were decent godless people: their
only monuments the asphalt road and a thousand lost golf balls.
                                                           T.S. Eliot   ☿ ♑ 5

Drop kick me Jesus through the goal-posts of life.   *Country Song* ♂ ♓ 10

Necessity is not a fact, it is an interpretation.   *Nietzsche*   ♄ ♊ 3

Dust is more than dirt, it is the calling card of the past.
                                                           Emily Dickinson ♄ ♋ 4

Let boredom be your opportunity to visit the boardroom of
possibility.   *D.H.*   ♄ ♌ 12
                                                                           ♄ ♐ 5

I wasted time, and now doth time waste me.
                                          Shakespeare, <u>Richard II</u> ♄ ♏ 1

One may know the whole of a continuum from one segment of its
arc. Indeed, people who seem to know the past and the future
well have a habit of conceiving of them as forms of present time.
                                                           Robert Grudin ♄ ♒ 1

A skeptic is a failed romantic.   *Anon*   ♄ ♓ 5
                                                                           ♇ ♑ 5

Some people say my program to reduce the federal government
goes too far, that it throws out the baby with the bath water. But
we have no choice ... this is Rosemary's Baby we're talking about.
                                                           Harry Browne ☽ ♏ 10

The 1960's were unique as the first time elders acquiesced to the tantrums of youth.

Dennis Prager | ♄ Ⅱ

Worry robs today of its energy
but never its problems.

Anon | ♄ ♍ 1
♄ ♑ 6

Moses coming down the mountain reading the stone tablets:
"Oh God, is this another one of those self-responsibility deals?"

Cartoon--Anon | ☉ ♑ 9

Too often we seem slaves to striving and hostages to the future.

D.H. | ♄ ♑ 11
♄ ♒ 12

Since thou are not sure of a minute, throw not away an hour.

Ben Franklin | ♄ 1

Do our experiences become more marvelous with age, or is it just that we don't realize when they occur how really beautiful and precious they are?

Joseph Campbell | ♀ ♑ 4

You know you're getting older when: You join a health club and then don't go; you know all the answers but nobody asks you the questions; you regret all those mistakes resisting temptation.

Joseph Campbell | ☿ ♑

How has it come about, that we use the highly emotive word "stagnation," with all its malodorous and malarial overtones, for what other ages would have called "permanence?"

C.S. Lewis | ♄ ♏ 4

If a man begin with certainties, he shall end in doubts; but if he will be content to begin with doubts, he shall end in certainties.

Francis Bacon | ♄ ♐ 1

Being your slave, what should I do but tend upon the hours and
       times of your desire?
I have no precious time at all to spend, nor services to do, til you
       require,
Nor dare I chide the world-without-end hour
Whilst I, my sovereign, watch the clock for you.

Shakespeare | ♄ ♎ 6

I think what we're really facing are a bunch of people who want no limits, moral or otherwise, on their behavior.

Michael Medved | ♃ ♒ 1

History is the science of something that never happens twice.

Paul Valéry | ♄ ♒ 1

Government has become too large and oppressive to help one group without visibly harming several others. *Harry Browne* | ♄ ♏ 11

Saying "none of your business" to various government organizations doesn't mean anarchy. It means having laws that are limited and clearly enough defined that they are not just blank checks for busybodies. *Thomas Sowell* | ♄ ♍ 10

Political correctness is counterfeit respect, and like faked love is a form of contempt. *Anon* | ♀ ♓ 10

An example from the monkey: the higher it climbs the more you see of its behind. [Monkeys are ruled by ♊.] *St. Bonaventure* | ☿ ♏ 10

A fall from the air of high romance to the ground of realism.

Gonnaud | ♄ ♎ 5

Government has lost the latitude to promise benefits while hiding costs. *Harry Browne* | ♃ ♑ 12

Guilt seeks punishment, self-criticism locks in old patterns.

Louise Hay | ♄ ♏ 12

God cannot alter the past, but historians can. *Samuel Butler* | ♄ ♓ 4

Antipathy to excellence is a benchmark of modern government.

D.H. | ♄ ♐ 10

Not if I <u>get</u> time, but when I <u>make</u> time. *D.H.* | ♄ ♌ 6

Federal matching funds equals welfare for politicians.

Harry Browne | ♃ ♑ 12

Mediocrity is unnatural in nature and man, and can only be sustained by coercion. *D.H.* | ♄ ♏ 10

The result of government social engineering is not a level playing field, but rather a swamp of mediocrity. *D.H.* | ♄ ♏ 4

The power we give other people over our lives will last long beyond that moment. (Pluto in Libra approximately 1971 to 1984.)

Thomas Sowell | ♇ ♎ 1

Government is now responsible for politicizing and delivering meaning.   *Ted Forstmann*   ♄ ♊ 9

We have legalized confiscation, consecrated sacrilege, and condoned high treason.   *Disraeli (mid 1800's)*   ♄ ♏ 10

Life is a rock <u>and</u> a hard place.   *Anon*   ☉ ♑ 12

Take away the free market and you have the black market.
                                                                Winston Churchill   ♃ ♑ 12

Respect tradition then make up your own.   *Antero Alli*   ♄ ♒ 4

Memory is just frozen time.   *Deepak Chopra*   ♄ ♏ 4

Reality is an ocean, but we take it away in teacups.
                                                                   Deepak Chopra   ♄ ♓ 7

Skepticism is a hedge against vulnerability.   *Charles Samuels*   ♄ ♋ 3

You cannot have integrity without consistency, yet consistency of itself has little value.   *D.H.*   ♃ ♑ 2

Naivete is the belief that the next government program will work.
                                                                     Harry Browne   ♅ ♑ 10
                                                                                                          ☿ ♓ 10

Well done is soon enough. (Joseph Campbell found this in a fortune cookie when overloaded with work and deadlines.)
                                                                (Joseph Campbell)   ♃ ♑ 6

Politically correct hypocrisy: those that felt oppressed in the past are now silencing others.   *John Caldara*   ♄ ♓ 7

What one does is what counts, and not what one had the intention of doing.   *Picasso*   ♄ ♑ 5

A government formed to protect us from government has become our greatest threat.   *D.H.*   ♀ 10

Character is that which can do without success.   *Emerson*   ☉ 10

Mother Teresa on the possible failure of a newly opened mission: "I'm not in the business of success."   *Mother Teresa*   ☉ ♍ 10

The appearance of character makes the state unnecessary. *Emerson*   ☉ ♑ 1

All great men come out of the middle class.   *Emerson*   ♃ ♑ 10

Make yourself necessary to the world, and mankind will give you bread.   *Emerson*   ☉ ♑ 2

Fear has a smell, as love does.   *Margaret Atwood*   ♄ ♊ 5

Fear of losing is what makes competitors so great. Show me a gracious loser and I'll show you a perennial loser.   *O.J. Simpson*   ♄ ♎ 5

The only way to get rid of my fears is to make films about them.   *Alfred Hitchcock*   ♄ ♓ 5

Nothing is more despicable than respect based on fear.
    Albert Camus   ♄ ♑ 12

The truth is that once he was in an environment where he could work, Dylan was extremely disciplined, writing to a strict routine no matter where he was, and that continued right to the end. [Dylan Thomas was ☉♏5 with Pluto conjunct Saturn in 1st.]   *Caitlin Thomas*   ♄ ♏ 1

DEMOSCLEROSIS: Loss of flexibility on the part of government to solve problems.   *Jonathan Rausch*   ♄ ♍ 10

The only time there is is the one you are aware of.   *Deepak Chopra*   ♄ 1

Who will protect us from the protectors?   *Ayn Rand*   ♃ ♋ 10

If Moses had been a committee the Israelites would still be in Egypt.   *J.B. Hughes*   ♄ ♒ 10

Saturn is the lord of the morning after.   *Anon*   ♄ ♓ 12

He who is sad, saddens others.   *St. Exupéry*   ♄ ♋ 11

Lessons are not given, they are taken.   *Pavese*   ♄

Malice drinks half of its own poison.   *Seneca*   ♄ ♏ 12

Bored people, unless they sleep a lot, are cruel.   *Renata Adler*   ♄ ♊ 12

To be a man is to feel that one's own stone contributes to the edifice of the world. *St. Exupéry* | ☉ ♑ 10

Humility is being a chosen chairman; to set them up and put them away. *Anon* | ♄ ♌ 6 / ♄ ♍ 11

Better to be late in this world than early in the next. *Israeli Proverb* | ♄ ♈ 8

The source of (East) Indian devotion is a bottomless pessimism. *Kafka* | ♃ ♑ 12

I most emphatically advocate a black and white (good vs. evil) view of the world. There is no justification ever for choosing any part of what you know to be evil. *Ayn Rand* | ♄ ♏ 10

Government spending is like a transfusion from one arm to the other with half of it spilt in the middle. *Jesse Helms* | ♃ ♓ 10

We live in an age where victims parade around in their diapers seeking comfort from a "Nanny-State" run by ethical infants. *D.H.* | ☽ ♓ 10

A saint and a sinner are the same after two hours of mountain climbing. *Binswanger* | ♄ ♏ 9

The teeth are the bones of the stomach. *Ann Ree Colton* | ♄ ♋ 1

One marches through the streets as if through dark canals of times dishwater. *Kafka* | ♄ ♋ 3

A free mind and a free economy are corollaries; one can't exist without the other. *Ayn Rand* | ☿ ♒ 10

The greatest problem facing the world is population growth. *Al Gore* | ♃ ♋ 10

The greatest problem facing the world is too many bad people. *Dennis Prager* | ♄ ♋ 10

Government turns people into hirelings. *Burgess Owens* | ♄ ♋ 6

To a young man Macbeth is a character part; to an older man it is a straight part. *Laurence Olivier* | ♂ ♓ 5

The revolution evaporates, and leaves behind only the slime of a new bureaucracy. The chains of tormented mankind are made out of red tape.   *Kafka*   ♀ 10

A creator builds bridges, a victim walls.   *D.H.*   ♄ ♌ 3
    ♄ ♓ 12

The way to prove non-racism is to apply the same moral and intellectual standards to all.   *Dennis Prager*   ☽ ♐ 10

Continuity without a starting point is time.   *Chuang-Tzu*   ♄ ♓ 1

Choose not to identify persistence with struggle.
    Bashar   ♂ ♑ 6

Political correctness is a fear-based projection into the future, an attempt at healing personal wounds of the past by diapering the collective for tomorrow.   *D.H.*   ♄ ♋ 11

'Tis a pity we should leave with the children all the romance, all that is daintiest in life, and reserve for ourselves as we grow old only the prose. Goethe fell in love in his old age, and I would never lose the capacity of delicate and noble sentiments.   *Emerson (1839; age 36)*   ♄ 5

One sad reflection arises on all the course of the narrative, of wonder, namely, at the depravity of men in power, and at the shocking tameness with which it is endured.   *Emerson (1849, age 46)*   ♀ 10

The past is gone, washed away by time's sea.
The future is but a dream, yet to be.
Now is your gift and your eternity.   *Kyros*   ♄ ♓ 1

By definition integrity must be holographic.   *D.H.*   ♄ ♓ 3

Sorrow makes us all children again.   *Emerson*   ♄ ♋ 5

If adversity purifies man, why not nations?   *Jean Paul Richter*   ♄ ♏ 10

The time which we have at our disposal every day is elastic; the passions that we feel expand it, those that we inspire contract it; and habit fills up the rest.   *Marcel Proust*   ♄ ♓ 6

The tyranny of the tick is the squawk of the clock.   *D.H.*   ♄ ♏ 1

You know you're getting old when you stoop to tie your shoes
and wonder what else you can do while you're down there.

George Burns ♄ ♊ 1

The duties of a writer as a writer and a citizen are not the same.
The only duty a writer has as a citizen is to defend language.
And this is a <u>Political</u> duty. Because, if language is corrupted,
thought is corrupted. This leads to violence. *W.H. Auden* ♄ ♊ 10

**Few things help an individual more than to place
responsibility upon him, and to let him know that
you trust him.**

Booker T. Washington ☽ ♑ 7

Cynicism is the dishonest businessman's substitute for conscience.

Russell Jones ♄ ♏ 12

Be on guard against:
Science without humanity
Politics without principle
Knowledge without character
Wealth without work
Commerce without conscience
Worship without sacrifice. *Gandhi* ♄ 9

... All the time in everything you do, whatever you are doing,
is the time for politics. *Plutarch* ♄ ♐ 10

All history becomes subjective, in other words there is properly
no history, only biography. *Emerson* ♄ ♌ 3

If you can't take their money and drink their booze and screw
their women and then vote against them, you don't belong here.
(Ickes is an advisor to President Clinton.) *Harold Ickes* ♄ ♏ 10

We now have less people making widgets than regulating
and taxing them. *Stephen Moore, James Carter* ♃ ♑ 8

Sell when you can; you are not for all markets. *Shakespeare* ♅ 10

Necessity never made a good bargain. *Ben Franklin* ♄ ♊ 2

When you strike at a king, you must kill him. *Emerson* ♂ ♏ 10

Whatever you hold onto is dead because it is past. *Deepak Chopra* ♄ ♏ 4

The heart of making a temptation that is greater than you can
resist is that you do not wish to be held responsible for your choice.
Gary Zukov ♄ ♏ 12

Tomorrow and tomorrow and tomorrow
Creeps in this petty pace from day to day
To the last instant of recorded time.
And all our yesterdays have lighted us
The way to dusty death. *Shakespeare, <u>Macbeth</u>* ♄ ♏

Victimhood sees discipline as punishment. *D.H.* ♄ ♏ 12

I will waste time before it wastes me. *Lagowski & Mumma* ♄ ♏ 12

Time: That which man is always trying to kill, but which ends
in killing him. *Herbert Spencer* ♄ ♏ 8

The religious world has too many taboos, the secular world
has none. *Dennis Prager* ♄ ♑ 9

Doubt is the shabby emperor of Samsara (the cycle of rebirth).
Sogyal Rinpoche ♄ ♌ 8

The ancient civilizations who built the extra-terrestrial
monuments (on Mars and the Moon) are us before the Fall.
Richard Hoagland ♄ ♐ 4

I don't deserve this award, but I have arthritis and I don't deserve
that either. *Jack Benny* ♄ ♍ 10

There's no such thing as old age, there is only sorrow.
Edith Wharton ♄ ♋ 12

Never face facts; if you do you'll never get up in the morning.
Marlo Thomas ♄ ♍ 1

Cynic: An idealist whose rose-colored glasses have been removed,
snapped in two, and stomped into the ground, immediately
improving his vision. *Rick Bayan* ♄ ♓ 3

Only a cynic can see viruses in the milk of human kindness.
[Viruses are ruled by Pluto.] *Anon* ♄ ♏ 6

A cynic thinks it's right that divorce should cost more than
marriage because it's worth more. *Anon* ♄ ♎ 8

To the cynic, what is, is no better than it ought to be.
("God's will is what's happening.")   *Anon*   ♄ ♐ 1

More harm is done to infants in infancy than to adults in adultery.
                                                       Anon   ♄ ♋

> **Humility is not renunciation of pride but the
> substitution of one pride for another.**
>   *Eric Hoffer*   ♄ ♌

What do you do when humility leads to still greater glory?   *Anon*   ♄ ♐ 10
                                                                          ♃ ♓ 10

It is God, not man, who should be humble when he reflects
upon the indifferent job he has made of a human being.
                                           Somerset Maugham   ♄ ♐ 11

The earth, though grievously abused, still suffers me to tread
its surface.   *Marcus Aurelius*   ♂ ♑ 1

Be as positive as you have allowed yourself to be negative.   *Anon*   ♃ ♑ 12

And although we may be sorry for people who suffer, we only
"feel their pain" when we're full of baloney and running for office.
                                           P.J. O'Rourke   ☿ 10
                                                                ♆ ♑

Addictive/compulsive people "SHOULD" on themselves.   *Anon*   ♄ ♏ 1

In elections Democrats run like Republicans and Republicans
run like Libertarians.   *Harry Browne*   ♆ 10

The Constitution contains a plan for representative democracy
that has, over the years, been successful in luring some of our
most egregious national characters out of the private sector,
where they would have done no end of damage to industry and
commerce, and into public office, where they can be watched.
                                           P.J. O'Rourke   ♄ ♏ 10

Responsibility must proceed from the bottom up, from the
individual outward, never from the top down, never from the
outside in, with the individual as the squeezed cream filling
of that giant Twinkie which is the State.   *P.J. O'Rourke*   ☉ ♑ 1

To walk into history is to be free at once, to be at large among
people.   *Elizabeth Bowen*   ☿ ♑ 11

At twelve noon the natives swoon
and no further work is done.
But mad dogs and Englishmen
go out in the midday sun.   *Noel Coward*   ☉ ♈ 10

The consumer's side of the coffin lid is never ostentatious.
[Coffins are ruled by Saturn.]   *Stanislaw Lec*   ♄ ♌ 8

It's so much easier to pray for a bore than to go and see one.
                                             C.S. Lewis   ♄ ♊ 9

There is no present or future, only the past, happening over
and over again, now.   *Eugene O'Neill*   ♄ ♋ 1

As far as the laws of mathematics refer to reality, they are not
certain; as far as they are certain, they do not refer to reality.
                                             Albert Einstein   ♄ 9

If women can sleep their way to the top, how come they aren't there?
                                             Ellen Goodman   ☽ ♏ 10

Fame lost its appeal for me when I went into a public restroom
and an autograph seeker handed me a pen and paper under the
stall door.   *Marlo Thomas*   ☿ ♋ 10

In the face of an obstacle which is impossible to overcome,
stubbornness is stupid.   *Simone de Beauvoir*   ♄ ♉ 1

In the burrows of the nightmare where justice naked is,
Time watches from the shadows and coughs when you would kiss.
                                             W.H. Auden   ♄ ♎ 12

Too bad all the people who know how to run the country
are busy driving taxi cabs and cutting hair.   *George Burns*   ☿ ♑ 6

No country can be destroyed by a mere conspiracy; it can be
destroyed by ideas.   *Ayn Rand*   ☿ ♏ 10

No matter how big a business is, you don't have to deal with it;
there's always an alternative. But government forces you to
accept what it wants ... whether or not you agree.   *Harry Browne*   ♀ 10
                                                                            ♂ ♑

The reason there is so little crime in Germany is that it is against
the law.   *Alex Levin*   ♄ ♏ 10

Culture is on the horns of this dilemma: if profound and noble it must remain rare, if common it must become mean.

George Santayana — ♄ ♒ 10

Problems are the cutting edge that distinguishes between success and failure. Problems call forth our courage and our wisdom; indeed, they create our courage and our wisdom.

Scott Peck — ♄ ♍ 9

We live in an age when pizza gets to your home before the police.

Jeff Marder — ♄ ♋ 6

A historian is a prophet in reverse.

Friedrich von Schlegel — ♅℞ ♑

One grows very cautious when living across the border from malevolent rivals.

Baltasar Gracian — ♄ ♑ 7

The more substances controlled by the government, the more people controlled by the government.

Bob Beckler — ☿ ♑ 10 / ☽ ♏ 10

Politics is supposed to be the second oldest profession. I have come to realize that it bears a very close resemblance to the first.

Ronald Reagan — ☿ 10

Political correctness is counterfeit compassion and the bastardization of Liberalism.

D.H. — ♃ ♓ 10

The world hangs on a thin thread, and that is the psyche of man.

Carl Jung — ☿ 10

Private faces in public places are wiser and nicer than public faces in private places.

W.H. Auden — ♃ ♏ 10

A government big enough to give you everything you want is big enough to take it away from you.

Anon — ☿ 10

Convenience talks, commitment walks.

D.H. — ♂ ♑

Heaven help us if government ever gets into the business of protecting us from ourselves.

Ronald Reagan (1973) — ♄ ♍ 6

Old Pond,
Frog Jump,
Plop.

Basho   ♄ ♋

      Old Man,
      Peeing,
      Drip.

D.H.   ♄ ♏

But above all do not make yourself important by doubting.

Kierkegaard   ♄ ♌ 9

ELEVENTH HOUSE

The House of Friendships
'fun with others'

the sphere of goals and
objectives
friends
detached or impersonal
relationships
clubs and social groups
objectives in life
social connections and
spheres of influence

URANUS

Influence:
progress
originality
extremism
freedom
the unexpected
rebellion
simultaneity

Examples:
activists
radicals
social scientists
innovators
channelers
prophets

AQUARIUS

ingenious
individualistic
energetic
independent
scientific

antagonistic
erratic
eccentric
inflexible
insensitive

Life purpose to:
awaken
invent
confront
change
equalize

11

Who gives to all a helping hand,
But bows his head to no command --
And higher laws doth understand?
Inventor, Genius, Superman --
Aquarius.

I didn't throw myself into life -- I threw my astrologer. *G.B. Shaw* ♅ ♈ 7

Whoso would be a man must be a nonconformist. *Emerson* ♅ ♒ 1

The body is the only part of us in present time. *Anon* ♄ ♒ 1

All originality is relative. *Emerson* ☿ ♒

With New Age workshops for everything from coping with chronic crab grass and preparing for post-partum wealth to learning to live with junk mail and establishing compassionate relationships with adult children of extraterrestrials, it's a wonder there are still women who can apply lipstick without a workshop support group. *Hester Mundis* ♒ 6

Where there are humans there are flies and Buddhas. *Issa* ☿ ♐ 11

Contentment -- the smother of invention. *Anon* ☽ ♒

I think we have obligations to society, not just privileges <u>from</u> society; that's why I'm not a Libertarian. *Dennis Prager* ♄ ♒ 10

Nervous as a long-tailed cat in a room full of rocking chairs. *Anon* ♅ ♍ 3

Much of what we call miraculous is simply grace given in synchronicity, thus making it more recognizable; a present from non-local reality. *D.H.* ♃ ♒ 1

The finger of God never leaves identical fingerprints. *Stanislaw Lec* ☿ ♒ 1

Individuals are smarter than groups, as anybody who is a member of a committee or of a large Irish family after six in the evening can tell you. *P.J. O'Rourke* ☉ ♊ 1

For a society to function truth is the most important virtue. *Dennis Prager* ♃ 11

"The Quickening" -- Karmupence becoming chaos. *D.H.* ♂ ♒ 12

Successful artists do have their clusters; they move ahead tribally; it's not "The Lone Ranger." *Anon* ♀ ♑ 11

Every exit is an entrance somewhere else. *Zen Saying* ♅ 12

Liberty is indivisible. You can't pick and choose among a list of freedoms, fight for the ones you like and let the others be suppressed.   *Rick Thompkins* | ♃ ♒ 10

Everything that has happened and will happen is here now. Our limited perception keeps us from seeing or experiencing it in the present.   *Courtney Brown* | ♄ ♒ 1

Elitism: To restrict the freedom of the many for the privilege of the few.
                    David Hayward | ♄ ♒ 10

Altruism does not necessitate self-esteem.   *Pearl & Sam Oliner* | ♃ ♒ 2

The best way to predict your future is to create it.   *Anon* | ♃ ♒ 5

The future is the present all the time.   *Chogyam Trungpa* | ♄ ♒ 1

Multiculturalism is the politicizing of community.   *Ted Forstmann* | ♄ ♒ 4

No central planner can match the sheer genius of the marketplace.
                    Ted Forstmann | ♄ ♒ 8

Any victim demands allegiance.   *Graham Greene* | ☽ ♓ 11
 ♀ 11

Drop expectations and be surprised by life.   *Dennis Prager* | ♄ ♒ 1

The health of a Democratic society can be measured by the quality of functions performed by its private citizens.
                    De Tocqueville (1805-1859) | ♃ ♒ 4

There's no point in making plans for the future if you can't fully enjoy the results when they, in turn, become part of the present.
                    Alan Watts | ♀ ♒ 1

Friendship is far more tragic than love. It lasts longer.
                    Oscar Wilde | ♄ ♒ 12

Friendship is like money, easier made than kept.   *Samuel Butler* | ♀ ♒ 2

It's been said that love is blind. Friendship, on the other hand, is clairvoyant.   *Philippe Soupault* | ♀ ♓ 11

A friend is one who dislikes the same people you dislike.

Anon   ♄ ♎ 11

The friends of freedom still have much work to do on the issue of no-knock raids. (4th Amendment to Constitution.)   *James Bovard*   ♅ ♑ 4

Computer jargon: Floppy now, hard later. (Graffito, Silicon Valley.)
(M. Rose Pierce)   ♂ ♒ 8

Anything of great value -- creation, a new idea -- carries its shadow zone with it. You have to accept it that way. Otherwise there is only the stagnation of inaction. But every action has an implicit share of negativity. There is no escaping it. The genius of Einstein leads to Hiroshima.   *Picasso*   ♂ ♒ 12

Yesterday's miracles are today's sciences.   *Deepak Chopra*   ♄ ♒ 9

What is a committee? A group of the unwilling, picked from the unfit, to do the unnecessary.   *Richard Harkness*   ♄ ♒ 10

The ideal committee is one with me as the chairman and two other members in bed with flu.   *Lord Milverton*   ☉ ♒ 6

A camel is a horse designed by a committee.
[Camels are ruled by Saturn, horses by Sagittarius.]   *Anon*   ♄ ♐ 11

Originality is the art of concealing your sources.   *Anon*   ♅ 12

The sign of an intelligent people is their ability to control emotions by the application of reason.   *Marya Mannes*   ☽ ♒ 9

Is it progress if a cannibal uses a fork?   *Stanislaw Lec*   ♅ 6

The highest goal: to make one's life a periscope for the soul.   *D.H.*   ♀ ♐ 11

There are two ways to live your life -- as though nothing is a miracle, or everything is.   *Einstein*   ♅ 9

I'm no advocate of the purely Uranian society myself. I mean, I certainly don't want to live ONLY with queers.   *W.H. Auden*   ♄ ♒ 11

If spending money on social programs would reduce crime, America would be the safest country on Earth.   *Anon*   ♄ ♒ 8

Progress is our present power. Perfection is our future fiction.

D.H.   ☿ ≈ 1

Live to the real future by living to the real present.   *Emerson*   ⛢ 1

Multiculturalism creates hyphenated Americans, our new
separatism, or racism.   *Anon*   ☽ ≈ 10

A preoccupation with the future not only prevents us from seeing
the present as it is, but often prompts us to rearrange the past.

Eric Hoffer   ♄ ≈ 1

Life is always insecure. The only choice is between liberty and
insecurity on the one hand, and insecurity and enslavement on
the other.   *Jacob Hornberger*   ☽ ≈ 12

SYNTROPY -- the tendency of life-energy to move towards
greater association, communication, cooperation and awareness.

Howard Sasportas   ♃ ≈ 11

In the heaven of Indra, there is said to be a network of pearls,
so arranged, that if you look at one you see all the others reflected
in it.   *A Hindu Sutra*   ☽ 11

A truth once seen, even by a single mind, always ends by
imposing itself on the totality of human consciousness.

Pierre Teilhard de Chardin   ♃ ≈ 12

The virtue in most request is conformity.   *Emerson*   ♃ ♎ 11

Underlying most arguments against the free market is a lack
of belief in freedom itself.   *Milton Friedman*   ♄ ≈ 9

People enslave themselves when all that freedom requires
is the word "no."   *Wendy McElroy*   ♄ ≈ 3

On the Internet: "Who do you want to talk to? All those morons
who are living across the world somewhere? You don't even want
to talk to them at home.   *Ray Bradbury*   ♄ ≈ 3

Socialism is an adult fairy tale.   *David Horowitz*   ♆ ≈ 3

Our Congress is the best money can buy.   *Will Rogers*   ♀ 11

Going against the grain gives you splinters.   *Bashar*   ♄ ≈ 1

I hold that while man exists it is his duty to improve not only his own conditions, but to assist in ameliorating mankind. I am for those means which will give the greatest good to the greatest number. [Spoken like a true Aquarian!]   *Abraham Lincoln*   ♃ ≈ 11

New-agers remind me of kids who discover sex and think they invented it, then get bent out of shape to find out their parents must have known about it too.   *Joseph Silveira de Mello*   ♅ 8

It isn't black or white, it's wrong or right.   *Anon*   ♃ ≈

False friendship is like a parasitic plant; it kills the tree it embraces.   *Anon*   ♄ ≈ 8
♇ ≈ 8

He who hath too many friends, hath as many candidates for enemies.   *Anon*   ♀ 11

A penny saved is a congressional oversight.   *Hal Lee Luyah*   ♀ ♓ 11

When the American people give up their freedom for security, they shall have neither.   *Ben Franklin*   ♄ ≈ 4

Who knows what form the forward momentum of life will take in the time ahead or what use it will make of our anguished searching. The most that any one of us can seem to do is to fashion something -- an object or ourselves -- and drop it into the confusion, make an offering of it, so to speak, to the life force.   *Ernest Becker (1973)*   ♅ ≈

Once respect for the individual is lost, then what do a few million dead individuals matter? Especially if their deaths are for the collective good? Fifty million were killed in the war the Nazis started. Soviet purges and persecutions killed 20 million more. As many as 30 million died in Chinese famines caused by forced communization of agriculture. That's 100 million dead from collectivism, not counting Korea, Indochina, Angola, Cuba, Nicaragua, and so on.   *P.J. O'Rourke*   ♄ ≈ 8

The test is to live a new paradigm, a visionary rather than fearful perspective.   *Inspired by David Pond*   ♅ ≈ 9

The women's movement is no longer a cause, but a symptom.   *Joan Didion*   ☽ ≈ 6

Culture in its higher forms is a delicate plant.   *Einstein*   ♀ ♉ 11

For precocity some great price is always demanded sooner or later in life. *Margaret Fuller (1884)*

♄ ≈ 1

Friendship is honey -- but don't eat it all. *Moroccan Proverb*

♄ ♎ 11

When a friend speaks to me, whatever he says is interesting. *Jean Renoir*

☿ ♊ 11

Anything one man can imagine, other men can make real. *Jules Verne*

☉ ≈ 5

Science as it is today, is severely limited in its potential by the very criterion that it has imposed upon itself -- namely, that it will accept as real only those phenomena that can be weighed or measured. *Caroline Norris*

♄ ≈ 9

> **I was over thirty before, for the first time,
> I heard somebody say that he did not think
> of himself as masculine or feminine, but
> merely as a person attracted to other persons
> with male sexual organs.**
> *Quentin Crisp*

♂ ≈ 8

Life is a drag, you know -- then you become one! *Charles Pierce, American female impersonator*

♄ ≈ 8

It's much easier for men to do drag. For a woman to be in male drag and claim that power, it's not funny. For boys to be girls is hysterical. *Peggy Shaw*

♅ ≈ 8

Every man should own at least one dress, and so should lesbians. *Jane Adams Spahr*

♀ ≈ 8

It's the daylight you gotta watch out for. Face it, a thing of beauty is a joy till sunrise. *Harvey Fierstein, gay playwright, actor*

♀ ≈ 1

Queers United Against Closets (or QUAC) (American Protest Organization) *Anon*

♅ ♑ 8

Why do motorcyclists wear leather? Because chiffon wrinkles too easily, that's why. *Paul Lynde*

♀ ≈ 3

I'd like any role that would stretch me, where I was credible. But I'm not about to drag myself up in leather or in chiffon. *Rock Hudson*

♄ ≈ 1

It is indeed a burning shame that there should be one law
for men and another for women. I think there should be no law
for anybody.   *Oscar Wilde* | ⍫ 10

You've heard of my case? Don't distress yourself. All is well.
The working classes are with me ... to a boy.   *Oscar Wilde* | ☿ ≋ 6

Military Tribunal enquirer: Tell me, Mr. Strachey, what would
you do if you saw a German soldier attempting to rape your sister?
Lytton Strachey: I should try and come between them.
                    Lytton Strachey, WWI conscientious objector | ♂ ≋ 8

Judges realize that putting a homosexual into prison is like
trying to cure obesity by incarceration in a candy shop.
                                                   Martin Hoffman | ♀ ≋ 12

There is no monument dedicated to the memory of a committee.
                                                 Lester J. Pourciau | ♄ ≋ 3

I'm sick of hearing about twelve-step programs for healing and
recovery. What we need are fewer twelve-step programs and
more twelve-gauge shotguns.   *Anon* | ♂ ♍ 11

Would you like to know the great drama of my life?
It is that I've put my genius into my life;
I've only put my talent into my works.
                                                    Oscar Wilde | ⍫ ♌ 1

I have sometimes almost wished it had been my destiny to be born
two or three centuries hence.   *Ben Franklin (1788)* | ♆ ≋

My friends are the wellspring of my life.   *George Eliot* | ☉ ≋ 11

Laughter is the shortest distance between two people.
                                                  Victor Borge | ♃ ♊ 11

One man's cosmic revelation is another's gobbledygook.
                                                 Roger Woolger | ⍫ 9

The perception of the comic is a tie of sympathy with other men.
                                                       Emerson | ☿ ♓ 11

Television is a medium of entertainment which permits millions
of people to listen to the same joke at the same time, and yet
remain lonesome.   *T.S. Eliot* | ⍫ 12

Nothing is really real unless it happens on television.

Daniel Boorstin | ♅ ♑

Television: the bland leading the bland. *Anon* | ♄ ♒ 10

Your friend is the one who knows all about you, and still likes you.

Elbert Hubbard | ♃ ♎ 11

You are free and that is why you are lost. *Franz Kafka* | ♅ ♒ 12

Television is an invention that permits you to be entertained
in your living room by people you wouldn't have in your house.

David Frost | ♄ ♒ 4

I must say I find television very educational. The minute
somebody turns it on, I go to the library and read a good book.

Groucho Marx | ☿ ♒ 12

Imitation is the sincerest form of television. *Fred Allen* | ♅ ♎ 7

But once one has tasted the intensity of an inner life that
contains brotherly love, one desperately demands the conditions
that create it. *Saint Exupéry* | ♀ ♏ 11

The astrologer sees the client's wholeness from the inside out.
The psychologist sees the client's wholeness from the outside in.

Anon | ♅ 8

A radical is one who thinks he votes right when he votes left.

Anon | ♅ 10

When one is living as a spiritual being they become a unique
innovator of manifested soul. *D.H.* | ♅ ♓ 1

You cannot become thorough Americans if you think of yourselves
in groups. America does not consist of groups. A man who thinks
of himself as belonging to a particular national group in America
has not yet become an American. *Woodrow Wilson (1915)* | ♄ ♒ 10

An American in the 1990's who does not think of himself as
belonging to the multi-cultural group-think mentality has no
identity. A Balkanized America has no place for the traditional
American. Sadly, the "melting pot" is an old idea. *D.H.* | ♄ ♒ 10

Friends are born, not made. *Henry Adams* | ♒ 8

Friendship, n. A ship big enough to carry two in fair weather, but only one in foul.   *Ambrose Bierce*   ♄ ♒ 3

The future is much like the present, only longer.   *Don Quisenberry*   ♄ ♒ 1

An associate producer is the only guy in Hollywood who will associate with a producer.   *Fred Allen*   ♀ ♒ 5

Television has proved that people will look at anything rather than each other.   *Ann Landers*   ♒ 7

You ask what hope is? A waking dream.   *Aristotle*   ♆ 11

Happy are the men whom nature has buttressed with indifference and cased in stoicism.   *Guy de Maupassant*   ♀ ♑ 11

Scientists hate paradox. It is a threshold over which their logic won't go.   *Joseph Chilton Pierce*   ♄ ♒ 9

What a vast difference there is between the barbarism that precedes culture and the barbarism that follows it.   *Frederick Hebbel*   ⚲ 11

> **A man who wants to lead the orchestra
> must turn his back on the crowd.**
>   *James Crook*   ♄ ♒ 5

Hope is a slave's virtue.   *E.M. Cioran*   ♄ ♐ 11

A friend in need is what most of us have.   *Anon*   ♄ ♒

Genius is eternal patience.   *Michelangelo*   ⛢ ♑

We are headed toward an event ... something ... at an ever increasing speed ... "The Quickening."   *Art Bell*   ♂ ♒ 10

They were such a progressive couple they tried to adopt a gay baby.   *Anon*   ☽ ♒ 7

Cease being the slave of a political party and you become its deserter.   *Jules Simon*   ♄ ♒ 10

Friends are like melons, shall I tell you why? To find one good, you must a hundred try.   *Claude Mermet*   ♄ ♋ 11

There is a sense of entitlement that seems to be overwhelming our society. Things that used to be privileges have become rights. People feel entitled to free medicine, free retirement benefits, every kind of disaster relief, protection from bad luck and from bad weather, and on and on, never asking themselves, "What have I done for society that would make society want to do anything for me? What have I even tried to do?"   *P.J. O'Rourke* | ♃ ♑ 11

Pick your friends, but not to pieces.   *Anon* | ♍ 11

You not only can [buy friendship], you must ... Everything worthwhile has its price.   *Robert J. Ringer* | ♀ ♉ 11

Make new friends, but keep the old;
those are silver, these are gold ...
For 'mid old friends, tried and true,
Once more we our youth renew.   *Anon* | ☿ ♑ 11

My best consolation is the hope that the things I failed to get weren't really worth having.   *Ashleigh Brilliant* | ☽ ♉ 11

There is a sort of hatred which is never extinguished;
it is the hatred that superiority inspires in mediocrity.   *Paul Bourget* | ♄ ♒ 11

The more I see of men the more I like dogs.   *Marie de Sévigné* | ♍ 11

There's always something about your success that displeases even your best friends.   *Mark Twain* | ♄ ♑ 11

When I get over on the other side, I shall use my influence to have the human race drowned again, and this time drowned good, no omissions, no Ark.   *Mark Twain* | ♆ 11
♒ 8

Any sufficiently advanced technology is indistinguishable from magic.   *Arthur C. Clarke* | ♆ ♒

The danger is not that a particular class is unfit to govern. Every class is unfit to govern.   *Lord Acton* | ♄ ♒ 10

The socialist distrust and hatred of private ownership is not just a fatal flaw. It is also a serious misunderstanding of that yearning for freedom with which all human beings are endowed.   *Rush Limbaugh* | ♄ ♒ 2

There is nothing so compelling, so potent, as a rugged individual pursuing excellence. It is the force that has moved history. An individual with passion, conviction, drive, has always confounded and frightened those obsessed with making regulations for "fairness" -- that is, mediocrity. Such rugged individuals cannot, ultimately, be controlled or crushed. *Rush Limbaugh* | ♃ ♒ 1

To silence criticism is to silence freedom. *Sidney Hook* | ♄ ♊ 11

Unless men are free to be vicious they cannot be virtuous. *Frank Meyer* | ♂ ♐ 11

Liberty is the only thing you cannot have unless you are willing to give it to others. *William Allen White* | ♃ ♒ 11

The fact is that government cannot produce equality, and any serious effort to do so can destroy liberty and other social goods. *Jeanne Kirkpatrick* | ♄ ♎ 11

If we survey history and compare the lofty aims, in the name of which revolutions were started, and the sorry end to which they came, we see again and again how a polluted civilization pollutes its own revolutionary offspring. *Arthur Koestler* | ♅ ♏ 5

The difference between Socialism and Communism is the difference between seduction and rape; either way you've had it in the end. *Anon* | ♅ ♏ 10

He who confronts the paradoxical exposes himself to reality. *Friedrich Dürrenmatt* | ♅ 1

I've always been interested in people, but I've never liked them. *Somerset Maugham* | ♄ ♊ 11

Race and gender-based quotas are another example of a society devolving from meritocracy to mediocrity. *D.H.* | ♆ ♑ 11

It is the duty of us men of the spirit to defy the steamroller of standardization and not to generalize but to differentiate. *Hermann Hesse* | ♒ 9

70% of the black population has managed to live above the poverty level, but only those black Americans in our community on government assistance are portrayed by the media. *Mason Weaver* | ☿ ♑ 11

(170) aquarius - uranus - eleventh house

What is an A.A. meeting but a group of the unwilling, picked
from the unfit, to do the impossible.   *D.H.*   ♄ ≈ 12

Any sufficiently advanced technology is indistinguishable
from magic.   *James C. Maxwell*   ♅ ♓ 8

Feminists will not be satisfied until every abortion is performed
by a gay black doctor under an endangered tree on a reservation
for handicapped Indians.   *Florence King*   ♅ ♏ 4

Cherish forever what makes you unique,
'cuz you're a yawn if it goes!   *Bette Midler*   ♀ ≈ 1

TWELFTH HOUSE

The House of Seclusion
'what I won't show you'

the sphere of unseen causes
subconscious mind
repressions
self-undoing
limitation
deception
confinement
hidden enemies
karma

NEPTUNE

Influence:
imagination
fantasy
spirituality
charisma
unreality
idealism

Examples:
dancers / musicians
artists
spies
mystics
drug-takers
alcoholics

PISCES

compassionate
intuitive
forgiving
trusting
poetic

unstable
addictive
self-deceptive
self-pitying
deceitful

Life purpose to:
empathize
sacrifice
absorb
dream
help / heal

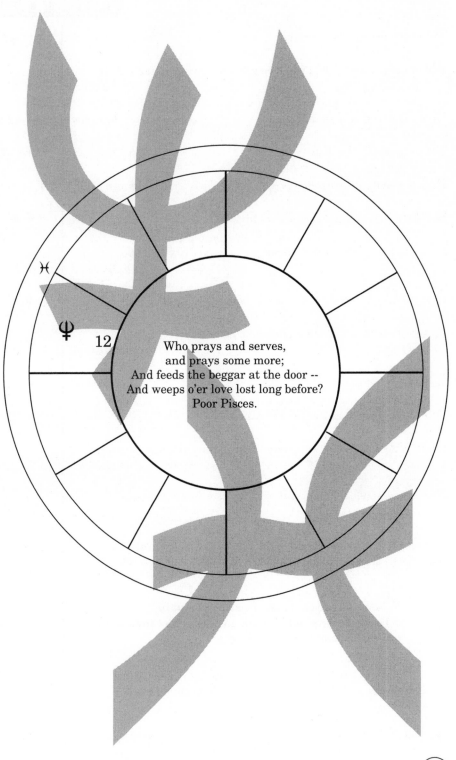

Who prays and serves,
and prays some more;
And feeds the beggar at the door --
And weeps o'er love lost long before?
Poor Pisces.

(173)

There is a dream dreaming us.	*African Bushman*	♆ ≈ 11
What is this life if, full of care, we have no time to stand and stare?	*W.H. Davies*	♄ ♓ 6
Chaos is paradise dislocated.	*Emerson*	☿ ♓ 12
Too pure water -- no fish.	*Ts'ai Ken Tan*	♃ ♏ 12
Pain is inevitable, suffering is optional.	*M. Kathleen Casey*	♄ 12
He that pities another remembers himself.	*Mark Twain*	☽ ♓ 7
I went to bed at two with a 10 and woke up at 10 with a two.	*Country Song*	♀ ♓ 5
God created you so that everything wouldn't happen to me.	*Anon*	☉ ♓ 7
listen, there's a hell of a good universe next door; let's go.	*e.e. cummings*	♃ ♊ 12
Escape via inscape.	*D.H.*	♃ ♓ 12
One foot in spirit and one on a banana peel.	*D.H.*	♆ ♓ 1
Oh that my head were waters and mine eyes a fountain of tears.	*Jeremiah 9:1*	♂ ♋ 12
The only real tragedy is to suffer without learning the lesson.	*Emmet Fox*	♄ ♐ 12
Jung said the dream was always going on in the unconscious, but it needs sleep and inattentiveness to come to the surface.	*Barbara Hannah*	♆ 12
When your fear touches someone's pain it becomes pity; when your love touches someone's pain it becomes compassion.	*Vauvenargues*	♄ ♓ 12 ♆ 5
Let the waters settle, you will see stars and moon mirrored in your being.	*Rumi*	☽ ♓ 12
Addicts do ABZ, not ABC.	*Heather Hayward*	♂ ♊ 12

He has seen but half the universe who never has seen
the house of pain. *Emerson* | ♄ ♋ 12

The greater the soul's desire to heal addiction,
the greater the cost of keeping it. *Gary Zukov* | ♀ 12

Sustained joy takes great courage, suffering none. *Joy Gilbert* | ♃ ♈ 12

The difference between a mystic and a schizophrenic
is the mystic knows who not to talk to. *Anon* | ☿ ♓ 12
♄ ♊ 12

A.A. is a gaggle of guzzlers that meets in a sacred circle
in the "damaged goods department." *D.H.* | ♆ 11

Prisoners of the past can't acknowledge that power
is only of the present. *D.H.* | ♄ ♋ 12
☉ 12

It was always easy to find an unhappy woman
'til I started looking for mine. *Country Song* | ♄ ♋ 12

It's hard to fight an enemy that has outposts in your head.
Sally Kempton | ♂ ♎ 12

The sin is to suffer passively. *Nathaniel Branden* | ☽ ♓ 12

Disequilibrium is where the magic is. Creativity springs
more from failure than success. *Dana Gerhardt* | ♄ ♌ 12
♄ ♓ 12

I have made a captive of myself and put me in a dungeon
and now I cannot find the key to let myself out.
Nathaniel Hawthorne | ☉ 12
♄ ♌ 12

The morphogenetic field. *Andrew Patterson* | 12

I drank for two reasons: to feel good when I felt bad
and to feel better when I felt good. *Anon (A.A.)* | ♆ 1
♃ ♓ 12

Misery no longer loves company; nowadays it insists on it. *Anon* | ☽ ♎ 12
♄ ♓ 11

Emerson's voice was disembodied.   *Gonnaud*   ☿ ♓ 1

> **The shadow is both the awful thing that needs**
> **redemption and the suffering thing that can**
> **provide it.**
>   *Liz Greene*   ♀ 12

My personal experience is that without transcendence,
life has no beauty.   *Deepak Choprah*   ♃ ♓ 1

Nothing is so like God as stillness.   *Meister Echart*   ♃ 12

In the presence of silence, the conditioned self rattles and scratches.
                                                    Joan Halifax   ♄ ♊ 12

How do you find a lion that has swallowed you?   *Carl Jung*   ♀ ♌ 12

Suffering is pain multiplied by resistance.   *Shinzen Young*   ♀ 12

One seeks solitude to know relatedness.   *Joan Halifax*   ☽ ♎ 12

The more possibilities for interpretation through fantasy the better.
                                                    Kandinsky   ♆ 5
                                                                       ♃ ♓ 5

GLAMOROSE: A self-pitying reclusive. Used by the famous to
appear more interesting that they are, i.e., Garbo and Hemingway.
                                                    Carole Seborovski ♀ ♌ 12

Suicide is often justifiable, but very rarely admirable;
you can't praise a man for going to bed early.   *Robinson Jeffers* ♄ ♋ 12
                                                                        ♀ ♌ 12

LACTITUDE: An indifference regarding effort at following a dream.
                                                    Carole Seborovski ♄ ♓ 1

Ecstasy means ("EC") to stand outside of ("STATIC") the body.
                                                    Anon   ♓ 1

Venus is to glamour what Neptune is to enchantment --
the beautiful woman or beautiful angel -- lower and higher
octaves of transcendence.   *D.H.*   ♀ ♓ 12

Books come from trees; that's why we have branch libraries.
                                                    Anon   ♊ 12

Downloading in cosmic soup. *Anon* ♅ 12

Penetrating so many secrets we cease to believe in the unknowable.
But there it sits nevertheless calmly licking it's chops.
H.L. Mencken ♀ 12

The most terrifying thing is to accept oneself completely.
Carl Jung ☉ 12

In meditation the breath at the nostrils becomes gatekeeper
to the mind. *D.H.* ♄ ♊ 12

The unconscious produces impossible situations to bring out
the best in us. *Carl Jung* ☉ 12

Drowsiness shall clothe a man in rags. *Proverbs 23:21* ♄ ♍ 12

Gluttony is not a secret vice. *Orson Welles* ♃ ♋ 12

Victimhood is the neighborhood and infrastructure of the
Nannystate. *D.H.* ♄ ♋ 12

Eco-Fascists are coercive Utopians with green illusions. *D.H.* ♄ ♉ 12

By working with our shadow we draw darkness out of the
collective shadow. *Alice Howell* ♄ ♏ 12

We do not get enlightened by imaging beings of light,
but by making the darkess conscious. *Carl Jung* ♃ 12
☿ ♏ 12

Follow poet, follow right, to the bottom of the night ...
Sing of human unsuccess in a rapture of distress ...
In the prison of his days teach the free-man how to praise.
W.H. Auden ♃ ♓ 12

If you sip the sea just once, you will know the taste of the oceans
of the world. *Zen Saying* ☽ ♓ 2

The wound that does not heal can be a well of cures. *Anon* ♀ 12

We are fishing for minnows while standing on a whale.
Polynesian Saying ♃ ♓ 12

Like a struggling spiritualist slipping her card into a passing coffin.

Derek Marlowe   ♄ ♓ 8

Those that don't understand symbols are like diners
in a restaurant eating the menu.   *Joseph Campbell*   ♆ ♐ 6

Poetry is the shorthand of the soul.   *Ann Ree Colton*   ☉ ♓ 3

(Alcoholism is) like treating a pimple on your face with a guillotine.

Claire Booth Luce   ♂ ♏ 12
   ♀ ♈ 12

Who let Claire Booth Luce?   *Anon*   ☿ ♐ 12

The opposite of the present is not past or future; it's absent.

George Sheehan   ♆ 1

The surest cure for vanity is loneliness.   *Thomas Wolfe*   ♀ 12

Isolation must precede society.   *Emerson*   ♒ 12

At 3:00 a.m. the veil between the worlds is thin.   *D.H.*   ♆ ♓ 2

Almost every in evil the world today is caused by people
who view themselves primarily as victims.   *Dennis Prager*   ♇ 12

Remember discouragement is the only illness.

George Bernard Shaw   ♄ ♈ 12

Teach us to care and not to care. Teach us to sit still.

T.S. Eliot   ♄ ♐ 12

Freud pointed out that during bouts of melancholy
the outer life may look empty, but at the same time
inner work may be taking place at full speed.   *Thomas Moore*   ☽ ♈ 12

Immature poets imitate; mature poets steal.   *T.S. Eliot*   ☿ ♓ 7
   ♄ ♓ 7

I think we are in rat's alley where the dead men eat their bones.

T.S. Eliot   ♄ ♏ 12

Nothing is more difficult for Americans to understand than the
possibility of tragedy.   *Henry Kissinger*   ♄ ♊ 12

Proof of a poet is that his country absorbs him as affectionately
as he absorbed it.   *Walt Whitman*   ♆ 12

Honesty is praised and starves.   *Juvenal*   ♃ ♋ 12

When man found the mirror he began to lose his soul. *Anon*   ♀ ♏ 12

Depression is when you've spent your life climbing the corporate,
or whatever, ladder and you finally reach the top and find it's
against the wrong wall.   *Joseph Campbell*   ♄ ♑ 12

Aum (Om) is the sound the universe makes when it is pleased
with itself.   *Carl Jung*   ♆ ♓ 12

I meditate by underlining sentences.   *Joseph Campbell*   ♆ 3

The most beautiful thing we can experience is the mysterious.
It is the source of all true art and science.   *Einstein*   ♆ ♏ 12

Sacred or sacrificial grace gathered from former lives of martyrdom
or selfless works which were devoid of thought of reward.
                                                      Ann Ree Colton   ♃ ♓ 12

Music that gentler on the spirit lies,
Than tir'd eyelids upon tir'd eyes.   *Tennyson*   ♆ ♓ 1

Most people live their lives like a man winding
his watch on the way to the guillotine.
                                                      Alan Watts   ♄ ♏ 12

Few understand the world of Cummings,
and few James Joyce's mental slummings,
and few young Auden's coded chatter;
But then it is the few that matter. (Written at 19.) *Dylan Thomas*   ☿ ♓ 3

Myths are public dreams. Dreams are private myths.
Myths are vehicles of communication between the conscious
and the unconscious, just as dreams are.   *Joseph Campbell*   ♆ ♓ 12

We in the 20th century have been completely snookered by this
myth of the alienated artist, the idea that the only worthwhile art
is made by poor people starving in garrets, hounded by critics
and censored by authoritarian people.   *Michael Medved*   ♀ ♓ 12

Schizophrenia is the exclusive domain of past lives. *Dr. Peebles*   ♅ 12

Through inner work the Satanic may become the Saint's tonic.

D.H. ♄ ♓ 12

They'll make me bake cookies back in Ole' Arkansas
and be forced to listen to Rush Limbaugh if I'm busted.

Hillary (Country Song) ♄ ♋ 12

Compulsive, addictive people have two choices: expand or expire.

D.H. ♀ ♏ 12

Emotions respond to belief. Those who see themselves as victims
have no choice but to resent the rest of us. *D.H.* ☽ ♏ 12

At Dirty Dick's and Sloppy Joe's we drank our liquor straight;
Some went upstairs with Marjorie and some, alas, with Kate;
And two by two like cat and mouse
The homeless played at keeping house. *W.H. Auden* ☽ ♏ 12

Sanskrit-based languages have 96 terms for love, Persian 80,
Greek three; we have one. No differentiated language for a
subject means it is an unconscious area in the consciousness
of that people. Eskimos have 50 terms for snow because
they have to deal with it -- we have one. *Joseph Campbell* ☿ ♊ 12

Mighty poets are cradled forth in wrong, they learn in suffering
what they teach in song. *Shelley* ♄ ♓ 12
♃ ♋ 12

Poor me can become pour me when the wounded child
doesn't meet the Divine Child. *D.H.* ☽ ♓ 12

Responsibility is the answer to addiction recovery and is the
challenge to merely being a survivor. Insight isn't change.
Recognition demands responsibility. *D.H.* ♄ ♏ 12

We are God in disguise pretending not to be Himself.

Upanishads ♃ ♓ 1

We are masters of limitation blocked by an illusion of separation.

Bashar/Dr. Peebles ♄ ♒ 12

Compassion is environmental generosity. *Chogyam Trungpa* ♃ ♓ 2
♆ 1

A good conscience is the hemisphere of virtue. *Baltasar Gracian* ♃ ♋ 12

All sins are attempts to fill voids.   *Simone Weil*   ☽ ♏ 12

The devil's boots don't creak.   *Scottish Proverb*   ♄ ♏ 12

The new compassion provides excuses for failure.   *Rush Limbaugh*   ♅ ♑ 12

The fat lady is vocalizing in the back room.   *Anon*   ♇ 12

Time is quantified infinity.   *Deepak Chopra*   ♄ ♓ 12

It is not unlikely that the least clearly foreseen way in the end
may be the most important. (At age 27.)   *Joseph Campbell*   ♇ 9

If you connect the dots backwards, you may see there are
no victims, only volunteers.   *D.H.*   ☿ ♏ 12

Ask nothing, expect nothing, and accept everything.   *Anthony Hopkins*   ♓ 9

Because of myself I am nothing, and of myself I've been nothing.   *Anthony Hopkins*   ☉ 12

**My epitaph, if ever I have one, will be,
"What was that all about?"**   *Anthony Hopkins*   ☉ 12

Robin Hood, the moral leader of the new liberalism:
confiscate wealth in the name of compassion.   *D.H.*   ♄ ♉ 12

Every man is a divinity in disguise, a God playing the fool.   *Emerson*   ☉ ♓ 9
   ☿ ♓ 1

The worst of charity is that the lives you're asked to preserve
aren't worth preserving.   *Emerson*   ♇ 12

A nation never fails but by suicide.   *Emerson*   ♄ ♏ 12

Nine in ten are suicides.   *Ben Franklin*   ♂ ♏ 12

Mystery is the only addiction I wholeheartedly recommend.   *Scott Peck*   ♏ 12

Once men are caught up in an event they cease to be afraid.
Only the unknown frightens men.   *St. Exupéry*   ♂ ♈ 12

Molly Yard looks like a stubbed toe.
Florence King — ♄ ♓ 1

You are forever the eternal creator, never the victim.
Dr. Peebles — ☉ ♌ 12

Darkness within darkness.
The gateway to all understanding.
Lau Tzu — ♀ 12

Things pass for what they seem, not what they are.
Baltasar Gracian — ♀ ♓ 3

What is to give light must endure burning.
Victor Frankl — ♂ ♏ 12

Every man lives behind bars which he carries with him.
Kafka — ♂ ♑ 12

Every generation is a secret society and has incommunicable
enthusiasms, tastes and interests which are a mystery both to
its predecessors and posterity.
John Jay — ♒ 12

The God whom I worship placed my soul with a thousand voices,
like a resounding echo, at the center of everything.
Victor Hugo — ☿ ♓

The question is whether suicide is the way out, or the way in.
Emerson — ♀ 12

A clear conscience is often the sign of a bad memory.
Anon — ♄ ♊ 12

Inside everyone there's a poet who died young.
Stefan Kanfer — ☿ ♓ 8

Discernment lies hidden in retirement so as to be more esteemed
by the wise and discreet.
Emerson — ♃ 12

Victimhood parades itself in it's diapers.
D.H. — ☽ ♏ 12

Time wounds all heals.
Jane Ace — ♄ ♓ 1

There's one advantage to being poor -- a doctor will cure you faster.
Kin Hubbard — ♃ ♍ 12

Loss in all of its manifestations is the touchstone of depression --
in the progress of the disease and, most likely, in its origin.
William Styron — ♄ ♋ 12

I have felt the wind of the wing of madness.
Baudelaire — ☿ ♓ 12

Most distressing of all the instinctual disruptions was that of sleep, along with a complete absence of dreams.   *William Styron*   ♄ 12

To live alone one must have within himself either much of God, or much of the jungle beast.   *Baltasar Gracian*   ☉ ♋ 12

The poet Rilke once defined love as the capacity of two solitudes to "protect and border and greet each other," and that kind of love is the key to the paradoxical relationship of solitude and community.   *Parker Palmer*   ♀ ♒ 12

The only thing we have to bring to community is ourselves, so the contemplative process of recovering our true selves in solitude is never selfish. It is ultimately the best gift we can give to others.   *Parker Palmer*   ☉ ♒ 12

God can only be present in the creation in the form of absence.   *Simone Weil*   ♆ 1

What is behind your eyes holds more power than what is in front.   *Gary Zukov*   ☿ 12

Mystics can never be politically correct.   *Joy Hayward*   ♄ ♓ 10

The purity of mysticism is lost in the dogma of the church.   *D.H.*   ♄ ♓ 9

Our very defects are but shadows of our virtues.   *Emerson*   ♃ 12

Communists define peace as the absence of opposition.   *Rush Limbaugh*   ♆ 7

Mud has rained down on me so long I do not attempt even to open my umbrella.   *Mme. Blavatsky*   ♄ ♋ 12

Nothing could embitter her. She was not tragic in the Greek sense. (Speaking of Mme. Blavatsky -- a true ♌ -- in the late 1880's.)   *Edmund Russell*   ♄ ♌ 12

The most beautiful and profound emotion we can experience is the sensation of the mystical. It is the sower of all true science.   *Einstein*   ♆ 9

Our greatest pretenses are built up not to hide the evil and the ugly in us, but our emptiness. The hardest thing to hide is something that is not there.   *Eric Hoffer*   ♏ 12

Music has the privilege of expressing all while excluding nothing.

Nadia Boulangér ♆ 5

Music can be made anywhere and does not smell.   *W.H. Auden* ♆ ♏ 5

When I was a boy I would have visions; now I'm too busy.

Dalai Lama ♄ ♓ 5

Dreams are real as long as they last; can we say more of life?

Havelock Ellis ☉ 12

If the doors of perception were cleansed, everything would
appear to man as it is: infinite.   *William Blake* ♄ ♐ 12
                                                    ♏ 12

God is alone -- but the devil, he is far from being alone;
he sees a great deal of company; he is legion.   *Thoreau* ♆ 12

They are compassionate, and not only with beggars and cats,
for they grieve in their soul for what the naked eye does not see.
(One of six qualities of the educated person according to Chekhov
in a letter to his brother.)   *Chekhov* ⚳ 12

Through music and poetry "I spit in the face of time."

D.H., inspired by Yeats ♄ ♓ 5

Love ceases to be a pleasure when it ceases to be a secret.

Aphra Bein ♀ ♏ 12

So far as ideas are concerned, meditation on any theme,
if positive and honest, inevitably separates him who does
the meditating from the opinion prevailing around him,
from that which ... can be called "public" or "popular" opinion.

Ortega y Gassett ♅ 12

Welfare should be repealed in the name of those who have had
their property taken away and given to people who have not
earned it. That is all the justification needed.   *Sheldon Richman* ♄ ♉ 12

I laugh when I hear the fish in the water is thirsty.

Rabindranath Tagore ♄ ♋ 12

Silence is agreement.   *Talmud* ♄ ♊ 12

Silence is the field of infinite co-relation.   *Deepak Chopra* ♄ ♊ 12

(184) pisces - neptune - twelfth house

Those who are compassionate when they should be cruel
will be cruel when they should be compassionate.   *Talmud*   ♂ ♏ 12

Come unto me, all of you who labor and are heavy laden
and I will give you rest. Take my yoke upon you, and learn of me,
for I am meek and lowly in heart and you shall find rest unto your
soul. For my yoke is easy, and my burden is light.   *Jesus*   ♄ ♓ 6

Our language has wisely sensed the two sides of being alone.
It has created the word "loneliness" to express the pain of
being alone. And it has created the word "solitude" to express
the glory of being alone.   *Paul Tillich*   ☿ ♋ 12

A midget psychic who just escaped from jail: small medium at large.
                                                         Anon   ♄ ♓ 12

Without Karma, no fisherman could catch a fish;
outside of Karma, no fish would die on dry land,
or in boiling water.   *Gems from the East* (Blavatsky)   ♏ 12

Everyone talks about going <u>up</u> the ladder --
no one talks about going <u>down</u> the ladder.   *Thomas Moore*   ♇ ♏ 12
                                                                          ♄ ♊ 12

We've created a society of woundology;
a tribal reflection of the victim.   *Caroline Myss*   ♂ ♋ 12
                                                                          ♓ 11

Don't think that suffering always ennobles -- it sometimes degrades.
                                                       Dennis Prager   ♄ ♏ 12

Music is the best means we have of digesting time.   *W.H. Auden*   ♄ ♓ 6

I thank you, rusty prison grating,
and you, sharp glinting bayonet blades,
For you have given me more wisdom
Than learning over long decades.
              (Song from a Soviet prison camp in the mid-1980's)
                                              Tatyana Mikhailovna   ♄ ♐ 12

It is a fact about our culture that a poet can earn much
more money writing or talking about his art than he can
by practicing it.   *W.H. Auden*   ♄ ♓ 3

Poetry is a way of taking life by the throat.   *Robert Frost*   ♂ ♓ 3

Good cognac is like a woman. Do not assault it. Coddle and warm
it in your hands before you sip it.   *Winston Churchill*   ☽ ♓ 3

                                                             ☽ ♓ 5

It's the poet's role to maintain the sacredness of language.
                                                    W.H. Auden   ♃ ♓ 3

Dwelling on tales of woe can be as useless as
telling of toes on whales.   *D.H.*   ♄ ♓ 3

The surest sign that intelligent life exists elsewhere
in the universe is that it has never tried to contact us.
                       Bill Watterson (Calvin & Hobbes)   ☿ ♐ 12

Life is full of misery, loneliness, and suffering --
and it's all over much too soon.   *Woody Allen*   ♄ ♏ 12

I'm worried that the universe will soon need replacing.
It's not holding a charge.   *Edward Chilton*   ♅ 12

Maybe this world is another planet's hell.   *Aldous Huxley*   ♀ ♐ 12

I wish people wouldn't say, "Excuse me," when I want them
to step on my feet.   *Karen Gordon*   ♄ ♓ 1

A dyslexic agnostic insomniac is someone who stays up all night
wondering if there is a dog.   *Anon*   ♆ ♐ 6

Poets are the unacknowledged legislators of the world.   *Shelley*   ♄ ♓ 11

Poetry readings and Bach concerts at Auschwitz were not only
aesthetic activities, but moral ones as well, for in making the
world better than it had been before, they also improved and
enriched the lives of those who took part in them.   *Tzvetan Todorov*   ♃ 12

Moses dragged us for forty years through the desert to bring us
to the place in the Middle East where there was no oil.
                                                Golda Meir   ♄ ♓

Poets, like whores, are only hated by each other.
                                        William Wyncherley   ♄ ♓ 11

Reincarnation may be our most unconscious addiction.
Perhaps we could benefit from E.A.A. -- Earth Addicts
Anonymous, a haven for gravity junkies.   *D.H.*   ♆ ♏ 11

(**M**usic is) an agreeable harmony for the honor of God
and the permissible delights of the soul.   *J. S. Bach*   ♀ ♓ 9

Alternate lives are landscapes reflected in window-glass ...
they're as real as our daily lives, but not so clearly seen.
                                                  Richard Bach   ☽ ♓ 1

What is valuable is a certain ordering of things. Civilization is
an invisible tie, because it has to do not with things but with the
invisible ties that join one thing to another in a particular way.
We shall have perfect musical instruments (mass-produced),
but where shall we find the musician?   *Saint Exupéry*   ☿ ♓ 2

Parables are unnecessary for recognizing the blatant absurdity
of everyday life. Reality is lesson enough.   *Jane O'Reilly*   ♄ ♓ 1

Life is full of disappointments. Nothing ever comes off but buttons.
                                                  Anon   ♅ ♍ 12

A loonie is praying in a room, and another loonie asks,
"What are you doing?"
"Keeping the elephants away."
"There are no elephants here."
"See?"   *Anon*   ♃ ♓ 12

Neurosis is always an excuse for legitimate suffering.
                                                  Carl Jung   ☿ ♋ 12

Be sober, be vigilant, because your adversary the devil,
as a roaring lion, walketh about seeking whom he may devour.
                                                  Peter 15:8   ♀ ♌ 12

          Tears are round,
          The sea is deep.
          Roll them overboard,
          And sleep.   *W.H. Auden*   ☽ ♓ 12

We are such stuff as dreams are made of,
And our little life is rounded with a sleep.   *Shakespeare*   ☉ ♓ 8

The poor don't know that their function in life
is to exercise our generosity.   *Jean-Paul Sartre*   ♃ ♓ 7
                                                              ♃ ♉ 12

Music is grace made audible, and a rainbow over suffering.   *D.H.*   ♀ 9

A Baptism of Bewilderment

Battalions of Barbarians
Beseeching and Bartering
Barmaids Befogged and
Beguiled By a Bedlam
Of Beneficent Benefactors
While Beasts of Burden and
Barrenness Beg Beauty for
Beaver in a Baptism
Of Bewilderment   *D.H.*   ♂ ♏ 12

The chart of Winston Churchill is presented as an example of how Astrological Aphorisms can work when applied to a personal horoscope. I chose Winston Churchill as an example not only as a world famous personality and historical figure, but because he was a writer and wit and thus I could avail myself of the added fun of letting his own words illuminate his chart.

This is the reverse of my usual process in the body of this book. Normally I have been attracted to a quotation, poem, maxim, etc. and then later I've added my Astrological translations, so to speak, of planets, signs and houses. Here, I am going through the planets in order with aphorisms as I feel they apply to the chart.

To give a brief example of how I assign importance to what I emphasize in looking for Aphorisms that fit the chart: Venus Retrograde in Sagittarius in the 3rd House is a key for my thought process. Venus also rules Mars, Jupiter and South Node as well as Pluto. This is an interesting planet to have so prominent a place in the horoscope of a Warrior, Statesman, Writer and Artist.

As I've stated elsewhere, nothing in this technique is written in stone. For the most part, I trust the process will be clear with a little familiarity and one that will be fun and informative astrologically, biographically and historically.

Churchill, Sir Winston Leonard Spencer, 1874-1965. Born at Blenheim Palace. British statesman and author; elder son of Lord Randolph Churchill. Educated Harrow and Sandhurst; served in Cuba with Spanish forces (1895), in India (1897), in Sudan (1898); present at Khartoum (1898); as war correspondent, captured by Boers but escaped (1899), and engaged in battles up to capture of Pretoria.

He entered Parliament in 1900 and thereafter held the offices of, among others, Home Secretary (1910-11), First Lord of the Admiralty (1911-15), Secretary of State for War (1918-21), Chancellor of the Exchequer (1924-9), and Prime Minister (1940-5 and 1951-5). He published several historical studies including The World Crisis 1916-18 (6 vols., 1923-31), The Second World War (6 vols., 1948-54) and A History of the English-Speaking Peoples (4 vols., 1956-8). His biographies include Lord Randolph Churchill (1906) and Marlborough: His Life and Times (4 vols., 1933-8). He also wrote a novel, Savrola (1900), and several books dealing with his early career, among them My African Journey (1908) and My Early Life (1930). He was awarded the Nobel Prize for Literature in 1953.

Winston Churchill biographical information from Webster's Biographical Dictionary.

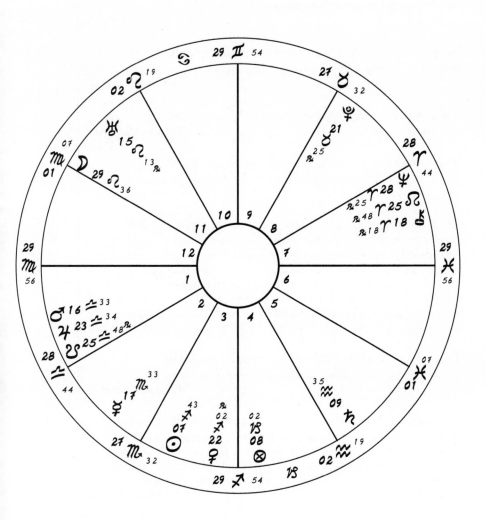

Winston Churchill
b. 30 November 1874, 01:30 GMT, Woodstock, UK (51N52, 01W21)
Source: John Addey quotes a letter from Churchill's father. Koch Houses.

It was the nation and race dwelling all around the globe
that had the lion's heart. I had the luck to be called upon
to give the roar. *Winston Churchill*

Reading is to the mind what exercise is to the body.
Richard Steele

Books in all their variety are often the means by which
civilization may be carried triumphantly forward.
Winston Churchill

Mr. Gladstone read Homer for fun, which I thought served
him right. *Winston Churchill*

It is a good thing for an uneducated man to read books of
quotations ... The quotations when engraved upon the memory
give you good thoughts. *Winston Churchill*

After the miraculous deliverance of the British Army in June
1940 at Dunkirk, Churchill inspired the House of Commons to
thunderous ovation. One member described the speech as "the
most magnificent words ever heard in the English language."
When President Roosevelt heard the words on radio, he said to his
aide, "As long as that old bastard is in charge, Britain will never
surrender." He then committed the previously neutral United
States to send needed military aid to Britain. *James Humes*

There is a great deal of difference between a tired man
who wants a book to read and the alert man who wants
to read a book. *Winston Churchill*

Those who wish to savor the full majesty of Churchill's oratory
cannot find it in a quoted sentence or two. The array of words,
the cadence of line, the mounting of sentences, the crescendoing
culmination can be sensed only by reading aloud the addresses
as a whole. Of course, listening to his recorded addresses is
even better. *James Humes*

No inhibition bridled this colossal personality. He freely
expressed his tastes and opinions on everything from alcohol
to Zionism. *James Humes*

Of all the talents bestowed upon men, none is so precious
as the gift of oratory. He who enjoys it wields a power more
durable than that of a king. *Winston Churchill*

Of course, I am an egotist. Where do you get if you aren't?
Winston Churchill

We have no assurance that anyone else is going to keep
the British Lion as a pet. *Winston Churchill*

If I have been of any service to my fellow men, it has never been
by self-repression, but always by self-expression.
Winston Churchill

How vain are human calculations of self-interest.
Winston Churchill

Follow your heart, <u>then</u> your feelings. *Barbara Sher*

Egoism is the very essence of a noble soul. *Nietzsche*

Let me have my own way exactly in everything, and a sunnier
and pleasanter creature does not exist. *Thomas Carlyle*

Winston Churchill was the greatest public figure of our time.
Harry Truman

It is wonderful how men can keep secrets they have not been told.
Winston Churchill

If you destroy a free market you create a black economy.
Winston Churchill

I am astonished to see how few people are afraid to defend the
capitalist system. The politicians are afraid, the newspapers
are afraid ... as a matter of fact the capitalist system is capable
of sustained and searching defense. *Winston Churchill*

The idea that a nation can tax itself into prosperity
is one of the cruelest delusions which has ever befuddled
the human mind. *Winston Churchill*

Taxes are a grave discouragement to enterprise and thrift.
Winston Churchill

I prefer landscapes. A tree doesn't complain that I haven't
done it justice.   *Winston Churchill*

We Conservatives see private enterprise as the sturdy horse
that pulls along our economy.   *Winston Churchill*

Do not hesitate to be blunt ... this is better done by manner
and attitude than by actual words which can be reported.
[♀ gives a mediating and softening factor to a perhaps too
blunt, shoot- from-the-hip, ⚹ tendency. Also the appreciation
of painting and culture in general is greatly heightened in this
case by the Venusian influence.]   *Winston Churchill*

Once, in a flight of philosophic gloom, Margot Asquith turned
to her dinner partner and said, "Winston, in terms of infinity,
we are cosmic dust -- we are just worms." "Perhaps, Margot,"
Churchill replied, "but I am a glow worm."   *James Humes*

The commander must try, above all, to establish personal and
comradely contact with his men, but without giving away an inch
of his authority.   *Field Marshall Erwin Rommel*

One mark of a great man is the power of making lasting
impressions upon the people he meets.   *Winston Churchill*

To change your mind is one thing; to turn on those who have
followed your previous advice is another.   *Winston Churchill*

Use soft words and hard arguments.   *English Proverb*

The German people, in spite of all their brains and courage,
worship power and let themselves be led by the nose.
                                                    Winston Churchill

Germany must be beaten; Germany must feel like she is beaten.
No compromise with the main purpose, no peace till victory,
no pact with unrepentant wrong.   *Winston Churchill*

I like a man who grins when he fights.   *Winston Churchill*

It is hard, if not impossible, to snub a beautiful woman;
they remain beautiful and the rebuke recoils.

Winston Churchill

Battles are won by slaughter and maneuver. The greater the
general, the more he contributes in maneuver, the less he
demands in slaughter. *Winston Churchill*

Nothing in life is so exhilarating as to be shot at without result.
[These last two quotations also work for Churchill's North Node in
Aries in the 7th House.] *Winston Churchill*

Great countries... must not allow resentment or caprice or imitation
or vengeance to enter into their policy. *Winston Churchill*

My hatred died with their surrender. *Winston Churchill*

At Blenheim I took two very important decisions: to be born
and marry. I am content with the decision I took on both
occasions. *Winston Churchill*

The most precious thing I have in life is your love for me.
[Written in 1920 to his wife.] *Winston Churchill*

I love you more each month that passes and feel the need of you
and your beauty ... I am so devoured of egoism that I would like to
have another soul in another world and meet you in another
setting and pay you all the love and honor of the great romances.
[Written in a letter to his wife from the World War I trenches in
France in 1916.] *Winston Churchill*

One ought to be just before one is generous. *Winston Churchill*

It is a mistake to look too far ahead. Only one link in the chain
of destiny can be handled at a time. *Winston Churchill*

In the past we had a light which flickered; in the present we
have a light which flames; and in the future there will be a light
which shines over all the land and sea. *Winston Churchill*

We've reached a point in the journey where ... it must be world
anarchy or world order. *Winston Churchill*

If the present tries to sit in judgement of the past,
it will lose the future. *Winston Churchill*

Is it the only lesson of history that mankind is unteachable?
Winston Churchill

It is difficult to find new interests at the end of one's life.
Winston Churchill

(On punctuality): I am a sporting man. I always like to give
trains and airplanes a fair chance of getting away.
Winston Churchill

Socialism assails the preeminence of the individual ... I have never
taken the view that individuals exist to serve a state or system.
Winston Churchill

Whenever socialism has been tried, it has failed.
Winston Churchill

No Socialist system can be established without a political police.
Winston Churchill

In sport, in courage, and in the sight of Heaven,
all men must meet on equal terms. *Winston Churchill*

What greater tragedy can there be than is presented by the
spectacle of a child whose life prospects and hopes are smashed
at the very outset of its existence? *Winston Churchill*

What is the use of living, if it be not to strive for noble causes
and to make this muddled world a better place to live in
after we are gone? *Winston Churchill*

The human story does not always unfold like a mathematical
calculation ... the element of the unexpected and the unforeseeable
is what gives some of its relish and saves us from falling into the
mechanical thralldom of the logicians. *Winston Churchill*

Individualism offers an infinitely graduated and infinitely varied system of records for genius, for enterprise, for exertion, for industry, for faithfulness, for thrift. Socialism (☿) destroys all this.   *Winston Churchill*

Innovation of course involves experiment. Experiments may or may not be fruitful.   *Winston Churchill*

It is not possible to draw a hard-and-fast line between individualism and collectivism. You cannot draw it either in theory or in practice. No man can be a collectivist alone or an individualist alone. He must be both an individualist and a collectivist ... collectively we light our streets and supply ourselves with water. But we do not make love collectively and the ladies do not marry us collectively.   *Winston Churchill*

I have no fear of the future. Let us go forward into its mysteries, let us tear aside the veils which hide it from our eyes and let us move onward with confidence and courage.   *Winston Churchill*

Have some whiskey and soda water. It is a good drink to draw a sword on.   *Winston Churchill*

It is human nature to dislike the wretch who dispels the delightful mirages and speaks roughly to the dupes.
                                              Winston Churchill

It is a crime to despair. We must learn to draw from misfortune the means of future strength.   *Winston Churchill*

For each and for all, as for the Royal Navy, the watchword should be, "Carry on, and dread naught."   *Winston Churchill*

We are waiting for the long-promised invasion. So are the fishes.
                                              Winston Churchill

The destiny of mankind is not decided by material computation. When great causes are on the move in the world ... we learn that we are spirits, not animals, and that something is going on in space and time, and beyond space and time, which, whether we like it or not, spells duty.   *Winston Churchill*

From Stettin in the Baltic to Trieste in the Adriatic
an iron curtain has descended across the continent.

Winston Churchill

One night, after a few drinks, Churchill stumbled into Bessie
Braddock, a corpulent Labourite member of the House of
Commons. An angry Bessie straightened her clothes and
addressed the British statesman. "Sir Winston," she roared,
"You are drunk, and what's more, you are disgustingly drunk."
Churchill, surveying Bessie, replied, "And might I say, Mrs.
Braddock, you are ugly, and what's more, disgustingly ugly.
But tomorrow," Churchill added, "I shall be sober."   *James Humes*

It is no use leading other nations up the garden path
and then running away when the dog growls.

Winston Churchill

When you have to kill a man it costs nothing to be polite.

Winston Churchill

The Hun is always at your throat or on his knees.

Winston Churchill

(On nuclear war): The Dark Ages may return -- the Stone Age
may return on the gleaming wings of science; and what might
now shower immeasurable material blessing upon mankind
may even bring about its total destruction. Beware, I say!
Time may be short.   *Winston Churchill*

Noel Tyl is one of the foremost astrologers in the world. His twenty-two textbooks have led the teaching of astrologers for two generations. Tyl has written the professional manual for the field, the 1,000 page text *Synthesis & Counseling in Astrology* that has securely placed astrology in pace with the most sophisticated disciplines of humanistic studies extant today.

In 1998, his study *Astrological Timing of Critical Illness* appeared, establishing a breakthrough position between astrology and medical diagnosis.

His book *The Creative Astrologer* (January 2000) takes modern astrology into the new century with a newly forged alliance, in theory and technique, between astrology and the modality of Single Session PsychoTherapy.

Tyl is a graduate of Harvard University in Social Relations (Psychology, Sociology, and Anthropology). He lectures constantly throughout sixteen countries and maintains a client list of individuals and corporations throughout the world. His office and home are in the Phoenix, Arizona area in the United States.

In May 1998, Tyl was honored at the United Astrology Congress , the world convention for astrology, as the recipient of the Regulus Award for establishing and maintaining professional image in the field. As well, he has been designated Director Principal of MilleyDome/Johannesburg, a 42,000 square feet domed edifice now under construction in South Africa as the Noel Tyl Learning Center for Astrology and New Age Exploration.

Tyl is in his twelfth year as Presiding Officer of AFAN (Association for Astrological Networking), astrology's world organization.

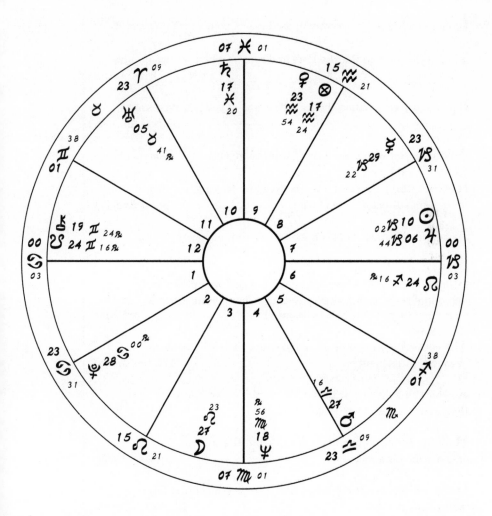

Noel Tyl
b. 31 December 1936, 15:57 EST, West Chester, PA, USA (39N58, 75W36)
Source: Birth Certificate. Koch Houses.

(There is) a tremendous focus and absorption in my life ...
to administer my performer's personality to attract notice
and appreciation, to express my sense of drama, to make
things happen and get credit for it -- within a spirit of
optimism and success.   *Noel Tyl*

In married life three is company and two is none.   *Oscar Wilde*

Time watches from the shadows and coughs when you would kiss.
                                                        W.H. Auden

If you and your partner always agree, one of you is unnecessary!
                                                    Robert Anthony

Anything that won't sell, I don't want to invent.   *Thomas Edison*

It is not looking into each other's eyes, but looking together
in the same direction. (On love.)   *Saint Exupéry*

At 64 the difference between monotony and monogamy blurs.
                                                            Anon

Seldom, or perhaps never, does a marriage develop into an
individual relationship smoothly and without crisis; there is
no coming to consciousness without pain.   *Carl Jung*

The power we give other people over our lives will last long
beyond that moment.   *Thomas Sowell*

A cynic thinks it's right that divorce should cost more
than marriage because it's worth more.   *Anon*

Humility is not renunciation of pride but the substitution
of one pride for another.   *Eric Hoffer*

One grows very cautious when living across the border from
malevolent rivals.   *Baltasar Gracian*

If men knew how women pass the time when they're alone,
they'd never marry.   *O. Henry*

All unhappiness is caused by comparison.   *Anon*

A change of heart is the essence of all other change
and it is brought about by a re-education of the mind.

Emmeline P. Lawrence

Every child is an artist. The problem is how to remain
an artist once he grows up.

Picasso

A tremendous amount of emotional drama propels my
communication always, from the kitchen to the stage!
... The management of my personal needs MUST BE
through communication.

Noel Tyl

... We find our childhood selves, and our present differences
from these selves, in the pages of the books we long ago read
as children.

Wendy Lesser

Forgiveness in the heart comes about when the walls
of separation in the mind fall.

Deepak Chopra

One stops being a child when one realizes that telling one's
troubles does not make it better.

Cesare Pavese

But still I dream that somewhere there must be the spirit
of a child that waits for me.

Bayard Taylor

Unlike grown-ups, children have little need to deceive themselves.

Goethe

Some writers confuse authenticity, which they ought always
to aim at, with originality, which they should never bother about.

W.H. Auden

Life can only be understood backward, but it must be lived forward.

Niels Bohr

I need to take an emotional breath, step back, and remind
myself who's actually in charge of my life.   *Judith M. Knowlton*

The kingdom of thought is a proud aristocracy.   *Emerson*

Our ancestors knew the world by proper name, but we recognize
it only in analytical description. They were so acutely aware of
the personality of nature and of things that they could easily
give names and faces to things we consider inanimate, and they
could even imagine embodied spirits hiding in and near rocks,
rivers, mountains, and forests.   *Thomas Moore*

In a culture that tries to preserve a sexless surface for daily life,
erotic life is also chased into the underground toilets, where its
poetry and art appear as graffiti.   *Thomas Moore*

A cynic is a man who, when he smells flowers, looks around
for a coffin.   *H.L. Mencken*

Carlos Castaneda was told by Don Juan, "The trouble with you
is you think you have time."   *Carlos Castaneda*

Necessity relieves us from the embarrassment of choice.
                                                                   Vauvenargues

Lines of age sleep on the stones till trumpeting dawn. Time
buries the spring weather that belled and bounded with the
fossil and the dew reborn.   *Dylan Thomas*

My choices (and my horoscope) reflect the reconciliations made
with The Choice to have another physical experience: "choose
what you've chosen and get on with it!"   *D.H.*

If your lips would keep from slips,
Five things observe with care;
To whom you speak, of whom you speak,
And how, and when, and where.   *W.E. Norris*

An obituary is a final summation of our lives that, for most of us,
occupies about three inches of space in what will shortly become
cage liner for our neighbor's parakeet.   *Rick Bayan*

Gossip is the only thing that travels faster than E-mail.
Michael Levine

A friend dislikes the same people you dislike.   *Anon*

Happy are the men whom nature has buttressed with
indifference and cased in stoicism.   *Guy de Maupassant*

Scientists hate paradox. It is a threshold over which their logic
won't go.   *Joseph Chilton Pierce*

Why do motorcyclists wear leather? Because chiffon wrinkles
too easily, that's why.   *Paul Lynde*

A man who wants to lead an orchestra must turn his back
on the crowd.   *James Crook*

The same people who deny values want more laws.   *Dennis Prager*

Our faith comes in moments; our vice is habitual. Yet there is a
depth in those brief moments which constrains us to ascribe
more reality to them than to all other experiences.   *Emerson*

Some persons are likable in spite of their unswerving integrity.
Anon

I tore myself away from the safe comfort of certainties through
my love for truth; and truth rewarded me.   *Simone Weil*

Prayer acknowledges universal partnership.   *Anon*

Out beyond ideas of right-doing and wrong-doing there is a field;
I'll meet you there.   *Rumi*

Non-judgmentalism is often just an exchange of moral blank checks.
Ayn Rand

Humor is God laughing at itself.   *D.H.*

The true traveler loves something just because it is different.
Aldous Huxley

The trouble with foreign aid is that it enables too many countries
to live beyond our means.   *Anon*

So, to remember our changing garden,
We are linked as children in a circle dancing.   *W.H. Auden*

A lover without indiscretion is no lover at all.   *Thomas Hardy*

In the act of loving someone you arm them against you.   *Anon*

Familiarity breeds contempt -- and children.   *Mark Twain*

The world is full of double beds
      And sweet young things with maidenheads,
This being so, there's no excuse,
      For sodomy or self-abuse.   *Hilaire Belloc*

Among those whom I like or admire, I can find no common
denominator, but among those whom I love, I can: all of them
make me laugh.   *W.H. Auden*

Love is not the opposite of hate. Being whole, love has no opposites.
Deepak Chopra

I don't even know what I'm thinking, but there's a rich round
fullness in the air like living inside Beethoven's piano on a day
when he was particularly energetic.   *Sujata Bhatt*

He can look at a girl and tell what kind of past she's going to have.
Anon

Hide not your talents, they for use were made.
Benjamin Franklin

Give all thou canst; high Heaven rejects the lore of
nicely-calculated less or more.   *Wordsworth*

Believe those who are seeking the truth; doubt those who find it.
André Gide

If we treat those who do bad good, how will we treat those
who do good?   *Confucius*

Without commitment, you cannot learn to see others as your
soul sees them -- as beautiful and powerful spirits of Light.

Gary Zukov

By practicing forgiveness I'm spared the burden of others
living rent-free in my head.

D.H.

A sound marriage is not based on complete frankness;
it is based on a sensible reticence.

Morris Ernst

A sense of duty is useful in work but offensive in personal relations.

Bertrand Russell

Love-making is radical, while marriage is conservative.

Eric Hoffer

An insatiable satyr name Bruce
Likes his women delightfully loose.
          He finds 'em out dancing,
               And twisting and prancing,
And puts 'em to very good use.

Anon

If you cry "Forward!" you must without fail make plain in what
direction to go. Don't you see that if, without going so, you call
out the word to both a monk and a revolutionary, they will go
in directions precisely opposite?

Anton Chekhov

CYNIC: An idealist whose rose-colored glasses have been
removed, snapped in two, and stomped into the ground,
immediately improving his vision.

Rick Bayan

Remember discouragement is the only illness.

George Bernard Shaw

They are slaves who fear to speak for the fallen and the weak.

James Russell Lowell

Time is quantified infinity.

Deepak Chopra

The chains of tormented mankind are made out of red tape.   *Kafka*

I always wanted to be somebody, but I should have been more
specific.

Lily Tomlin

What do you call a midget psychic that just committed a crime?
A small medium at large. *Anon*

Life is something that happens when you can't get to sleep.
Fran Lebowitz

With the farming of a verse
Make a vineyard of the curse.
Sing of human unsuccess
In a rapture of distress;
... In the prison of his days
Teach the free man how to praise. *W.H. Auden*

Through music and poetry "I spit in the face of time." (Yeats)
D.H.

Music begins to atrophy when it departs too far from the dance;
... poetry begins to atrophy when it gets too far from music.
Ezra Pound

The soul's attachments are as nails in the cross of commitment
that keeps us here. *D.H.*

Housed in hamlets of heaven ... (and)
Humble in all his planets. *Dylan Thomas*

Why do elephants drink? To forget. *Anon*

Nature has neither kernel nor shell; she is everything at once.
Goethe

Successful artists do have their clusters, they move ahead
tribally; it's not "The Lone Ranger." *Anon*

Liberty is indivisible. You can't pick and choose among a list
of freedoms, fight for the ones you like and let the others be
suppressed. *Rick Thompkins*

Unity in diversity -- "the coat of many colors." *John Jocelyn*

There's no point in making plans for the future if you can't fully
enjoy the results when they, in turn, become part of the present.
Alan Watts

No central planner can match the sheer genius of the marketplace.
Ted Forstmann

Culture in its higher forms is a delicate plant. *Einstein*

Queers United Against Closets (QUAC). *Anon*

You cannot become thorough Americans if you think of
yourselves in groups. America does not consist of groups.
A man who thinks of himself as belonging to a particular
national group in America has not yet become an American.
Woodrow Wilson

Do not do unto others as you would that they should do unto you.
Their tastes may not be the same. *George Bernard Shaw*

Cease being the slave of a (political) party and you become its
deserter. *Jules Simon*

In friendship nobody has a double. *Friedrich Schiller*

True friendship is a plant of slow growth, and must undergo
and withstand the shocks of adversity before it is entitled to
the appellation. *George Washington*

Know how to sell your wares. Intrinsic quality isn't enough.
Not everyone bites at substance or looks for inner value.
... Everybody goes for something unique. Uniqueness appeals
both to the taste and to the intellect. *Baltasar Gracian*

He that pities another remembers himself. *Mark Twain*

The only real tragedy is to suffer without learning the lesson.
Emmet Fox

The most remarkable thing about my mother is that for
30 years she served the family nothing but leftovers.
The original has never been found. *Calvin Trillin*

If God lived on Earth people would break His windows.
Yiddish Proverb

Water which is too pure has no fish. *T'sai Ken Tan*

One of life's major mistakes is being the last member of the
family to get the flu -- after all the sympathy has run out.   *Anon*

The moon peered through (rain clouds) as if she were
an old woman opening a drawer to find something lost
in the bottom of it -- me.   *Alice Howell*

Everyone is a moon and has a dark side which he never shows
to anybody.   *Mark Twain*

Families break up when people take hints you don't intend
and miss hints you do intend.   *Robert Frost*

Those that don't understand symbols are like diners
in a restaurant eating the menu.   *Joseph Campbell*

Discernment lies hidden in retirement so as to be more
esteemed by the wise and discreet.   *Emerson*

Loss in all of its manifestations is the touchstone of depression
-- in the progress of the disease, and most likely, in its origin.
       William Styron

God can only be present in the creation in the form of absence.
       Simone Weil

Loss is the universe rearranging itself. It personalizes the
impersonal.   *D.H.*

A.F.G.O. -- another fucking growth opportunity.   *Anon*

In the 60's the manifesto of the raised fist was, "We want yours."
In the 90's the message of the raised phallus is, "Where's mine?"
       (After) Malcolm Muggeridge

The lust for comfort murders the passion of the soul.   *Gibran*

I sit and worry about money who very soon will have to die.
       Peter Porter

GENEALOGY -- Remembrance of Flings Past. Man does not
live by bred alone.   *M. Rose Pierce*

Luxury is more deadly than any folly. *Juvenal*

He that is of the opinion that money will do anything,
may well be suspected of doing anything for money.
Benjamin Franklin

He festooned the dung heap on which he had placed himself
with sonnets as people grow honeysuckle around outdoor privies.
Quentin Crisp on Oscar Wilde

Earth first; we'll strip-mine the rest of the planets later.
Bumper Sticker

CONFISCATED -- Rendered unto Seizer. Subjected to a hostile
takeover. *M. Rose Pierce*

Any man who has to ask about the annual upkeep of a yacht
can't afford one. *J.P. Morgan*

A casino is a house of shill repute. *M. Rose Pierce*

Our society has suffered from the disappearance of family
businesses and the spread of impersonal, massive, anonymously
owned and operated supermarkets and other stores. These
changes in social patterns suck the soul from everyday life
... somewhere in the differences you can detect a loss of
enchantment. *Thomas Moore*

Born in Germany, raised and schooled in Switzerland, Marion March came to the US in 1941 and acted in films as well as on the stage. Married in 1948, she has two grown children and three grandchildren. A teacher and professional astrologer since 1970 with a large international clientele, Marion speaks 5 languages and is an eagerly sought lecturer all over the world as well as writer for magazines here and abroad.

With Joan McEvers, in 1975, she founded Aquarius Workshops, a school of Astrology whose magazine Aspects is still one of the most respected in the astrological community. Together they wrote the best-selling six volume The Only Way to... Learn Astrology series, translated into 8 languages.

Marion served on AFAN's Steering Committee, coordinated UAC `86 and `92, Program Chairman for `89, and was assistant coordinator and Hotel Liaison for `95. She is the recipient of numerous awards, including the PAI 1990 annual award, and two prestigious Regulus awards: for Education and Community Service, and the Robert C. Jansky award. She has been given a Life Achievement Award from UAC. Marion is named in Who's Who in America.

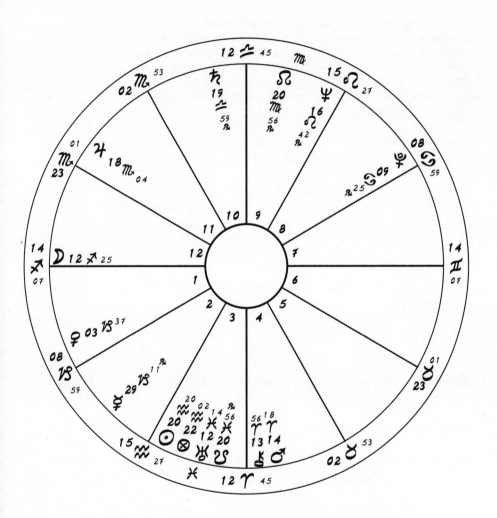

Marion March
b. 10 February 1923, 03:46 MET, Nürnberg, Germany (49N27, 11E04)
Source: Lois Rodden quotes March. Koch Houses.

All originality is relative. *Emerson*

Words lead to deeds ... they prepare the soul, make it ready,
and move it to tenderness. *Saint Teresa*

Do what excites you <u>with integrity</u> -- which means functioning
as a whole idea, and not stopping to think of yourself as a
collection of parts, or compartments, that is scattered here and
there. Recognize that all the different things that have your
attention are all part of the same whole idea, and will all fall
into place automatically when you act on the one that represents
your strongest intention. *Bashar*

A woman's ability to speak several languages is often combined
with her inability to hold her tongue even in one. *Anon*

The ratio of literacy to illiteracy is constant, but nowadays
the illiterates can read and write. *Alberto Moravia*

A combination of Little Nell and Lady Macbeth (on Dorothy Parker).
Alexander Woollcott

Don't shoot too high. Aim low, and the common people will
understand you. *Abe Lincoln*

listen, there's a hell of a good universe next door; let's go.
e.e. cummings

Beware when the great God lets loose a thinker on this planet.
Emerson

It's co-existence or no-existence. *Bertrand Russell*

Only on the basis of individual rights can any good --
private or public -- be defined and achieved. *Ayn Rand*

It's a nervous work. The state that you need to write in is the state
that others are paying large sums to get rid of. *Shirley Hazzard*

Any writer overwhelmingly honest about pleasing himself
is almost sure to please others. *Marianne Moore*

It is not often that someone comes along who is a true friend
and a good writer. *E.B. White*

What lies behind us and what lies before us are small matters
compared to what lies within us.   *Emerson*

What is more important: actual experiences, or the memories
that remain when the experiences are over?   *Gregory Stock*

Emotion is defined by belief and trust is the thrust of faith.   *D.H.*

Participate joyfully in the sorrows of the world. We cannot cure
the world of sorrows.   *Joseph Campbell*

Now the day is over
Night is drawing nigh,
Shadows of the evening
Steal across the sky.   *S. Baring-Gould*

If you could script the basic plot for the dream you will have
tonight, what would the story be?   *Gregory Stock*

I'm careful of the words I say,
To keep them soft and sweet,
I never know from day to day
Which ones I'll have to eat.   *Anon*

Somewhere in the heaven of lost futures
The lives we might have lived
Have found their own fulfilment.   *Derek Mahon*

The discovery of a new dish does more for human happiness
than the discovery of a new star.   *Brillat-Savarin*

Would you give up half of what you now own for a pill
that would permanently change you so that one hour
of sleep each day would fully refresh you?   *Gregory Stock*

Though restraining tongue and pen,
There's a time to let them go ...
Watch the Lunar Cycle, then,
Let vituperations flow.   *D.H.*

Now at length we're off to Turkey,
        Lord knows when we shall come back!
Breezes foul and tempests murky
        May unship us in a crack.
But, since life at most a fest is,
        As philosophers allow,
Still to laugh by far the best is,
        Then laugh on-- as I do now.   *Lord Byron*

Do you feel you have enough time? If not, what would give you
that feeling? How much has your attitude about time changed
as you've aged?   *Gregory Stock*

If writers were good businessmen, they'd have too much sense
to be writers.   *Irving S. Cobb*

Each person is born with one possession which out-values all
others -- his last breath.   *Mark Twain*

Now, having read Jung, Ficino, Yeats, Rilke, and Dickinson,
I've discovered how to listen meditatively. It has taken me
thirty years to learn how to stop talking, to wait and really listen.
(Mercury is retrograde <u>and</u> unaspected.)   *Thomas Moore*

Youth sees an endless hourglass; age hears the grains running out.
                                                                                           D.H.

Writing is like walking in a deserted street. Out of the dust
in the street you make a mud pie.   *John Le Carre*

It's true that money talks, but in these days a dollar doesn't
have enough cents to say anything worthwhile.   *Anon*

Finance is the art of passing currency from hand to hand
until it finally disappears.   *Robert Sarnoff*

Keep in mind that abundance is a general idea, whereas money
is a TOOL. Abundance is the ability to do what you need and
want to do when you want to do it. Period!   *Bashar*

That breath I draw was first exhaled
By diesel and incinerator;
I should have wakened not at all,
Or, were it feasible, even later.
Walls of the world close in one me,
Threats equatorial and polar;
Twixt pit and pendulum I lie;
Another day, another dolor.   *Ogden Nash*

Non-judgementalism is often an exchange of moral blank checks.
                                                                                      Ayn Rand

Selective hearing guards the door to selective remembering,
and both are fear-based.   *D.H.*

Mingle occasional pleasures with your care that you with
courage any task may bear.   *Cato*

Do you prefer being around men or women? Do your closest
friends tend to be men or women?   *Gregory Stock*

If you could spend one year in perfect happiness but afterward
would remember nothing of the experience would you do so?
If not, why not?   *Gregory Stock*

Love's commitments are the nails in the cross that keeps us here.
                                                           D.H.

It is by going down into the Abyss that we recover the treasures of
life. Where you stumble, there lies your treasure.   *Joseph Campbell*

There once was a dentist named Stone
Who saw all his patients alone.
          In a fit of depravity
          He filled the wrong cavity,
And my, how his practice has grown!   *Anon*

Narcissism is the handmaiden of materialism.   *D.H.*

What actors learn is how to get out of the trap of their mask.
Why? Because otherwise they become what is called the
type-cast actor and they get stuck in one role. Indeed, Hollywood
in its heyday in the 30's and 40's kept lists of actors by their
Ascendant sign.   *Richard Idemon*

Diplomacy is the art of letting someone else have your way.   *Anon*

The object of art is to give life shape.   *Jean Anouilh*

How many loved your moments of glad grace,
And loved your beauty with love false or true,
But one man loved the pilgrim soul in you,
And loved the sorrows of your changing face.   *W.B. Yeats*

Do our experiences become more marvelous with age, or is it
just that we don't realize when they occur how really beautiful
and precious they are?   *Joseph Campbell*

The world hangs on to its ancient sanity
And orders another round of vanity.   *Ogden Nash*

There was a young man of Khartoum,
The strength of whose balls was his doom.
> So strong was his shootin',
> The third law of Newton
Propelled the poor chap to the moon.   *Anon*

Courage is not simply one of the virtues, but the form of every
virtue at the testing point. (Marion's Mars is conjunct the I.C.
in the Fourth House, which could be called "the testing point
of the soul.")   *C.S. Lewis*

The end of man is an action, not a thought, though it were the
noblest.   *Thomas Carlyle*

The end is where we start from.   *T.S. Eliot*

Do not go gentle in that good night,
Old age should burn and rave at close of day.
Rage, Rage against the dying of the light.   *Dylan Thomas*

For all we have and are,
For all our children's fate,
Stand up and take the war,
The Hun is at the gate.   *Rudyard Kipling (1914)*

Life is lived forward, and understood backward.
                                                   Sören Kierkegaard

Action minus integrity is an abuse of power. Power with
integrity is soul in action.   *D.H.*

Every conflict that has not been suffered to the end and
been resolved will recur.   *Herman Hesse*

They sicken of the calm that know the storm.   *Dorothy Parker*

The home is the only place of liberty, the only spot on earth
where a man can alter arrangements suddenly, make an
experiment or indulge in a whim.   *G.K. Chesteron*

My Youth I shall never forget,
But there's nothing I really regret,
Wotthehell Wotthehell,
There's a dance in the old dame yet.   *Don Marquis*

Friendship is like money, easier made than kept. *Samuel Butler*

Liberty is indivisible. You can't pick and choose among a list
of freedoms, fight for the ones you like and let the others be
suppressed. *Rick Thompkins*

Our Congress is the best money can buy. *Will Rogers*

Pick your friends, but not to pieces. *Anon*

Never do your best card tricks for the group you play poker with.
 Anon

A truth once seen, even by a single mind, always ends by
imposing itself on the totality of human consciousness.
 Pierre Tielhard de Chardin

He seemed to feel a need to find the minutest chinks in his
friends' armor, wherein to insert a poisoned needle.
 John Keats (On Alexander Woollcott)

Since the days when old Adam and Noah
Had a corner on spermatozoa,
    Those wee potent critters
    Have given girls jitters,
But they keep right on beggin' for moah! *Anon*

When bad men combine, the good must associate; else they will
fall, one by one, an unpitied sacrifice in a contemptible struggle.
 Edmund Burke

The men of the sign Sagittarius
Have customs obscene and barbarious.
    They sow their wild oats
    With girls, boys, and goats,
In postures ingenious and various. *Anon*

If God had meant us to have group sex, he'd have given us
more organs. *Malcolm Bradbury*

While shepherds watched their flocks by night,
    All shitting on the ground,
An angel of the Lord came down
    And handed paper all around. *Anon*

The fact is that government cannot produce equality, and any serious effort to do so can destroy liberty and other social goods.

Jeanne Kirkpatrick

One grows very cautious when living across the border from malevolent rivals.

Baltasar Gracian

All unhappiness is caused by comparison.

Anon

Love without power is rust. Power without love is tyranny.
He who polices his love is threadbare, naked.

Ann Ree Colton

The one who loves the least controls the relationship.

Anon

My success is contingent on the quality of my loving.

D.H.

There was an announcer named Herschel
Whose habits became controversial,
      Because when out wooing
      Whatever he was doing
At ten he'd insert his commercial.

Anon

Once we could have made the docks,
Now it is too late to fly;
Once too often you and I
Did what we should not have done;
Round the rampant rugged rocks
Rude and ragged rascals run. (January 1941)

W.H. Auden

It is not the business of politicians to please everyone.

Margaret Thatcher

The nine most terrifying words in the English language are,
"I'm from the government and I'm here to help." *Ronald Reagan*

Astrologers tell clients Uranus going into their Twelfth House
is going to open them up to spirituality and mystery; we don't
tell them someone's going to throw a radio in their bathtub.

Michael Lutin

What is a committee? A group of the unwilling, picked from the
unfit, to do the unnecessary. *Richard Harkness*

The world would not be in such a snarl
Had Marx been Groucho instead of Karl. *Irving Berlin*

Today musical greeting cards, which contain disposable
music-making chips, have more computer power than the
computers that existed before 1950. *Michio Kaku*

Socialism is an adult fairy tale. *David Horowitz*

Any sufficiently advanced technology is indistinguishable
from magic. *Arthur C. Clarke*

Television is a medium of entertainment which permits millions
of people to listen to the same joke at the same time, and yet
remain lonesome. *T.S. Eliot*

Being a musician and a confirmed spoonerist, I always wondered
when "Strike Up The Band" became "Bike Up The Strand?" *D.H.*

The astrologer sees the client's wholeness from the inside out.
The psychologist sees the client's wholeness from the outside in.

Anon

I must say I find television very educational. The minute
somebody turns it on, I go to the library and read a good book.

Groucho Marx

Cognitive dissonance is the term for a divided mind, or, a mind
whose local space is bifurcated -- producing a "house divided."
Glimpses of multiple, simultaneous realities are thus made
possible. *D.H.*

An invented language is a form of poetry, for it's obliged to
name everything, to create and populate a new universe.

W.H. Auden

The soul sees opportunity, the ego counts the cost.   *D.H.*

The universe always supports you 100% in whatever idea you
believe yourself most to be.   *Bashar*

The exploration of one's beliefs is primary to the understanding
of Power. Atheists are Egoists; power stops at the boundary of
intellect and ego. But, one who believes his essential identity to be
divine must then deal with the dilemma of power as a fundamental
aspect of divinity, or spirituality, if you will. This is where the talk
becomes the walk.   *D.H.*

In the deserts of the heart
        let the healing fountains start.
In the prison of his days
        teach the free man how to praise.   *W.H. Auden*

Speak to me spirit
As you always have,
And help me to listen
As I never have.   *D.H.*

Music is grace made audible.   *D.H.*

Malt does more than Milton can
To justify God's ways to man.   *A.E. Housman*

It is only with the heart that one can see rightly; what is
essential is invisible to the eye.   *Antoine de St. Exupéry*

We have the power to be with God in heaven by touching Him
in His distressing disguise.   *Mother Teresa*

Love of God is pure when both joy and suffering inspire gratitude.
                                                            Simone Weil

That singular command I do not understand;
Bless what there is for being,
For what else am I made for --
Agreeing or disagreeing?   *W.H. Auden*

The average taxpayer works from January 1st until May 6th to pay federal, state, and local taxes. This means that for five months out of a year we do not have the rights to decide how the fruits of our labor will be used ... this is an example of a working definition of slavery. *Walter Williams*

Some are born to greatness, some achieve greatness, and some have greatness thrust within them. *Hal Lee Luyah*

How do your feelings about death influence the way you lead your life? *Gregory Stock*

Prostitution is a game where the man gets a little fun and the woman gets a little fund. *Anon*

All passions produce prodigies. *Simone Weil*

A little house well filled, a little field well tilled, and a little wife well willed, are great riches. *Ben Franklin*

Titillation results when pubic goes public. *D.H.*

Most people sell their soul and live with a good conscience on the proceeds. *Logan Pearsall Smith*

You fall out of your mother's womb, you crawl across open country, and you drop into your grave. *Quentin Crisp*

Bibliography

Books on Astrological Rulership:

The Rulership Book by Rex Bills (Macoy Publishing, 1971)

Horary Astrology by Anthony Louis (Llewellyn, 1991)

Astrological Thesaurus: House Keywords by Michael Munkasey (Llewellyn, 1992)

The Horary Reference Book vol. 1 by Anne Ungar and Lillian Huber (ACS Publications, 1984)

The Concept Dictionary by Michael Munkasey (Arcturus Press, 1991)

Key Words for Astrology by Hajo Banzhaf & Anna Haebler (Samuel Weiser, 1996)

Appendix

For those who wish to delve further into the study of astrological symbolism, over the next couple of pages I have presented a more elaborate array of key-word tables for the Twelve Houses, and for the Planets.

	Economic	Political	Sociological	Entrepreneurial	Meteorological
First House	prosperity and health of the people	the voters	country's citizens and self-image	action to be taken during the period	earth's ecology and its atmosphere
Second House	equities, treasury notes, bonds, commodities, stock exchanges, banks	GNP, tax revenue, currency, trade	national earned income, the arts	purchasing power of the population	calm, wooded areas
Third House	copyrights and patents	public opinion, the media, neighbouring nations	basic education, teachers, all land travel, advertising	licenses, communication instruments, mail	breezes, weather in general
Fourth House	real estate values, mines, hotels, natural resources	opposition political party	families, builders, farmers, cemeteries	land, owners of land, agriculture	property damage from weather
Fifth House	public speculation and investments, gambling	national public figures	fertility, children, recreation	theaters, concerts, sporting events and arenas	weather conditions in resort areas
Sixth House	workers and employees	public health, armed forces, civil servants, thieves	unions. health workers, pets and small animals	resource centers, computer programs, employment	food production, weather for farms
Seventh House	competitors, mergers, fair exchange, public relations, business partnerships, sales	foreign affairs, civil war, diplomatic relations, battles, fugitive criminals, arbitrators	marriage, divorce	shoppers or buyers, organization of charities	air quality
Eighth House	frozen assets, loans, trusts, interest rates, mortgages insurance, charge accounts	national debt, FBI, IRS, organized crime	birth control, mortality, death, latrines, sewers, surgeons, weapons	public income, bequests, estates, pension funds, stockholders, prostitutes	underground activity
Ninth House	corporations	courts of law, foreign affairs and trade, immigration	religion, clergy, ceremonies, festivals, astrology, colleges	overseas traffic sea and air, science	coastal weather conditions
Tenth House	national credit and trade, power, achievements, chairman of the board	chief executive, national reputation, party in power, law enforcement, senators	famous people, scandal	business, utilities	whirlwinds, weather in mountainous areas
Eleventh House	stock exchanges, profits, management, commodity exchange	legislatures, councils, will of the people, foreign alliances, national treasury, parliament	organizations, social clubs, juries	business plan, perks	electric storms, erosion
Twelfth House	cattle, drugs, unemployment strikes and labor troubles, fuel	hospitals, jails, spies, crimes, mental asylums, assassins	charity groups, witchcraft, secret religions, clinics	smuggling, personal journeys and writings of those in power	remote places

	Economic	Political	Sociological	Entrepreneurial	Meteorological
Sun	CEO, gold	president, head of state, public officials	fame, famous people, men	money	dry weather, sunny, warm
Moon	dealers, occupations, retail trade	public opinion, water transportation	daily routine, food, home, women, crowds	subjects or objects of popular interest	oceans, rain, land, crops, environment
Mercury	transportation, communication	ambassadors, post office, educators, Secretary of State	youth, speakers, the press, literary world, intelligentsia	media, autos, signing papers	wind, cold, changeable weather
Venus	money, profit, luxury items, lenders, financial gain	revenue, treasury, goodwill ambassadors, preservers of the peace	artists, fashion, females, musicians, theaters, births, marriages, children	disposable income, movable possessions	fair, balmy
Mars	construction, steel, manufacturing	armed forces, wars, criminals military leaders, agitators	surgeons, guns, epidemics	engineers	heat, dry weather
Jupiter	industrialist, capitalist	tariffs, diplomats, judiciary, legislature, foreign ministry	clergy, voyages, metaphysics long-distance travel, religion educational institutions	peace, prosperity, plenty	balmy
Saturn	financial affairs, property, businesses	law enforcement, government civil service, public buildings	common people, history, senior citizens	mine operators, farming, scarcities, land owners	national calamities, dry cool weather
Uranus	air and rail transport	strikes, riots, explosions	labor organizations	inventions, radio and electrical industry	lightning, earthquakes
Neptune	oil, chemicals	political movements	service organizations, hospitals, charities	art, craftsmanship, movies	fog, floods, humidity
Pluto	insurance, taxes	underworld, organized crime	mob psychology	chain stores, mines	ice, earthquakes mud flows, volcanoes

The tables overleaf are designed to help the reader ascertain their Sun Sign. For those born 'on the cusp' (ie. around the period when the Sun changed sign), you may need to know your birth time to calculate your true Sun Sign. All the times are in Greenwich Mean Time (GMT), so if you were born during daylight saving time (roughly from late March/April to early October each year), please subtract one hour from your birth time. Those born in Great Britain between the following dates will need to subtract two hours from their birth time (Greenwich War Time):

> 4 May - 10 August 1941
> 5 April - 9 August 1942
> 4 April - 15 August 1943
> 2 April - 17 September 1944
> 2 April - 15 July 1945

In addition, all those born in Great Britain between 18 February 1968 and 31 October 1971 will need to subtract one hour from their birth time to obtain GMT.

Time changes before 1981 were made at 02:00 GMT. Time changes after 1981, and changes from one hour of Daylight Saving Time to two hours (during War Time - see above), were made at 01:00 GMT.

With thanks to David Fisher and his leaflet, Time Changes in Great Britain (AA, 1991).

	♒︎ Aquarius begins JAN	♓︎ Pisces begins FEB	♈︎ Aries begins MAR	♉︎ Taurus begins APR	♊︎ Gemini begins MAY	♋︎ Cancer begins JUN
1920	21 (08:04)	19 (22:29)	20 (22:00)	20 (09:39)	21 (09:20)	21 (17:38)
1921	20 (13:53)	19 (04:19)	21 (03:51)	20 (15:32)	21 (15:16)	21 (23:34)
1922	20 (19:47)	19 (10:15)	21 (09:48)	20 (21:29)	21 (21:10)	22 (05:26)
1923	21 (01:37)	19 (16:01)	21 (15:30)	21 (03:08)	22 (02:48)	22 (11:05)
1924	21 (07:32)	19 (21:55)	20 (21:23)	20 (09:01)	21 (08:43)	21 (17:02)
1925	20 (13:21)	19 (03:45)	21 (03:14)	20 (14:53)	21 (14:34)	21 (22:52)
1926	20 (19:12)	19 (09:36)	21 (09:03)	20 (20:39)	21 (20:18)	22 (04:33)
1927	21 (01:11)	19 (15:34)	21 (15:01)	21 (02:35)	22 (02:11)	22 (10:26)
1928	21 (06:56)	19 (21:18)	20 (20:43)	20 (08:16)	21 (07:54)	21 (16:09)
1929	20 (12:43)	19 (03:06)	21 (02:32)	20 (14:07)	21 (13:45)	21 (22:00)
1930	20 (18:34)	19 (09:00)	21 (08:29)	20 (20:04)	21 (19:40)	22 (03:51)
1931	21 (00:19)	19 (14:43)	21 (14:08)	21 (01:41)	22 (01:15)	22 (09:27)
1932	21 (06:07)	19 (20:29)	20 (19:55)	20 (07:29)	21 (07:07)	21 (15:22)
1933	20 (11:50)	19 (02:14)	21 (01:42)	20 (13:18)	21 (12:57)	21 (21:11)
1934	20 (17:35)	19 (07:59)	21 (07:26)	20 (18:59)	21 (18:35)	22 (02:49)
1935	20 (23:30)	19 (13:52)	21 (13:17)	21 (00:50)	22 (00:26)	22 (08:40)
1936	21 (05:15)	19 (19:35)	20 (18:59)	20 (06:31)	21 (06:07)	21 (14:22)
1937	20 (11:03)	19 (01:23)	21 (00:47)	20 (12:19)	21 (11:56)	21 (20:11)
1938	20 (16:59)	19 (07:21)	21 (06:46)	20 (18:17)	21 (17:51)	22 (02:03)
1939	20 (22:51)	19 (13:10)	21 (12:31)	20 (23:59)	21 (23:30)	22 (07:41)
1940	21 (04:43)	19 (19:02)	20 (18:23)	20 (05:52)	21 (05:26)	21 (13:38)
1941	20 (10:33)	19 (00:55)	21 (00:19)	20 (11:50)	21 (11:23)	21 (19:35)
1942	20 (16:23)	19 (06:46)	21 (06:09)	20 (17:37)	21 (17:08)	22 (01:17)
1943	20 (22:19)	19 (12:41)	21 (12:04)	20 (23:33)	21 (23:04)	22 (07:14)
1944	21 (04:06)	19 (18:27)	20 (17:49)	20 (05:18)	21 (04:51)	21 (13:03)
1945	20 (09:52)	19 (00:13)	20 (23:36)	20 (11:06)	21 (10:40)	21 (18:52)
1946	20 (15:44)	19 (06:07)	21 (05:31)	20 (17:02)	21 (16:34)	22 (00:45)
1947	20 (21:34)	19 (11:54)	21 (11:13)	20 (22:40)	21 (22:10)	22 (06:20)
1948	21 (03:22)	19 (17:40)	20 (16:58)	20 (04:25)	21 (03:58)	21 (12:11)
1949	20 (09:10)	18 (23:29)	20 (22:49)	20 (10:17)	21 (09:50)	21 (18:01)
1950	20 (14:59)	19 (05:18)	21 (04:36)	20 (16:00)	21 (15:27)	21 (23:35)
1951	20 (20:51)	19 (11:09)	21 (10:26)	20 (21:50)	21 (21:17)	22 (05:26)
1952	21 (02:38)	19 (16:55)	20 (16:11)	20 (03:35)	21 (03:03)	21 (11:12)
1953	20 (08:22)	18 (22:40)	20 (21:58)	20 (09:22)	21 (08:50)	21 (16:57)
1954	20 (14:12)	19 (04:33)	21 (03:53)	20 (15:18)	21 (14:45)	21 (22:52)
1955	20 (20:02)	19 (10:21)	21 (09:38)	20 (21:00)	21 (20:25)	22 (04:31)
1956	21 (01:48)	19 (16:06)	20 (15:23)	20 (02:47)	21 (02:15)	21 (10:25)
1957	20 (07:36)	18 (21:55)	20 (21:16)	20 (08:42)	21 (08:12)	21 (16:22)
1958	20 (13:27)	19 (03:46)	21 (03:04)	20 (14:28)	21 (13:54)	21 (22:00)
1959	20 (19:21)	19 (09:39)	21 (08:55)	20 (20:17)	21 (19:44)	22 (03:54)
1960	21 (01:13)	19 (15:29)	20 (14:44)	20 (02:06)	21 (01:34)	21 (09:44)
1961	20 (07:03)	18 (21:19)	20 (20:34)	20 (07:56)	21 (07:22)	21 (15:30)
1962	20 (12:58)	19 (03:16)	21 (02:32)	20 (13:53)	21 (13:18)	21 (21:24)
1963	20 (18:54)	19 (09:09)	21 (08:21)	20 (19:38)	21 (19:00)	22 (03:05)
1964	21 (00:41)	19 (14:56)	20 (14:08)	20 (01:26)	21 (00:50)	21 (08:56)
1965	20 (06:29)	18 (20:46)	20 (20:02)	20 (07:23)	21 (06:47)	21 (14:53)
1966	20 (12:19)	19 (02:37)	21 (01:51)	20 (13:09)	21 (12:29)	21 (20:31)
1967	20 (18:07)	19 (08:24)	21 (07:37)	20 (18:55)	21 (18:17)	22 (02:22)
1968	20 (23:52)	19 (14:08)	20 (13:22)	20 (00:41)	21 (00:05)	21 (08:12)
1969	20 (05:36)	18 (19:52)	20 (19:07)	20 (06:26)	21 (05:49)	21 (13:54)

	♌	♍	♎	♏	♐	♑
	Leo begins JUL	Virgo begins AUG	Libra begins SEP	Scorpio begins OCT	Sagittarius begins NOV	Capricorn begins DEC
1920	23 (04:33)	23 (11:21)	23 (08:28)	23 (17:13)	22 (14:15)	22 (03:16)
1921	23 (10:28)	23 (17:13)	23 (14:19)	23 (23:02)	22 (20:05)	22 (09:08)
1922	23 (16:18)	23 (23:02)	23 (20:09)	24 (04:54)	23 (01:57)	22 (14:59)
1923	23 (22:02)	24 (04:52)	24 (02:03)	24 (10:51)	23 (07:55)	22 (20:56)
1924	23 (03:59)	23 (10:49)	23 (07:57)	23 (16:43)	22 (13:45)	22 (02:45)
1925	23 (09:47)	23 (16:34)	23 (13:43)	23 (22:29)	22 (19:33)	22 (08:35)
1926	23 (15:28)	23 (22:18)	23 (19:30)	24 (04:21)	23 (01:28)	22 (14:33)
1927	23 (21:20)	24 (04:09)	24 (01:21)	24 (10:11)	23 (07:17)	22 (20:20)
1928	23 (03:04)	23 (09:55)	23 (07:07)	23 (15:57)	22 (13:03)	22 (02:06)
1929	23 (08:53)	23 (15:41)	23 (12:52)	23 (21:41)	22 (18:48)	22 (07:54)
1930	23 (14:41)	23 (21:27)	23 (18:36)	24 (03:26)	23 (00:34)	22 (13:40)
1931	23 (20:21)	24 (03:10)	24 (00:24)	24 (09:16)	23 (06:24)	22 (19:29)
1932	23 (02:16)	23 (09:05)	23 (06:15)	23 (15:03)	22 (12:09)	22 (01:12)
1933	23 (08:04)	23 (14:50)	23 (11:59)	23 (20:47)	22 (17:53)	22 (06:57)
1934	23 (13:42)	23 (20:32)	23 (17:45)	24 (02:37)	22 (23:46)	22 (12:51)
1935	23 (19:35)	24 (02:25)	23 (23:39)	24 (08:30)	23 (05:37)	22 (18:40)
1936	23 (01:19)	23 (08:12)	23 (05:26)	23 (14:18)	22 (11:25)	22 (00:27)
1937	23 (07:07)	23 (13:58)	23 (11:13)	23 (20:05)	22 (17:15)	22 (06:20)
1938	23 (12:57)	23 (19:47)	23 (17:02)	24 (01:56)	22 (23:07)	22 (12:13)
1939	23 (18:37)	24 (01:31)	23 (22:50)	24 (07:47)	23 (05:00)	22 (18:06)
1940	23 (00:34)	23 (07:27)	23 (04:44)	23 (13:38)	22 (10:49)	21 (23:55)
1941	23 (06:27)	23 (13:16)	23 (10:30)	23 (19:24)	22 (16:36)	22 (05:43)
1942	23 (12:09)	23 (19:00)	23 (16:17)	24 (01:14)	22 (22:29)	22 (11:38)
1943	23 (18:07)	24 (00:58)	23 (22:14)	24 (07:10)	23 (04:21)	22 (17:28)
1944	22 (23:57)	23 (06:49)	23 (04:04)	23 (12:58)	22 (10:08)	21 (23:14)
1945	23 (05:46)	23 (12:36)	23 (09:51)	23 (18:46)	22 (15:57)	22 (05:05)
1946	23 (11:38)	23 (18:28)	23 (15:43)	24 (00:38)	22 (21:50)	22 (10:57)
1947	23 (17:16)	24 (00:10)	23 (21:30)	24 (06:28)	23 (03:41)	22 (16:46)
1948	22 (23:08)	23 (06:03)	23 (03:21)	23 (12:17)	22 (09:28)	21 (22:34)
1949	23 (04:56)	23 (11:48)	23 (09:05)	23 (18:02)	22 (15:14)	22 (04:21)
1950	23 (10:29)	23 (17:23)	23 (14:45)	23 (23:46)	22 (21:03)	22 (10:13)
1951	23 (16:21)	23 (23:16)	23 (20:37)	24 (05:38)	23 (02:53)	22 (16:01)
1952	22 (22:06)	23 (05:01)	23 (02:21)	23 (11:21)	22 (08:36)	21 (21:44)
1953	23 (03:50)	23 (10:43)	23 (08:03)	23 (17:03)	22 (14:20)	22 (03:31)
1954	23 (09:43)	23 (16:34)	23 (13:54)	23 (22:54)	22 (20:12)	22 (09:23)
1955	23 (15:24)	23 (22:19)	23 (19:41)	24 (04:42)	23 (02:00)	22 (15:09)
1956	22 (21:20)	23 (04:14)	23 (01:34)	23 (10:34)	22 (07:48)	21 (20:57)
1957	23 (03:15)	23 (10:07)	23 (07:25)	23 (16:24)	22 (13:39)	22 (02:48)
1958	23 (08:53)	23 (15:48)	23 (13:10)	23 (22:13)	22 (19:32)	22 (08:43)
1959	23 (14:50)	23 (21:47)	23 (19:11)	24 (04:13)	23 (01:29)	22 (14:37)
1960	22 (20:41)	23 (03:38)	23 (01:01)	23 (10:03)	22 (07:19)	21 (20:27)
1961	23 (02:25)	23 (09:21)	23 (06:45)	23 (15:49)	22 (13:08)	22 (02:19)
1962	23 (08:18)	23 (15:15)	23 (12:39)	23 (21:44)	22 (19:04)	22 (08:16)
1963	23 (13:59)	23 (20:58)	23 (18:25)	24 (03:31)	23 (00:52)	22 (14:04)
1964	22 (19:51)	23 (02:49)	23 (00:14)	23 (09:19)	22 (06:38)	21 (19:50)
1965	23 (01:46)	23 (08:40)	23 (06:02)	23 (15:06)	22 (12:26)	22 (01:39)
1966	23 (07:22)	23 (14:16)	23 (11:42)	23 (20:49)	22 (18:12)	22 (07:26)
1967	23 (13:15)	23 (20:12)	23 (17:37)	24 (02:43)	23 (00:03)	22 (13:14)
1968	22 (19:06)	23 (02:02)	22 (23:26)	23 (08:29)	22 (05:48)	21 (18:58)
1969	23 (00:46)	23 (07:41)	23 (05:05)	23 (14:10)	22 (11:31)	22 (00:44)

sun sign tables ⟨229⟩

	♒	♓	♈	♉	♊	♋
	Aquarius begins JAN	Pisces begins FEB	Aries begins MAR	Taurus begins APR	Gemini begins MAY	Cancer begins JUN
1970	20 (11:24)	19 (01:41)	21 (00:56)	20 (12:15)	21 (11:38)	21 (19:44)
1971	20 (17:16)	19 (07:30)	21 (06:41)	20 (17:56)	21 (17:17)	22 (01:22)
1972	20 (23:01)	19 (13:14)	20 (12:24)	19 (23:39)	20 (23:01)	21 (07:08)
1973	20 (04:48)	18 (19:03)	20 (18:15)	20 (05:33)	21 (04:56)	21 (13:02)
1974	20 (10:44)	19 (00:58)	21 (00:07)	20 (11:21)	21 (10:38)	21 (18:39)
1975	20 (16:34)	19 (06:48)	21 (05:56)	20 (17:08)	21 (16:26)	22 (00:29)
1976	20 (22:25)	19 (12:37)	20 (11:46)	19 (23:00)	20 (22:20)	21 (06:25)
1977	20 (04:14)	18 (18:29)	20 (17:39)	20 (04:53)	21 (04:10)	21 (12:11)
1978	20 (10:04)	19 (00:21)	20 (23:33)	20 (10:48)	21 (10:06)	21 (18:07)
1979	20 (16:00)	19 (06:15)	21 (05:24)	20 (16:36)	21 (15:53)	21 (23:55)
1980	20 (21:47)	19 (12:01)	20 (11:10)	19 (22:23)	20 (21:42)	21 (05:45)
1981	20 (03:33)	18 (17:49)	20 (17:01)	20 (04:17)	21 (03:39)	21 (11:43)
1982	20 (09:30)	18 (23:44)	20 (22:53)	20 (10:06)	21 (09:22)	21 (17:23)
1983	20 (15:19)	19 (05:32)	21 (04:39)	20 (15:49)	21 (15:06)	21 (23:09)
1984	20 (21:08)	19 (11:18)	20 (10:25)	19 (21:37)	20 (20:56)	21 (05:01)
1985	20 (02:58)	18 (17:09)	20 (16:15)	20 (03:26)	21 (02:41)	21 (10:42)
1986	20 (08:46)	18 (22:58)	20 (22:05)	20 (09:15)	21 (08:29)	21 (16:30)
1987	20 (14:39)	19 (04:50)	21 (03:53)	20 (15:00)	21 (14:13)	21 (22:13)
1988	20 (20:25)	19 (10:35)	20 (09:38)	19 (20:46)	20 (19:58)	21 (03:58)
1989	20 (02:06)	18 (16:19)	20 (15:26)	20 (02:37)	21 (01:52)	21 (09:52)
1990	20 (08:00)	18 (22:13)	20 (21:19)	20 (08:26)	21 (07:37)	21 (15:33)
1991	20 (13:46)	19 (03:58)	21 (03:03)	20 (14:09)	21 (13:21)	21 (21:20)
1992	20 (19:30)	19 (09:41)	20 (08:47)	19 (19:57)	20 (19:12)	21 (03:14)
1993	20 (01:21)	18 (15:32)	20 (14:38)	20 (01:47)	21 (01:01)	21 (08:59)
1994	20 (07:08)	18 (21:21)	20 (20:27)	20 (07:35)	21 (06:48)	21 (14:48)
1995	20 (13:04)	19 (03:14)	21 (02:16)	20 (13:22)	21 (12:34)	21 (20:35)
1996	20 (18:56)	19 (09:04)	20 (08:05)	19 (19:11)	20 (18:23)	21 (02:23)
1997	20 (00:42)	18 (14:53)	20 (13:56)	20 (01:04)	21 (00:17)	21 (08:18)
1998	20 (06:44)	18 (20:53)	20 (19:55)	20 (06:58)	21 (06:06)	21 (14:02)
1999	20 (12:35)	19 (02:44)	21 (01:44)	20 (12:46)	21 (11:53)	21 (19:50)
2000	20 (18:22)	19 (08:31)	20 (07:32)	19 (18:36)	20 (17:47)	21 (01:46)
2001	20 (00:16)	18 (14:26)	20 (13:28)	20 (00:31)	20 (23:40)	21 (07:34)
2002	20 (06:01)	18 (20:14)	20 (19:16)	20 (06:20)	21 (05:27)	21 (13:22)
2003	20 (11:53)	19 (02:02)	21 (01:03)	20 (12:05)	21 (11:14)	21 (19:10)
2004	20 (17:40)	19 (07:48)	20 (06:49)	19 (17:52)	20 (17:00)	21 (00:57)
2005	19 (23:19)	18 (13:29)	20 (12:32)	19 (23:38)	20 (22:49)	21 (06:47)
2006	20 (05:14)	18 (19:24)	20 (18:24)	20 (05:25)	21 (04:33)	21 (12:28)
2007	20 (11:02)	19 (01:10)	21 (00:07)	20 (11:07)	21 (10:13)	21 (18:09)
2008	20 (16:45)	19 (06:51)	20 (05:48)	19 (16:50)	20 (16:00)	20 (23:59)
2009	19 (22:39)	18 (12:46)	20 (11:43)	19 (22:43)	20 (21:49)	21 (05:43)
2010	20 (04:25)	18 (18:33)	20 (17:30)	20 (04:29)	21 (03:32)	21 (11:26)
2011	20 (10:17)	19 (00:23)	20 (23:18)	20 (10:15)	21 (09:19)	21 (17:14)
2012	20 (16:09)	19 (06:15)	20 (05:11)	19 (16:08)	20 (15:11)	20 (23:04)
2013	19 (21:50)	18 (11:59)	20 (10:58)	19 (21:58)	20 (21:04)	21 (04:58)
2014	20 (03:48)	18 (17:57)	20 (16:55)	20 (03:53)	21 (02:55)	21 (10:47)
2015	20 (09:40)	18 (23:48)	20 (22:44)	20 (09:41)	21 (08:43)	21 (16:35)
2016	20 (15:23)	19 (05:30)	20 (04:27)	19 (15:27)	20 (14:34)	20 (22:31)
2017	19 (21:19)	18 (11:27)	20 (10:24)	19 (21:24)	20 (20:28)	21 (04:22)
2018	20 (03:08)	18 (17:17)	20 (16:13)	20 (03:11)	21 (02:14)	21 (10:07)
2019	20 (09:01)	18 (23:05)	20 (21:59)	20 (08:55)	21 (07:59)	21 (15:54)

	♌ Leo begins JUL	♍ Virgo begins AUG	♎ Libra begins SEP	♏ Scorpio begins OCT	♐ Sagittarius begins NOV	♑ Capricorn begins DEC
1970	23 (06:37)	23 (13:34)	23 (10:59)	23 (20:05)	22 (17:26)	22 (06:38)
1971	23 (12:17)	23 (19:16)	23 (16:45)	24 (01:53)	22 (23:14)	22 (12:25)
1972	22 (18:04)	23 (01:04)	22 (22:33)	23 (07:40)	22 (05:00)	21 (18:11)
1973	22 (23:57)	23 (06:55)	23 (04:22)	23 (13:30)	22 (10:52)	22 (00:05)
1974	23 (05:32)	23 (12:31)	23 (10:02)	23 (19:13)	22 (16:40)	22 (05:55)
1975	23 (11:24)	23 (18:26)	23 (15:57)	24 (01:09)	22 (22:33)	22 (11:47)
1976	22 (17:19)	23 (00:19)	22 (21:48)	23 (06:58)	22 (04:22)	21 (17:36)
1977	22 (23:03)	23 (06:00)	23 (03:28)	23 (12:39)	22 (10:06)	21 (23:23)
1978	23 (04:59)	23 (11:57)	23 (09:26)	23 (18:37)	22 (16:04)	22 (05:20)
1979	23 (10:47)	23 (17:46)	23 (15:17)	24 (00:28)	22 (21:54)	22 (11:09)
1980	22 (16:39)	22 (23:38)	22 (21:07)	23 (06:17)	22 (03:41)	21 (16:55)
1981	22 (22:37)	23 (05:35)	23 (03:03)	23 (12:12)	22 (09:36)	21 (22:51)
1982	23 (04:15)	23 (11:14)	23 (08:45)	23 (17:58)	22 (15:25)	22 (04:40)
1983	23 (10:05)	23 (17:08)	23 (14:41)	23 (23:53)	22 (21:19)	22 (10:32)
1984	22 (15:58)	22 (23:00)	22 (20:32)	23 (05:43)	22 (03:08)	21 (16:22)
1985	22 (21:35)	23 (04:35)	23 (02:07)	23 (11:21)	22 (08:49)	21 (22:06)
1986	23 (03:23)	23 (10:25)	23 (08:00)	23 (17:15)	22 (14:45)	22 (04:01)
1987	23 (09:06)	23 (16:09)	23 (13:45)	23 (23:01)	22 (20:31)	22 (09:47)
1988	22 (14:51)	22 (21:52)	22 (19:26)	23 (04:41)	22 (02:10)	21 (15:27)
1989	22 (20:45)	23 (03:45)	23 (01:17)	23 (10:31)	22 (08:01)	21 (21:19)
1990	23 (02:23)	23 (09:22)	23 (06:56)	23 (16:13)	22 (13:45)	22 (03:05)
1991	23 (08:13)	23 (15:15)	23 (12:50)	23 (22:06)	22 (19:35)	22 (08:52)
1992	22 (14:09)	22 (21:11)	22 (18:44)	23 (03:58)	22 (01:26)	21 (14:42)
1993	22 (19:51)	23 (02:50)	23 (00:23)	23 (09:39)	22 (07:09)	21 (20:28)
1994	23 (01:42)	23 (08:45)	23 (06:21)	23 (15:38)	22 (13:09)	22 (02:26)
1995	23 (07:31)	23 (14:36)	23 (12:14)	23 (21:32)	22 (19:03)	22 (08:19)
1996	22 (13:18)	22 (20:23)	22 (17:59)	23 (03:17)	22 (00:47)	21 (14:05)
1997	22 (19:13)	23 (02:18)	22 (23:55)	23 (09:13)	22 (06:46)	21 (20:05)
1998	23 (00:54)	23 (07:58)	23 (05:37)	23 (15:00)	22 (12:35)	22 (01:56)
1999	23 (06:44)	23 (13:49)	23 (11:30)	23 (20:52)	22 (18:25)	22 (07:44)
2000	22 (12:41)	22 (19:46)	22 (17:24)	23 (02:44)	22 (00:17)	21 (13:37)
2001	22 (18:24)	23 (01:24)	22 (23:01)	23 (08:21)	22 (05:57)	21 (19:19)
2002	23 (00:13)	23 (07:16)	23 (04:55)	23 (14:17)	22 (11:52)	22 (01:13)
2003	23 (06:04)	23 (13:08)	23 (10:47)	23 (20:08)	22 (17:42)	22 (07:01)
2004	22 (11:49)	22 (18:52)	22 (16:29)	23 (01:48)	21 (23:20)	21 (12:40)
2005	22 (17:41)	23 (00:44)	22 (22:22)	23 (07:42)	22 (05:15)	21 (18:35)
2006	22 (23:20)	23 (06:24)	23 (04:04)	23 (13:27)	22 (11:03)	22 (00:24)
2007	23 (05:04)	23 (12:11)	23 (09:53)	23 (19:16)	22 (16:50)	22 (06:09)
2008	22 (10:56)	22 (18:05)	22 (15:46)	23 (01:08)	21 (22:43)	21 (12:02)
2009	22 (16:35)	22 (23:40)	22 (21:21)	23 (06:45)	22 (04:23)	21 (17:46)
2010	22 (22:19)	23 (05:26)	23 (03:10)	23 (12:37)	22 (10:16)	21 (23:39)
2011	23 (04:09)	23 (11:18)	23 (09:03)	23 (18:30)	22 (16:09)	22 (05:31)
2012	22 (09:56)	22 (17:02)	22 (14:44)	23 (00:09)	21 (21:47)	21 (11:10)
2013	22 (15:50)	22 (22:55)	22 (20:38)	23 (06:03)	22 (03:43)	21 (17:07)
2014	22 (21:37)	23 (04:42)	23 (02:25)	23 (11:53)	22 (09:34)	21 (22:59)
2015	23 (03:27)	23 (10:34)	23 (08:17)	23 (17:44)	22 (15:22)	22 (04:44)
2016	22 (09:27)	22 (16:34)	22 (14:17)	22 (23:42)	21 (21:19)	21 (10:40)
2017	22 (15:13)	22 (22:17)	22 (19:59)	23 (05:24)	22 (03:03)	21 (16:27)
2018	22 (21:00)	23 (04:07)	23 (01:52)	23 (11:21)	22 (09:01)	21 (22:23)
2019	23 (02:51)	23 (10:02)	23 (07:49)	23 (17:18)	22 (14:57)	22 (04:19)

Index

C

D

L

M

S

T

W

X•Y

Z

David Hayward

Dave Hayward, husband, father, and grandfather is a professional trumpet player, astrologer, massage therapist, and business owner. As a musician, he worked with Sonny Rollins, Stan Kenton, and Janis Joplin, to name a few, from 1965-70. He continues to be involved with music and plays the trumpet daily. He has been "putting plumbing on his face" for 46 years, and does not envision a trumpet-lamp in the near future. As much as he loves words, only music takes him beyond the verbal and into the midpoint of the soul.

In 1973, Dave experienced a transformation in which he left behind all chemical and alcohol abuse and went from being a card-carrying atheist to one who can't find a spot where God is not. His interest in metaphysics and the mystical aspect of life found a home in yoga, meditation, and most importantly, astrology.

In 1983, he became a licensed massage and Shiatsu therapist. This work continues to be greatly gratifying both to him and his clientele. With Jupiter, Saturn, Uranus and the Midheaven in Taurus, a Cancer Moon, and Scorpio Sun, this shouldn't be too surprising to fellow astrologers! That year, Dave recorded as leader of his own quartet.

In 1988, he became a consulting astrologer and since that time has conducted seminars on *Astrology and Addiction* as well as *Astrology and the Family Dynamic* with his daughter Heather, who is also a massage therapist, astrologer and published poet.

Dave and his wife Joy, reside in Topanga Canyon, in Malibu, CA, where they have flourished since 1960.

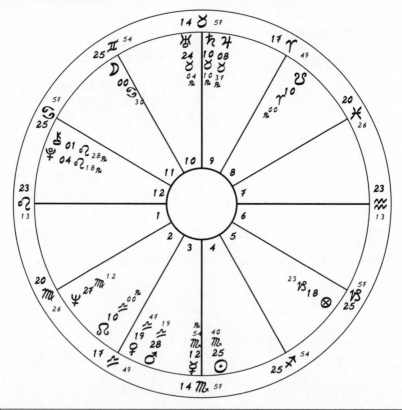

David Hayward
b. 17 November 1940, 22:50 EST, Winchendon, MA, USA (42N41, 72W03)
Source: Birth Certificate. Koch Houses.

photo by Heather Hayward

Astrology

"Your body's cells are exquisitely attuned to the cycles of the Moon, Sun, and stars" (Deepak Chopra). As a counselling astrologer since 1988, David has helped people to explore the map of the soul's intentions and to utilize planetary cycles for choices and timing. The planets help to plan it.

David sees each chart as a unique snowflake which will not be duplicated in a 25,000 year period. He believes our soul chose its moment of manifestation, how it wants to experience physical life. Being born into an envelope of forgetfulness, we have lost the authority of our own energies. Ignorance is not bliss, self-mastery brings self-empowerment.

Integrated Bodywork

David uses an integrated, multi-disciplinary approach developed over 14 years working as a fully licensed and accredited massage and Shiatsu therapist, Lic. 000628. He has worked on world-class athletes as well as invalids, and regular clients seeking relief from the daily stress of living.

To contact David Hayward, or to receive details of his astrological consultations, future seminars, tapes, or bodywork therapy, please write to: Hayward & Associates, 15237 Sunset Boulevard STE. 116, Pacific Palisades, CA 90272, USA, or e-mail: willisjoy@aol.com

Other Titles Published by Flare
(with their current UK prices)

Bookstores and internet bookshops stock most Flare titles,
but if you wish to keep informed of new books as they become available,
please write to us at:
Flare Publications, 29 Dolben Street, London SE1 0UQ, England
(or fill in the order form at the back of this book),
or call: +44 (0) 171 922 1123
or contact us at **flareUK.com**

The Draconic Chart - Rev. Pamela Crane

£16.99. Flare *Pioneer* Series

The fruit of 22 years' study and experience, Pamela Crane's important work is now available in a new, enlarged and revised edition. This trail-blazing volume unravels the history of Draconic and its meaning in the natal chart, in synastry, transits, progressions, directions and returns, in rectification and even horary with a host of examples, as well as revealing Pamela Crane's own impassioned journey to discovery. Acquire deeper insights into your life meaning, your driving principles, your spiritual purpose, your karma, and your vocation. (297x210.)

The Sun Sign Reader - Joan Revill

£9.99. Flare *Astro-Profiles* Series

Why do authors select a particular day for their characters to be born or for an event to take place? Are the characters comfortable in their zodiac signs? Do the events in their fictitious lives coincide with the movements of the planets? From a renowned astrology writer comes the ultimate birthday book of astrological characters and events for every day of the year. In her pithy, humorous manner, Joan Revill discovers what astrology reveals about authors, books and fictional characters. (228x152. 224 pp.)

British Entertainers - Frank C. Clifford

Special Price: **£5.99** (RRP: £9.99) Flare *Astro-Profiles* Series

This popular reference work combines astrology with concise biographies of over 700 prominent personalities from the worlds of film, theatre, television, comedy and music. It also uncovers the prime indicators of performing talent in birth charts. All data are meticulously researched and classified. (212x148. 224 pp. Flare, 1997. Revised edition.)

Teachers and Group Study Organisers: please enquire about our special discounts
for purchases of six or more copies of each title.

In 2000, **Flare** will be publishing titles in astrology, palmistry, and other Mind Body & Spirit disciplines (as well as publishing the first in a series of entertainment books) from a number of writers, including: Christeen Skinner, Richard J. Swatton, Frank C. Clifford, Peter Upton, and Jenni Dean.

PRIORITY ORDER FORM

	Quantity	Price	Total
The Draconic Chart ~ Rev. Pamela A. F. Crane		£16.99	
Shorthand of the Soul: the Quotable Horoscope ~ David Hayward		£12.99	
The Sun Sign Reader ~ Joan Revill		£9.99	
British Entertainers: The Astrological Profiles ~ Frank C. Clifford (revised edition)		£5.99	
Your Personal Draconic Chart Printout (in colour) - please give birth details below		£1.00	
Your Personal Natal Horoscope Printout (in colour) - please give birth details below		£1.00	
		p&p*	
		Total:	

Please send this order form with a cheque or postal order to:
Flare Publications,
29 Dolben Street,
London SE1 0UQ,
England
(credit card facilities available in 2000)

Please make ALL payments to:
Flare Publications.

International orders: please send payment in Sterling Pounds only

* Europe - please add 10%
* Rest of world - please add 20%

Tick here if you wish to receive details of forthcoming publications and special offers

Your delivery details:

Name:

Address:

Postcode:

Thank you for ordering with Flare Publications

Horoscope Printouts

Name (if different from order):

Birthdate:

Birthplace and country:

Birthtime (please specify am/pm):
(*Equal House used unless otherwise requested*)